MASS ATROCITIES, THE RESPONSIBILITY TO PROTECT AND THE FUTURE OF HUMAN RIGHTS

This book ambitiously weaves together history and politics to explain all of the major situations where mass atrocities have occurred, or been prevented, over the 15 years since the 'Responsibility to Protect' (R2P) was adopted at the 2005 UN World Summit.

The author provides a history of human rights, mass atrocities and the principle of the R2P from the perspective of someone whose day job has been to work with the UN Security Council, various governments and civil society groups to help ensure that the international community does not fail those who face the threat of genocide, war crimes and crimes against humanity today. It examines the implementation of the controversial principle of R2P since 2011. Using case studies from Iraq, Syria, Myanmar and Libya, the book offers a unique perspective regarding how we make 'never again' a living principle rather than a cliché and how we end the politics of impunity, indifference and inaction once and for all.

It will be of special interest to scholars, students and policy makers working in the fields of international politics or concerned about human rights, atrocities, the United Nations and international justice in the world today.

Simon Adams, PhD, is executive director of the Global Centre for the Responsibility to Protect, a human rights organisation that provides policy advice and carries out advocacy with the UN Security Council and Human Rights Council regarding crimes against humanity, war crimes and genocide. Dr Adams has worked extensively with civil society organisations in South Africa, Timor-Leste, Rwanda and elsewhere. He is the author of four books and regularly appears in the international media on matters related to the United Nations, human rights and conflict in the world today.

Routledge Global Institutions Series

Edited by Thomas G. Weiss
The CUNY Graduate Center, New York, USA
and Rorden Wilkinson
University of Sussex, Brighton, UK

MASS ATROCITIES, THE RESPONSIBILITY TO PROTECT AND THE FUTURE OF HUMAN RIGHTS

'If Not Now, When?'

Simon Adams

Routledge
Taylor & Francis Group

LONDON AND NEW YORK

First published 2021
by Routledge
2 Park Square, Milton Park, Abingdon, Oxon OX14 4RN

and by Routledge
52 Vanderbilt Avenue, New York, NY 10017

Routledge is an imprint of the Taylor & Francis Group, an informa business

British Library Cataloguing-in-Publication Data
A catalogue record for this book is available from the British Library

Library of Congress Cataloging-in-Publication Data
A catalog record has been requested for this book

ISBN: 978-0-367-55128-5 (hbk)
ISBN: 978-0-367-55129-2 (pbk)
ISBN: 978-1-003-09209-4 (ebk)

Typeset in Bembo
by MPS Limited, Dehradun

For Aislinn, Aidan and Siobhán

CONTENTS

LIST OF ABBREVIATIONS

ASEAN	Association of Southeast Asian Nations
AU	African Union
CAR	Central African Republic
DA	Democratic Alliance (South Africa)
ECOWAS	Economic Community of West African States
FFM	Independent International Fact-Finding Mission on Myanmar
FRELIMO	Frente de Libertação de Moçambique
FSA	Free Syrian Army
GDP	Gross domestic product
GNC	General National Congress (Libya)
ICC	International Criminal Court
ICISS	International Commission on Intervention and State Sovereignty
ICJ	International Court of Justice
ICTY	International Criminal Tribunal for the Former Yugoslavia
IDP	Internally displaced person
IIIM	International, Impartial and Independent Mechanism for Syria
IPCC	Intergovernmental Panel on Climate Change
ISF	Iraqi security forces
ISIL	Islamic State of Iraq and the Levant
NATO	North Atlantic Treaty Organization
NTC	National Transitional Council (Libya)
OHCHR	Office of the High Commissioner for Human Rights
OPCW	Organisation for the Prohibition of Chemical Weapons
PBC	UN Peacebuilding Commission
PMF	Popular Mobilization Forces (Iraq)
PSC	AU Peace and Security Council
RENAMO	Resistência Nacional Moçambicana

RwP	Responsibility while Protecting
SNHR	Syrian Network for Human Rights
SOHR	Syrian Observatory for Human Rights
UN	United Nations
UNAMI	UN Assistance Mission for Iraq
UNESCO	UN Educational, Scientific and Cultural Organization
UNITAD	UN Investigative Team to Promote Accountability for Crimes Committed by Da'esh/ISIL
UNSMIL	UN Support Mission in Libya
YPG	Kurdish People's Protection Units (Syria)

INTRODUCTION

It wasn't supposed to be this way

'We believe that mass killings and ethnic cleansing are underway across Rakhine State, and that there may be genocidal intent on behalf of the authorities.' That was my concluding comment at a briefing for members of the UN Security Council on the morning of 8 September 2017. The meeting took place in a building on Second Avenue, a short walk from UN headquarters and the Council's meeting room on the banks of New York's East River. From the expansive windows you could see the glistening skyscrapers of midtown Manhattan. The ambassadors and other diplomats who came to the briefing that morning drank coffee and ate muffins as they listened to our analysis and took notes.

Fifteen days earlier, thousands of miles away on the other side of the world, two of Myanmar's light infantry divisions, the 33rd and 99th, had launched so-called clearance operations against the ethnic Rohingya population of Rakhine State, in the northwest of the country, bordering Bangladesh. There were two colleagues beside me at the briefing table. One, from Human Rights Watch, provided satellite evidence that revealed the systematic burning of dozens of Rohingya villages during these operations. The images exposed the scorched outlines of incinerated mosques, huts and homes that had been the center of life for the local Rohingya population until 25 August, when Myanmar's military was unleashed upon them. Human Rights Watch was about to publicly release the images, and their briefer was able to compare before-and-after photos of villages that had been razed to the ground.

The other briefer was Matthew Smith from Fortify Rights, a human rights organisation based in Southeast Asia. Matthew's colleagues had been collecting testimony as tens of thousands of desperate Rohingya refugees staggered across the border into Bangladesh with stories of mass rape, systematic killings and even babies being thrown into burning huts by security forces. Many of the fleeing villagers exhibited signs of extreme emotional trauma, as well as untreated stab or bullet wounds. Matthew had flown straight to New York and come to the briefing. He was jet-lagged but opened his laptop and began reading from interview notes where the survivors of these atrocities told their stories. Again, the assembled diplomats took notes and asked questions.

The fifteen members of the UN Security Council represent the most powerful diplomatic body in the world. Together they form the only international institution mandated with the maintenance of global peace and security. They can authorise UN peacekeeping missions, impose sanctions, deploy crisis mediators, establish special international criminal tribunals and even authorise military intervention in a country if they deem it necessary. Of the diplomats assembled around the briefing table that morning, not one voiced any doubts about the veracity of the evidence we presented. Not one of them challenged the idea that atrocities were underway. And not one of them appeared to believe that they were capable of doing anything to stop it.

It wasn't supposed to be this way. The adoption of the principle of the 'responsibility to protect' (R2P) at the historic UN World Summit in 2005 was supposed to usher in a new era of commitment to preventing or halting the four 'mass atrocity crimes' – genocide, war crimes, ethnic cleansing and crimes against humanity. As a mobilising principle, R2P gained remarkable political traction in a short period of time. Dozens of states actively support the principle, and it has been invoked by the UN Security Council in more than eighty resolutions. In the first decade after R2P was adopted, international action halted atrocities in Côte d'Ivoire and in northern Iraq. International political pressure also helped prevent the worst from happening in Kenya, Burundi and the Gambia. Meanwhile, in the Democratic Republic of the Congo, South Sudan and the Central African Republic, action by the UN Security Council was belated and attenuated, but still saved lives. But R2P has also provoked enormous controversy, with the 2011 military intervention in Libya and the failure to act with regard to Syria causing bitter divisions. The UN Security Council also completely failed to halt atrocities in Sri Lanka, Myanmar and Yemen. While this is not an exhaustive list, it points to the magnitude of the challenge that faces us.

After the Myanmar briefing ended, several diplomats hung around to chat. Privately, they spoke about China's intransigence inside the negotiating rooms of the Security Council. Beijing, they said, had repeatedly threatened to veto any draft resolution seeking to impose targeted sanctions on Myanmar's generals for what they were doing in Rakhine State. The Chinese argued that the Security Council had no legitimate reason to interfere in Myanmar's domestic affairs, and facing a veto, the diplomats were unsure what, if anything, could be achieved. They reminded me that even a tersely worded presidential statement would be impossible without Beijing's consent.

But the struggle to end atrocities against the Rohingya and to punish those responsible did not end that morning. This book is about what I have learned leading an organisation dedicated to advancing the principle of R2P by working with governments, international civil society and the UN Security Council and

Human Rights Council, and trying to end genocide, crimes against humanity and war crimes in our world. The Global Centre for the Responsibility to Protect was formed in 2008 by several of R2P's architects – including former UN Secretary-General Kofi Annan, former Australian foreign minister Gareth Evans, former Irish president and former UN High Commissioner for Human Rights Mary Robinson and Roméo Dallaire, the Canadian general who led the failed UN peacekeeping mission during the Rwandan genocide. All of our founding patrons had direct experience of how inaction and indifference can create a political environment where mass atrocity crimes can be perpetrated. All were committed to the idea that R2P needed to become a mobilising principle around which the international community – meaning not just state powers but also intergovernmental organisations and global civil society – could rally whenever and wherever vulnerable civilians face the threat of the machete or the mass grave.

Fifteen years since the adoption of R2P at the historic UN World Summit in 2005, there are currently 79.5 million people in the world who have been forcibly displaced by conflict, persecution and mass atrocities – more than the number displaced following the genocide in Rwanda or during the peak of the wars in the former Yugoslavia during the 1990s.[1] Despite this expansion of human suffering, there has also been a crisis of compassion in many countries, with xenophobia, authoritarianism and religious extremism on the rise.

The ideas and institutions that are supposed to protect human rights and safeguard humanity are under threat. The United Nations, in particular, is facing severe challenges to its credibility. This book is about how we can overcome the current dismal state of international relations and consistently protect the world's most vulnerable populations.

The book is divided into seven chapters. Chapter 1 examines how disputes over national sovereignty and atrocity crimes reshaped international law and diplomacy during the second half of the twentieth century, presenting fresh challenges for governments and civil society alike. This introductory chapter also explores whether human societies are capable of ending the systematic infliction of cruelty, and establishes how and why R2P emerged as a mobilising principle to end atrocities once and for all.

Chapters 2, 3 and 4 explore case studies of success and failure over the last decade with regard to intervening to halt atrocities, with particular focus on, respectively, the contentious 2011 intervention in Libya, the deadly civil war in Syria and the way in which the world confronted the so-called Islamic State extremist group in Iraq. While these chapters examine the ongoing global debate about how and when the UN Security Council and other intergovernmental entities should deploy military force, they also explore other measures and means by which the world can prevent genocide, crimes against humanity and war crimes.

Chapter 5 examines the existential threat presented by global climate change and how it is reshaping Yemen and other contemporary armed conflicts. If climate change has indeed become a 'threat multiplier' for conflict and atrocities, how should the international community respond? Chapter 6 analyses the 2017 genocide against the Rohingya minority in Myanmar and the ongoing struggle to close the gap between words and deeds when it comes to upholding international law and defending human rights.

The final chapter of the book weighs up the successes and setbacks of the last fifteen years of R2P and the ongoing struggle for international justice. It argues that ideas, institutions and individuals remain crucial to human progress and provides recommendations on how governments, parliaments, the UN, civil society and individual activists can help prevent atrocity crimes. It argues that we need to build new networks and movements to jettison the failed politics of the past and uphold our collective responsibility to protect.

Finally, laced throughout the book are occasional personal interpolations relating to my work with the Global Centre for the Responsibility to Protect. I hope these add texture to the overall argument presented here. For example, in late December 2011, while on a family vacation, I received the following email regarding the situation in South Sudan from a contact inside the UN Department of Peacekeeping Operations:

> Simon, I hope you had a lovely Christmas and festive break. We are receiving news of an imminent attack by the Lou Nuer on the Murle community in Jonglei state. They have threatened to wipe out the 'Murle, the SPLA and the UN'. Aerial pictures of columns of Lou Nuer advancing on Pibor county are quite terrifying. Just wanted to let you know – possibility of a mass atrocity … Will keep you updated in case this turns nasty.[2]

I am part of a movement of people dedicated to making 'never again' a living principle rather than a cliché to whisper as we shuffle past the grim memorials and graves of those who died while the world sat in silence. Our job is to end the politics of impunity and inaction once and for all. This book is about how we do so.

Notes

1 United Nations High Commissioner for Refugees (UNHCR), "1 percent of humanity displaced: UNHCR Global Trends report," 18 June 2020, https://www.unhcr.org/en-us/news/press/2020/6/5ee9db2e4/1-cent-humanity-displaced-unhcr-global-trends-report.html.
2 Personal email to S. Adams from an anonymous source in the UN Department of Peacekeeping Operations, 26 December 2011.

1

WHY HUMANS COMMIT ATROCITIES AND HOW SOCIETIES CAN CHANGE

Contents

In January 2016, the fossils of twenty-seven humans from a Stone Age culture were unearthed at Nataruk in northern Kenya, in what is now semidesert but was once a fertile lagoon on the southern fringe of Lake Turkana. The skeletons belonged to primitive human ancestors who met grisly deaths approximately 10,000 years ago. Examining the site, paleoanthropologist Marta Mirazón Lahr's team concluded that the group of hunter-gatherers had been murdered before being dumped in the lagoon, where their bones were preserved in sediment. The researchers who excavated the skeletons described 'extreme blunt-force trauma to crania and cheekbones, broken hands, knees and ribs, arrow lesions to the neck, and stone projectile tips lodged in the skull and thorax of two men'. One woman, who was pregnant, had been tied up before being clubbed to death.[1]

The reason for the massacre is a mystery. These early human bands in Africa were made up of groups of extended families who hunted animals, foraged for plants and fished. While their lives were far from utopian or pacific, internal group dynamics tended towards cooperation and collaboration. The idea that a group could be deliberately exterminated therefore challenges our conception of prehistory.

Twenty-one of the skeletons belonged to adults and six were children. Perhaps, the scientists hypothesised, the massacre was the result of a conflict over resources, as the band expanded or accidentally roamed into another group's territory. Alternatively, perhaps this group was wiped out by invaders intent on seizing their hunting grounds. Or maybe the victims were simply humans who had become an unwelcome burden on a small group of primitive people with too many mouths to feed?

The evidence pointed to premeditated mass murder by a rival group. The Nataruk lagoon area was rich in food resources ten millennia ago, and Lahr pointed out that the killers used weapons that they would not have normally carried around with them just for hunting or fishing. Also, the remains of two arrow or spearpoints and a crude blade that were embedded within the skeletons were made from obsidian, a black volcanic rock that was worked to deadly sharpness. Lahr noted, 'Obsidian is rare in other late Stone Age sites of this area in West Turkana, which may suggest that the two groups confronted at Nataruk had different home ranges.' She argued that the 'Nataruk massacre' therefore stands as potentially our earliest scientific evidence of prehistoric deadly group conflict.[2]

Is there a historic blood trail that links the Nataruk massacre to our modern world? The widely held idea that all human beings have a potential mass murderer inside us contributes to the assumption that our societies are also innately cruel and murderous. It follows, therefore, that attempts to end atrocity crimes are futile. Unfortunately, events over the last century have seemed to confirm the view that extraordinary advances in science, technology and civilisation have not made our species more tranquil but have instead inspired us to more efficiently pursue the extinction of rivals and outsiders. The Holocaust, in particular, necessitated the creation of a whole new word – *genocide* – to explain the nature of the evil that humans do to one another. However, the development of human rights norms and laws indicates that it is possible to end mass atrocity crimes once and for all.

Genocide genesis

It was not until 1944 that Raphael Lemkin, a Polish Jewish lawyer and refugee, formulated the term *genocide* while intellectually grappling with the magnitude of the Nazis' destruction of European Jewry. Lemkin combined the Greek word for race or tribe, *genos*, with the French suffix for killing, Latin suffix. Lemkin wrote that the crucial thing was to capture the essence of the crime – the systematic and intentional destruction of a people.[3] Less than a year later, on 27 January 1945, the Red Army liberated the death camp at Auschwitz-Birkenau. It was not the first Nazi concentration camp to have its gates prised open – that had happened six months earlier, when a group of soldiers liberated Majdanek, also in Poland. But Auschwitz was clearly unique in the scale and scope of its industrialised mass killing.

Human rights would never be the same again. The end of the war, combined with revulsion regarding the Holocaust, helped make possible the creation of the United Nations. While its predecessor, the League of Nations, had collapsed in ignominy at the start of the Second World War, the UN was to prove successful in mediating the interests of the major powers and avoiding a direct armed conflict between them over the rest of the century. Another great achievement of the early UN was the 10 December 1948 adoption of the Universal Declaration of Human Rights, which articulated every human being's right to life and liberty, to privacy and freedom of movement, to a nationality, to freedom of conscience and religion and to an education, work and leisure. The declaration also proclaimed that all human beings have a right not to be subjected to arbitrary arrest or exile, or to be held in slavery or tortured. These rights were declared to be universal, that is to say, they were innate, unalterable and intrinsic to all the people of this planet.[4]

Lemkin's term also rose to prominence. The word *genocide* appeared in the indictment against Nazi war criminals by the International Military Tribunal at Nuremburg, and at the main trial between November 1945 and September 1946 it was invoked by several of the prosecutors. Lead prosecutor Benjamin Ferencz also mentioned genocide four times during his opening statement at the Einsatzgruppen Trial in September 1947 as a means of explaining how the 'extermination of whole categories of human beings, was a foremost instrument of the Nazi doctrine'.[5]

Genocide officially became an internationally recognised crime via the UN Convention on the Prevention and Punishment of the Crime of Genocide. That convention was adopted, not inconsequentially, on 9 December 1948, the day before the Universal Declaration of Human Rights. Article I confirmed that genocide, 'whether committed in time of peace or time of war, is a crime under international law' that the convention's signatories were committed 'to prevent and punish'.[6]

Lemkin's definition of genocide, outlined in Article II, included 'any of the following acts committed with intent to destroy, in whole or in part', members of a religious, ethnic, racial or national group. These acts included the obvious – 'killing members of the group' and 'inflicting on the group conditions of life calculated to bring about its physical destruction' – but also the policy of 'forcibly transferring children of the group to another group'.[7] In this regard, what was essential was not the lethality or injustice of the measures imposed but the intention to destroy the targeted group as a group.

That winter in Paris, after the UN General Assembly adopted the Genocide Convention, Lemkin checked himself into hospital. He joked that he was suffering from a new disease: 'genociditis: exhaustion from the work on the Genocide Convention'.[8] Lemkin, who lost 49 members of his extended family in the Holocaust, was also acutely conscious of past diplomatic failures. When he visited Geneva, he described walking through the hallways of the former League of Nations building as being like taking a stroll through a 'cultured cemetery of a dead world'.[9] Lemkin saw the Genocide Convention as an antidote to the meaningless diplomacy that had failed to prevent both the war and the Holocaust. What he most desired was practical action.

In the decades following Lemkin's untimely death in 1959, 149 states have ratified or acceded to the Genocide Convention. Other atrocity crimes – crimes against humanity and war crimes – were outlawed under the Geneva Conventions, prosecuted at Nuremburg, further defined via the International Criminal Tribunals for the Former Yugoslavia and Rwanda and codified in the 1998 Rome Statute of the International Criminal Court (ICC).[10] However, despite legal progress, in the half century after 1948 the international community's ability to make good on the post-Holocaust promise of 'never again' was dismal.

From the killing fields of Cambodia to the gassing of Iraqi Kurds during the Anfal campaign of 1988, signatories to the Genocide Convention failed to uphold or enforce it when it was needed most.

Rwanda marks a notoriously dark chapter of this ignoble history. Over 100 days between April and July 1994, a million people were systematically murdered at roadblocks, in the streets and even in churches where thousands sought sanctuary. Crucially, there was no determination at the UN Security Council in New York to forcibly halt the genocide. Instead, as the killing intensified, the small peacekeeping force in Rwanda, UNAMIR – commanded by the indomitable Canadian general Roméo Dallaire – had its resources depleted and many of its troops withdrawn. The Security Council provided polite excuses for inaction and retreat, ignoring Dallaire's pleas for reinforcement. As a result, when the genocide ended in July 1994 it was not because of an international intervention to protect people from machete-wielding killers, but because a rebel army led by Paul Kagame marched into Kigali and deposed the Hutu Power regime.

In Rwanda the *génocidaires* had loudly stated their intention to exterminate all ethnic Tutsi. The 1994 genocide was the culmination of a long process of systematic persecution. Genocidal intent was unequivocal. Not so in many other cases, where specific intent or the nature of the atrocities altered and deepened over time. And while the 'g-word' has talismanic power, other atrocity crimes – war crimes and crimes against humanity – are just as heinous and prohibited under international law. Determining the extent, intent and outcome of all atrocities therefore remains a question of evidence, argument and judgment.

Just as importantly, while Lemkin gave genocide a name, he left it to us to figure out how to prevent it. In the aftermath of Rwanda and a decade of war crimes and other atrocities in the former Yugoslavia, a number of international diplomats sought to do just that. In this undertaking they were not only challenging decades of inaction and indifference to atrocities around the globe, they were also inadvertently disputing our scientific understanding of human nature and society.

Those who kill and those who don't

Dutch sociologist Abram de Swaan escaped the Holocaust without even knowing it. He was just a baby when the Germans invaded the Netherlands and his Jewish parents gave him to a Christian family in their native Amsterdam to look after. Thus, Abram lived through the war with a surrogate family, just streets away from the secret hiding place of the most famous Jewish child of the Holocaust – Anne Frank. Seven decades later, de Swaan's book *The Killing Compartments* grapples with the social psychology of the atrocity perpetrator.

De Swaan deconstructs two widely held notions about mass killers. The first is the idea that only monsters commit genocide. De Swaan points out that scholarly studies of Nazi war criminals reveal that only about five percent displayed any serious psychopathologies. But he also rejects the countervailing argument that most perpetrators were just 'ordinary people in extraordinary circumstances' and that 'ordinary individuals, like you and me, under the same conditions would do the same thing'.[11] This he utterly rejects.

De Swaan attributes the genesis of this 'situationist argument' to Hannah Arendt and the famous subtitle to her book on the 1961 Adolf Eichmann trial, 'the banality of evil'. In de Swaan's words:

> Arendt and many others who reported on the trial were enthralled by the fashionable notion of the time that the Nazi (and the Soviet) state was a mighty machine, manned by countless nameless, faceless bureaucrats and soldiers who were no more than cogs in the apparatus, obediently and unthinkingly doing whatever they were told, without much conviction of their own, except for loyalty to the system.[12]

In Eichmann's case, this was 'an expedient masquerade', albeit one that failed to save him from the Israeli hangman. Nevertheless, the banality of evil became possibly 'the greatest bêtise in the small but widely quoted repertoire of clichés about the Holocaust and about genocide in general'.[13]

Genocide, crimes against humanity and other atrocity crimes, de Swaan emphasises, are neither banal nor ordinary. And neither, for the most part, are their perpetrators. For example, the majority of the two dozen defendants charged with responsibility for over one million murders and brought to Nuremburg for the Einsatzgruppen Trial were from the educated elite of German society. Eleven had studied law at university. But what bound them together was not profession, class or religion. They were all senior officials who had dedicated years of their lives to building the Nazi state, as well as being trained soldiers or police officers and venomous anti-Semites. Their responses to the developing genocide on the Eastern Front were diverse, with varying degrees of commitment, but they were an elite group who were deeply contemptuous of the Jewish civilians they were unleashed upon.[14]

De Swaan also questions the accepted logic of Stanley Milgram's hugely influential situationist experiments at Yale University. Milgram, who conducted his experiments three months after the commencement of the Eichmann trial in Jerusalem, famously had volunteers apply electric shocks of increasing voltage to other human subjects who were hidden from them. They did not know that the shocks were not real and that actors were only pretending to be in pain. The cries sounded real enough. A disturbing two thirds of participants kept applying the shocks, despite agonised pleas for mercy, when instructed to do so by fake scientists in white laboratory coats.[15]

Over the following decades Milgram's experiments penetrated deep into popular culture, resulting in a well-known documentary seen by generations of psychology students. Yet Milgram's methodology was questionable in parts, and at least one quarter of participants refused to administer the electric shocks once they believed they had reached a harmful level. No reassurance or insistence from a figure of authority, white laboratory coat or not, could induce them to continue.[16] The sociological opposite of the perpetrator, these are people who become potential rescuers and resisters. This is something that the historiography of atrocities should pay more attention to.

In recent years, social psychologists such as Alexander Haslam and Stephen Reicher have also questioned Milgram's conclusion that a disturbingly high proportion of people will inflict pain upon their fellow human beings if ordered to do so:

> All we take in is the evidence that people obey, not the particular circumstances in which this obedience occurs. Hence, we slip too easily from the evidence that ordinary people can obey even the most extreme of instructions to the conclusion that people cannot help but obey destructive authorities.[17]

Reexamining Milgram's data, they found remarkable variation in the responses of participants.[18] The highest compliance occurred when the mock electrocuters were carefully induced to identify with the faux scientists – meaning, when they believed that the experiment was providing crucial data, that the subject was not really in pain and that the scientists were from a renowned university. However, the more insistent the fake scientists became in ordering their subjects to continue, the less willing the subjects were to do so. The fourth prompt scripted by Milgram was 'You have no choice, you must go on'. But according to Reicher and Haslam:

> Tellingly, [Milgram] discovered that *on every single occasion* that the experimenter issued the fourth prompt, participants refused to continue. ... There is a powerful irony at play here. For, as we have noted, Milgram's studies are widely remembered as showing that people obey orders. However, upon closer inspection, it appears that one thing that they show unequivocally is that, when requests are framed as orders, people do *not* obey.[19]

Philip Zimbardo, whose notorious 1971 Stanford prison experiment has been linked to Milgram's work, has also written extensively about this area of social psychology and was called as an expert witness at the trial of one of the American guards responsible for torturing inmates at Abu Ghraib prison in Iraq. Zimbardo's 'sad conclusion' was that 'powerful situations corrupt most people', and that the line between good and evil is permeable, including the tolerance of 'evil through inaction or indifference'. But his work now focuses on the minority who make a conscious decision to resist malign institutions and harmful authority and 'act when most people are frozen'.[20]

The truth is that it actually takes a momentous effort to move people to commit mass atrocities. The genocide in Rwanda followed decades of persecution of the Tutsi. Even then, the perpetrators presented themselves as the victims. The Interahamwe argued that they were protecting the nation from *inyenzi* (cockroaches) who wanted to restore the oppressive Tutsi monarchy. Similarly, Walter Blume – a Nazi Einsatzgruppe commander who was sentenced to hang at Nuremburg – gave speeches to his men about how it was necessary to massacre unarmed Jewish civilians on the Eastern Front or else they would come to Germany and kill the soldiers' wives and children. The Khmer Rouge believed that the 'killing fields' were necessary to inoculate revolutionary Cambodia against spies, saboteurs and traitors. In all cases, some perpetrators 'participated eagerly, others reluctantly, still others indifferently'.[21] All relied on accomplices, who were themselves engaged as bystanders or enablers to varying degrees.

In short, what makes people kill is not their pathological monstrosity, nor their ordinariness or banality. Personal disposition and institutional authority are crucial, as are changing social norms regarding violence and organised cruelty.

Killer apes?

When Charles Darwin published *On the Origin of Species* in November 1859, his theories regarding 'natural selection' transformed our scientific understanding of the world. Of all the ideas attributed to Darwin, the one that created the greatest controversy at the time was the suggestion that human beings and apes share a common line of evolutionary descent. Scientists and theologians were drawn into a tumultuous public debate over the relationship between human and ape.[22]

The first documented discovery of gorillas had been made less than ten years earlier, in 1847, by Thomas Savage, a European missionary. It was – for European science, if not for the local Africans who were already aware of their existence – a remarkable find. Here was an animal so obviously similar to humans that it challenged our very notion of ourselves. The discovery excited scientific minds and inspired European artists. When French sculptor Emmanuel Frémiet displayed *Gorille enlevant une négresse* ("Gorilla carrying off a Negress") in 1859, it ignited a public scandal. Gorillas were popularly perceived as violent and more primitive versions of ourselves. All this despite the fact that gorillas are peaceful vegetarians who live in remote jungle far from human civilisation.

Colonialism and racism also played a role. In 1861 it appeared reasonable for someone like Richard Owen, superintendent of natural history at the British Museum, to lecture on "The Gorilla and The Negro." The popular magazine *Punch* published a cartoon in May 1861 mocking both the antislavery movement and supporters of Darwin's evolutionary theory, with an ape asking the reader, "Am I a Man and a Brother?" In 1864, Benjamin Disraeli, the future British prime minister, famously asked his audience, "Is man an ape or an angel?"[23] Such concerns troubled scientific and religious thinkers in Europe.

More than 150 years later, it is now an accepted scientific fact that humans are primates. More specifically, we are great apes, a taxonomic grouping of two species of orangutans, two species of gorillas, and chimpanzees, bonobos and humans. Like other great apes, humans are complex social animals. But *Planet of the Apes* and *King Kong* aside, Hollywood art and Western science have generally retreated from the idea that our gorilla cousins are truculent beasts who want to carry us off naked into the jungle. In fact, during the twentieth century it was widely assumed that what made humans unique was our predilection for murdering our own species. This view eventually fell into disrepute during the 1960s, when field studies by Jane Goodall and others documented that other primates also regularly murder one another.[24] According to Robert Sapolsky, a professor of biology and neuroscience:

> Males kill; females kill. Some kill one another's infants with cold-blooded stratagems worthy of *Richard III*. Some use their toolmaking skills to fashion bigger and better cudgels. Some other primates even engage in what can only be called warfare – organized, proactive group violence directed at other populations.[25]

Sapolsky spent years studying savanna baboons and was particularly interested in arguments about nature versus nurture. He believed that there was an unhealthy tendency to assume that high levels of violence amongst some primates (such as chimpanzees), or its relative absence amongst other species (like gibbons), was a matter of genetic destiny. If this was true, then the fact that chimpanzees – with whom humans share 98 percent of our DNA – had been documented participating in "an endless stream of murders, cannibalism, and organized group violence" had grim implications.[26]

Affairs in the baboon kingdom were no better. Despotic hierarchies among baboons are enforced with a violent intensity that would make the average military dictator blush. Food, sex and other resources are unequally divided. Power and privilege are male dominated, and establishing a high rank is usually the result of a ruthless campaign of physical cruelty.

During the 1980s Sapolsky famously studied two troops of savanna baboons with adjoining territories in Kenya – Forest Troop and Garbage Dump Troop. The territory of the latter, as the name implies, included a tourist lodge's garbage dump, and after discovering the half-eaten delicacies being thrown away by humans, the entire troop eventually moved into trees near the dump. Garbage Dump Troop became obese from their access to meat scraps, fatty food and discarded pastries.

Eventually a number of aggressive adult males from Forest Troop tried to seize Garbage Dump Troop's garbage. Battles between the males of Forest Troop and Garbage Dump Troop ensued. This state of hostilities continued until there was a catastrophic outbreak of bovine tuberculosis (a result of contaminated meat) that completely annihilated Garbage Dump Troop and killed all the males of Forest Troop who had been on raiding parties.[27] Forest Troop was fundamentally transformed. With only a few surviving males, aggression and violence decreased, hierarchy became 'looser', and 'affiliative behavior, such as males and females grooming each other', significantly increased. Some males even groomed each other from time to time, a behavior that Sapolsky described as 'nearly as unprecedented as baboons sprouting wings'.[28] What was truly unprecedented, however, was not discovered until years later.

In order to prevent inbreeding, male members of baboon troops relocate to another troop at puberty. Sapolsky's studies found that by the 1990s, all of Forest Troop's 'adult males had joined after the epidemic', but that the troop's 'unique social milieu persisted' for the following two decades. Males who were adopted into Forest Troop adapted to the low-aggression culture of their new society. In an article written for the influential *Foreign Affairs* magazine, Sapolsky pondered the implications of Forest Troop on debates over the peaceful transformation of human society. He wrote, 'Anyone who says, "No, it is beyond our nature," knows too little about primates, including ourselves'.[29]

Humans have a long tradition of projecting their social prejudices and biological assumptions onto our fellow primates. However, the one thing that truly makes us unique is that unlike baboons, we can consciously collaborate to foster alternative norms of behavior.

Cognitive psychologist Steven Pinker, for example, has spent much of his career using statistics to reveal how violence has declined in the modern world as literacy, health and life expectancy have improved for most of humanity.[30] He attributes the general – but not inexorable or irreversible – historical progress that has been made in decreasing war, atrocities and other forms of violence to a range of factors, including an 'international community which can propagate norms of non-violent cooperation' and 'humanistic counter-ideologies such as human rights, universal brotherhood, expanding empathy, and the demonization of war'.[31] In this context, Pinker notes:

> People tend to reduce human nature to a single essence, and then debate what that essence consists of. Are we nasty or noble, Hobbesian or Rousseauan, angel or ape? In this way of thinking, if we regularly engage in violence, we must be a violent species; if we are capable of peace, we must be pacifistic.[32]

In short, although humans have been responsible throughout history for unimaginable atrocities, we need not be prisoners to our past. Instead, we can challenge and fundamentally alter the way that people think and our governments act.

Kofi Annan and the responsibility to protect

Having unwillingly presided over two of the greatest failures in the history of UN peacekeeping – the Rwandan genocide in 1994 and the genocide at Srebrenica in Bosnia-Herzegovina a year later – Kofi Annan desired to make amends after he became UN secretary-general in 1997. In a series of speeches and articles he raised fundamental questions about the future of the United Nations and the importance of confronting mass atrocities in the world. By the late 1990s the United Nations appeared barely able to cope with what Annan described as 'problems without passports', such as poverty, AIDS, climate change and 'the persistence of deadly conflicts in which civilians are primary targets'. On the latter point, at the start of the new millennium Annan directly posed an awkward question to the UN General Assembly: 'If humanitarian intervention is, indeed, an unacceptable assault on sovereignty', he asked, 'how should we respond to a Rwanda, to a Srebrenica, to gross and systematic violations of human rights that offend every precept of our common humanity?'[33]

To answer these questions Annan turned to Algerian diplomat Mohamed Sahnoun, Australia's Gareth Evans and others. During the 1960s, when he was a university student, Evans had travelled throughout Asia, including Cambodia. Decades later, as Australia's foreign minister and one of the initiators of the Cambodian peace plan, he revisited the country. Evans tried to contact old friends but they had all perished or been dispersed by the Khmer Rouge's atrocities. The experience had a profound impact on Evans, who later reflected, 'It has taken the world an insanely long time, centuries in fact, to come to terms conceptually with the idea that state sovereignty is not a license to kill – that there is something fundamentally and intolerably wrong about states murdering or forcibly displacing large numbers of their own citizens, or standing by when others do so'.[34]

In 2001 Evans and Sahnoun were asked by the Canadian government to co-chair the International Commission on Intervention and State Sovereignty (ICISS). It was the ICISS that developed the concept of the responsibility to protect (R2P) as an answer to Annan's challenge. In Evans' words:

> We very much had in mind the power of new ideas, or old ideas newly expressed, to actually change the behavior of key policy actors. And a model we very much had in mind in this respect was the Brundtland Commission, which a few years earlier had introduced the concept of 'sustainable development' to bridge the huge gap which then existed between developers and environmentalists. With a new script, the actors have to change their lines, and think afresh about what the real issues in the play actually are.[35]

Specifically, the commissioners were seeking a term that avoided splitting people along partisan lines as promotors of 'humanitarian intervention' versus the paladins of inviolable sovereignty. Again, according to Evans:

> The whole point of the R2P doctrine, in the minds of those of us who conceived it, was above all to change the way that the world's policymakers, and those who influence them, thought and acted in response to emerging, imminent and actually occurring mass atrocity crimes. It was to generate a reflex international response that genocide, other crimes against humanity and major war crimes happening behind sovereign state walls were everybody's business, not nobody's.[36]

R2P was also a recognition of the fact that while the UN was established to stop wars between states, most conflicts were now within national borders. These internal conflicts or civil wars can have catastrophic consequences equal in devastating potential to invasion and conquest. For example, the current war in Syria has killed half a million people and wiped out the gains made in health and welfare over the previous 35 years.[37]

R2P was built upon the notion that sovereignty entails responsibility. This is largely an African concept in origin, drawing on the ideas of renowned South Sudanese scholar and diplomat Francis Deng and his collaborator Roberta Cohen. While working as Representative of the UN Secretary-General on Internally Displaced Persons (IDPs), Deng continually emphasised that with regard to upholding human rights, all governments had obligations to both their domestic constituents *and* the international community.[38]

The responsibility to protect was unanimously adopted at the UN's World Summit in 2005, the largest gathering of heads of state and government in human history. The historian Martin Gilbert famously described the adoption of R2P in paragraphs 138 and 139 of the World Summit Outcome Document as "the most significant adjustment to sovereignty in 360 years," since the Peace of Westphalia.[39] Journalistic hyperbole aside, the new idea was compressed into two exhaustively negotiated paragraphs of prosaic diplomatic prose. No commas were spared:

1. Each individual State has the responsibility to protect its populations from genocide, war crimes, ethnic cleansing and crimes against humanity. This responsibility entails the prevention of such crimes, including their incitement, through appropriate and necessary means. We accept that responsibility and will act in accordance with it. The international community should, as appropriate, encourage and help States to exercise this responsibility and support the United Nations in establishing an early warning capability.

2. The international community, through the United Nations, also has the responsibility to use appropriate diplomatic, humanitarian and other peaceful means, in accordance with Chapters VI and VIII of the Charter, to help to protect populations from genocide, war crimes, ethnic cleansing and crimes against humanity. In this context, we are prepared to take collective action, in a timely and decisive manner, through the Security Council, in accordance with the Charter, including Chapter VII, on a case-by-case basis and in cooperation with relevant regional organizations as appropriate, should peaceful means be inadequate and national authorities are manifestly failing to protect their populations from genocide, war crimes, ethnic cleansing and crimes against humanity. We stress the need for the General Assembly to continue consideration of the responsibility to protect populations from genocide, war crimes, ethnic cleansing and crimes against humanity and its implications, bearing in mind the principles of the Charter and international law. We also intend to commit ourselves, as necessary and appropriate, to helping States

build capacity to protect their populations from genocide, war crimes, ethnic cleansing and crimes against humanity and to assisting those which are under stress before crises and conflicts break out.[40]

The moral and political basis of R2P was that all humans have a right to be protected from mass atrocity crimes – genocide, war crimes, ethnic cleansing and crimes against humanity. The responsibility to protect people from these crimes falls, first and foremost, upon their sovereign government (pillar 1). Secondly, the international community has an obligation to assist any state that is struggling to uphold its protective responsibilities (pillar 2). And finally, if a government proves manifestly unable or unwilling to exercise its responsibility to protect, the international community is obligated to act (pillar 3).[41]

In the words of Ramesh Thakur, another ICISS commissioner, the responsibility to protect was a rejection of both 'institutionalized indifference and unilateral interference' with regard to mass atrocity crimes.[42] Speaking at the launch of the Global Centre for the Responsibility to Protect in New York in February 2008, the new UN secretary-general, Ban Ki-moon, described R2P and the launch of the Global Centre as a moment of 'great promise' in the struggle against mass atrocities and in moving 'from concept to actuality, from word to deed'. Until 2008, however, it was unclear if the R2P concept could provide a genuine rallying point for action.

Kenya and R2P in practice

On the last Monday of 2007, dozens of ethnic Kikuyu families crowded into the Assemblies of God church in Kiambaa, near Eldoret, seeking sanctuary from the violence engulfing Kenya. A disputed election and simmering resentment over decades of ethnic favouritism by the political elite had transformed the country from a perceived paragon of stability in East Africa into a killing zone. Just days after election results were released in late December, more than 250 people had been killed. The 400 people crowding into the church were terrified they might be next.

That Tuesday, in broad daylight, a mob surrounded the church, blocked the exits and set fire to the building. Most of the Kikuyu families inside were able to fight their way out and flee. However, at least 35 people were killed, including a number of women and children who were burned alive. As the international media came to document the horror at Kiambaa, an elderly professor spoke for many Kenyans when he said that the scene at the church 'reminds me of Rwanda'.[43] However, the horror of Kiambaa did not stop the internecine ethnic violence that eventually killed 1,133 Kenyans and displaced 663,000 others.

As the situation spiraled out of control in Kenya, the need for an international response became imperative. Former UN secretary-general Kofi Annan and a team of 'Eminent African Personalities' were deployed to interpose themselves between the main political rivals. Intervention took the form of high-level negotiations combined with the threat of international sanctions and isolation if the crisis was not resolved. Violence eventually ebbed as a result of a new power-sharing arrangement between the government and opposition.

The efforts of Annan and others were hailed as the first example of 'R2P in practice'. As Annan himself later argued, 'I saw the crisis in the R2P prism with a Kenyan government unable to contain the situation or protect its people. ... I knew that if the international community did not intervene, things would go hopelessly wrong'.[44]

After 2008 significant structural reforms were undertaken in Kenya – including investing in local peacebuilding and strengthening national institutions (often with international support) to avoid a recurrence of atrocities. These involved long-overdue reforms to the security sector, a rewriting of the constitution and measures designed to outlaw hate speech and incitement. Despite progress, political tensions and bitter ethnic rivalries remained. Unemployment, poverty and corruption continued to fuel distrust, and campaigning along ethnic lines remained standard operating procedure for many Kenyan politicians. But the dividends for the investment in structural prevention were enormous: the 2013 Kenyan elections were largely free, fair and transparent. Devastating ethnic violence was almost completely avoided.[45]

Kenya demonstrated that it was possible to have a successful nonmilitary response to an international crisis where atrocities were occurring. Coming just a few years after the UN World Summit, Kenya also provided a positive example of how to operationalise R2P.[46] But it also raised the question of whether support for R2P could be built in a more sustained manner to fundamentally challenge and change the way that people think about mass atrocity crimes.

As Kenya's convulsions subsided, Gareth Evans published his book on the origins and applicability of R2P. In the opening chapter, he concedes that throughout 'the nearly 400 years of more or less untrammeled operation of Westphalian sovereignty principles, it is hard to find examples where states looked beyond their own territorial and colonial borders, beyond their own immediate economic and security interests' to prevent or halt atrocities. One exception was the way that UN human rights bodies maintained a 'sustained focus on apartheid in South Africa'. Another was 'Britain's central role in the ending of the slave trade' during the nineteenth century. While Evans concedes that the world is 'full of cynicism, double standards, crude assertions of national interest' and other political dark arts, he remains convinced 'that ideas matter enormously, for good and for ill'. And few ideas hold more promise than the responsibility to protect.[47]

Eldorat, where the December 2007 Kiambaa church burning took place, and Turkana, where the first recorded human massacre was committed, are both in the Great Rift Valley of Kenya. Travelling a distance of approximately 400 km and 10,000 years between these two places and events, it would be easy to assume that they represent something deeply disturbing about our species. But mass atrocities are not a natural and unalterable part of the human condition. Genocide and other atrocity crimes do not just happen in human societies; they have to be incited and organised. This means that they can also be disrupted and prevented.

Conclusion

In April 2014 I was invited to Rwanda to represent the Global Centre for the Responsibility to Protect at numerous events commemorating the twentieth anniversary of the genocide against the Tutsi. At Amahoro Stadium in Kigali, President Paul Kagame presided over the country's official commemoration as I sat in respectful sunburnt silence. A few feet to my left were President Salva Kiir of South Sudan and ex-president Thabo Mbeki of South Africa. The UK's Tony Blair was there too, sitting alongside the US ambassador to the United Nations, Samantha Power.

As we all watched, a spectacular reenactment of Rwanda's history took place, with a jeep full of khaki-clad white people driving into the stadium. The white people got out of the vehicle and promptly started imposing racial science upon those young Rwandan performers chosen to represent the native population. Tutsi and Hutu were racially classified by the colonisers. Then, as other performers acted out the beginning of the genocide, the white people slipped off their pith helmets, replaced them with blue UN berets and retreated, leaving the Rwandans to be slaughtered. The middle of the stadium was littered with bodies as the performers lay prostrate, contorted and silent.

No less memorable were the very real cries of agonising grief from the crowd. Several women fainted during the commemoration and had to be carried out. No matter how many times it happened, the psychological effect of the wailing was haunting.

In his speech at Amahoro Stadium that day, UN Secretary-General Ban Ki-moon said that 'the shame still clings, a generation after the events' of 1994. Of the UN's failed mission in Rwanda, he said, 'We could have done much more. We should have done much more'. I thought immediately of Roméo Dallaire, who was shattered by his command over a denuded UN peacekeeping force that had been incapacitated by the UN Security Council. Dallaire and those UNAMIR troops who stayed in 1994 were heroes who saved many lives, including more than 10,000 Tutsi who took shelter at Amahoro Stadium. But they had neither the mandate nor the means to stop the genocide.

At Amahoro that day, Ban insisted that 'under the Responsibility to Protect principle states can no longer claim that atrocity crimes are only a domestic matter'. He detailed how he had initiated a 'human rights up-front' action plan and told all UN staff working in situations where atrocities may be threatened, 'Speak up, even if it may offend. Act! Our first duty must always be to protect people'.[48] He mentioned that in Syria, the Central African Republic and South Sudan, there would be an even greater shame in failing to defend those who face atrocities today.

Kofi Annan, Gareth Evans, Mohamed Sahnoun and their collaborators ensured that preventing atrocities was at the heart of R2P. Nevertheless, most subsequent public debate has focussed on those extreme cases where atrocities are already occurring and it becomes imperative to halt them. While the so-called Arab

Spring that swept across North Africa and the Middle East after December 2010 resulted in inspiring and tumultuous change in a number of countries, it quickly turned deadly in Libya and Syria. Civil wars and atrocities in those two countries would prove to be a crucible for the emerging norm of the responsibility to protect.

Notes

1 Brian Handwerk, "An Ancient, Brutal Massacre May Be the Earliest Evidence of War," The Smithsonian, 20 January 2016, http://www.smithsonianmag.com/science-nature/ancient-brutal-massacre-may-be-earliest-evidence-war-180957884/?no-ist. See also, M. Mirazón Lahr et al., "Inter-group violence among Early Holocene Hunter-Gatherers of West Turkana, Kenya," Nature, no. 529 (21 January 2016), 394–398, https://www.nature.com/articles/nature16477?platform=hootsuite#citeas; and James Gorman, "Prehistoric Massacre Hints at War Among Hunter-Gatherers," New York Times, 20 January 2016.
2 "Evidence of a Prehistoric Massacre Extends the History of Warfare," University of Cambridge: Research, 20 January 2016, http://www.cam.ac.uk/research/news/evidence-of-a-prehistoric-massacre-extends-the-history-of-warfare; and Handwerk, "An Ancient, Brutal Massacre May Be the Earliest Evidence of War."
3 The term genocide made its intellectual debut in Raphael Lemkin, Axis Rule in Occupied Europe: Laws of Occupation, Analysis of Government, Proposals for Redress (New York: Carnegie Endowment for International Peace, 1944).
4 Universal Declaration of Human Rights, http://www.un.org/en/universal-declaration-human-rights/index.html.
5 Notably, none of the Nazi defendants at Nuremburg was convicted of genocide. They were found guilty of war crimes, crimes against humanity and crimes against peace. John Q. Barrett, "Raphael Lemkin and 'Genocide' at Nuremburg, 1945–1946," in The Genocide Convention Sixty Years After Its Adoption, ed. Christoph Safferling and Eckart Conze (The Hague, Netherlands: T.M.C. Asser Press, 2010), 54; Opening Statement of the Prosecution in the Einsatzgruppen Trial, 29 September 1947, http://www.famous-trials.com/nuremberg/1917-einsatzopen; Henry T. King Jr, Benjamin B. Ferencz, and Whitney R. Harris, "Origins of the Genocide Convention," Case Western Reserve Journal of International Law 40, no. 1 (2007–2008), 17.
6 Convention on the Prevention and Punishment of the Crime of Genocide, https://treaties.un.org/doc/Publication/UNTS/Volume%2078/volume-78-I-1021-English.pdf.
7 Ibid.
8 Donna-Lee Frieze, ed., Totally Unofficial: The Autobiography of Raphael Lemkin (New Haven, CT: Yale University Press, 2013), 179.
9 Ibid, 134.
10 Rome Statute of the International Criminal Court, https://www.icc-cpi.int/NR/rdonlyres/ADD16852-AEE9-4757-ABE7-9CDC7CF02886/283503/RomeStatutEng1.pdf.
11 Abram de Swaan, The Killing Compartments: The Mentality of Mass Murder (New Haven, CT: Yale University Press, 2015), 14, 19.
12 Ibid, 22.
13 Ibid, 33.
14 Hilary Earl, The Nuremberg SS-Einsatzgruppen Trial, 1945–1958: Atrocity, Law, and History (New York: Cambridge University Press, 2010), 118–119.
15 De Swaan, The Killing Compartments, 24–25; Cari Romm, "Rethinking One of Psychology's Most Infamous Experiments," The Atlantic (28 January 2015).

16 De Swaan, *The Killing Compartments*, 26.

17 Stephen D. Reicher and S. Alexander Haslam, "After Shock? Towards a Social Identity Explanation of the Milgram 'Obedience' Studies," *British Journal of Social Psychology*, no. 50 (2011), 163, https://www.researchgate.net/publication/50265634_After_shock_ Towards_a_social_identity_explanation_of_the_Milgram_'obedience'_studies/citation/ download; S. Alexander Haslam and Stephen D. Reicher, "Questioning the Banality of Evil," *The Psychologist* 21, no. 1 (January 2008), 16–19.

18 Reicher and Haslam, "After Shock? Towards a Social Identity Explanation of the Milgram 'Obedience' Studies," 163–169.

19 Ibid, 168.

20 "Psychologist Investigates the Origins of Evil," National Public Radio (NPR), 30 June 2008, https://www.npr.org/templates/story/story.php?storyId=92021527; Philip Zimbardo, "The Psychology of Evil," *Ted Talk* (Transcript) (February 2008), https:// www.ted.com/talks/philip_zimbardo_on_the_psychology_of_evil/transcript; and Philip Zimbardo, *The Lucifer Effect: Understanding How Good People Turn Evil* (New York: Random House, 2007).

21 De Swaan, *The Killing Compartments*, 108, 111, 214, 234; Michael A. Musmanno, *The Eichmann Kommandos* (London: Peter Davies, 1962), 161–162; and *Trials of War Criminals Before the Nuernberg Military Tribunals Under Control Council Law No. 10* IV (October 1946–1949), 530.

22 Joel Mandelstam, "Du Chaillu's Stuffed Gorillas and the Savants from the British Museum," *Notes and Records of the Royal Society of London* 48, no. 2 (July 1994), 227–245; and Janet Browne, *Darwin's Origin of Species: A Biography* (Crow's Nest, Australia: Allen & Unwin, 2006), 66–67, 93–99.

23 Mandelstam, "Du Chaillu's Stuffed Gorillas and the Savants from the British Museum," 231–233; and Browne, *Darwin's Origin of Species*, 98–99.

24 Robert M. Sapolsky, "A Natural History of Peace," *Foreign Affairs*, January/February 2006, https://www.foreignaffairs.com/articles/2006-01-01/natural-history-peace.

25 Ibid.

26 Ibid; and Robert M. Sapolsky, "This Is Your Brain on Nationalism," *Foreign Affairs* (March/April 2019), 42–47.

27 Sapolsky, "A Natural History of Peace."

28 Ibid.

29 Ibid. The unfortunate postscript to this story is that after 20 years, the Forest Troop eventually moved into the garbage dump and their positive culture disintegrated. Sapolsky returns to the subject in Robert M. Sapolsky, *Behave: The Biology of Humans at Our Best and Worst* (New York: Penguin, 2018), 648–652.

30 Steven Pinker, *Enlightenment Now: The Case for Reason, Science, Humanism and Progress* (London: Allen Lane, 2018), 156–166.

31 Steven Pinker, "The Decline of War and Conceptions of Human Nature," *International Studies Review* 15, no. 3 (2013), 400–405.

32 Ibid.

33 Kofi Annan, "Problems without Passports," *Foreign Policy*, 9 November 2009, http:// foreignpolicy.com/2009/11/09/problems-without-passports/. The more immediate impetus for the debate had been the intervention in Kosovo. An important book mapping the transformation in Annan's thinking, and that of UN member states, is Thomas G. Weiss, *Humanitarian Intervention: Ideas in Action* (Malden, MA: Polity Press, 2007). Weiss also served as the Research Directorate for ICISS.

34 Gareth Evans, "The Responsibility to Protect: Creating and Implementing a New International Norm," Speech to Human Rights Law Resource Centre, Melbourne, 13 August 2007, http://www.gevans.org/speeches/speech235.html.

35 Gareth Evans, *The Responsibility to Protect: Ending Mass Atrocity Crimes Once and For All* (Washington, DC: Brookings Institution Press, 2008), 42. See also, Alex J. Bellamy and

Edward C. Luck, *The Responsibility to Protect: From Promise to Practice* (Medford, MA: Polity Press, 2018), 17–32.

36 Gareth Evans, "R2P: Looking Back, Looking Forward," Keynote to International Conference on the Responsibility to Protect at 10: Progress, Challenges and Opportunities in the Asia Pacific, Phnom Penh, Cambodia, 26 February 2015, http://www.gevans.org/speeches/speech568.html.

37 United Nations Development Programme, About Syria, http://www.sy.undp.org/content/syria/en/home/countryinfo.html.

38 Ramesh Thakur, "Kofi Annan, Africa, and the Responsibility to Protect," *The Baobab: A Journal of the Council on Foreign Relations-Ghana* 1, no. 1 (January 2020), 24–45.

39 Martin Gilbert, "The Terrible 20th Century," *The Globe and Mail*, 31 January 2007.

40 United Nations 2005 World Summit Outcome, A/60/L.1, http://www.globalr2p.org/resources/280.

41 The three-pillar approach was first articulated by UN Special Advisor on R2P Edward Luck, in the Secretary-General's 2009 annual report on R2P. Bellamy and Luck, *The Responsibility to Protect: From Promise to Practice*, 32–36.

42 Thakur has used several variations of this formulation. Ramesh Thakur, "Has R2P Worked in Libya?," *Canberra Times*, 19 September 2011; Ramesh Thakur, *Reviewing the Responsibility to Protect: Origins, Implementation and Controversies* (New York: Routledge, 2019), 5, 122.

43 Jeffrey Gettleman, "Mob Sets Kenya Church On Fire, Killing Dozens," *New York Times*, 2 January 2008.

44 Abdullahi Boru Halakhe, "'R2P in Practice': Ethnic Violence, Elections and Atrocity Prevention in Kenya," *GCR2P Occasional Paper*, no. 4 (December 2013), 3; Roger Cohen, "How Kofi Annan Rescued Kenya," *The New York Review of Books* 55, no. 13 (14 August 2008), 51.

45 Boru Halakhe, "'R2P in Practice': Ethnic Violence, Elections and Atrocity Prevention in Kenya."

46 On the downside, those responsible for inciting atrocities in 2007–2008 were not held accountable for their actions, either domestically or at the International Criminal Court.

47 Evans, *The Responsibility to Protect*, 7, 17–18, 20.

48 "In Kigali, Ban Marks 20th Anniversary of Rwandan Genocide Urging Vigilance to Prevent Future Atrocities," *UN News*, 7 April 2014, https://news.un.org/en/story/2014/04/465562-kigali-ban-marks-20th-anniversary-rwandan-genocide-urging-vigilance-prevent.

2

REGIME CHANGE IN LIBYA

Contents

UN Secretary-General Ban Ki-moon made a surprise visit to Tripoli in October 2014.[1] It was his second brief trip to Libya since the country's dictator, Muammar al-Qaddafi, was overthrown and murdered three years earlier. The secretary-general flew into a country divided east and west between two parliaments, two governments and rival coalitions of aspiring warlords battling for control of Libya's major cities, resources and political destiny. He gave a speech emphasising the importance of peacebuilding, met some local politicians and then quickly departed for Gaza, where another seemingly intractable conflict awaited him.

Three and a half years earlier, in February 2011, Ban had spoken to Qaddafi on the phone for forty minutes from UN headquarters in New York while Libyan security forces shot down unarmed demonstrators. Ban condemned these actions as possible crimes against humanity and in an unusually emotive statement to reporters afterwards said that those 'responsible for brutally shedding the blood of innocents must be punished'. He focussed on the personal role of Qaddafi: 'I have strongly condemned, again and again, what he has done. It is totally unacceptable.' Ban emphasised that the Libyan government 'must meet its responsibility to protect its people' and that 'the violence must stop – immediately'.[2]

A few days later the UN Security Council unanimously condemned the violence in Libya. Then on 17 March the Council authorised 'all necessary measures' to protect Libyan civilians, and an international military intervention began. Almost a decade later, debate over the consequences of these events continues.

The Arab Spring

On 17 December 2010, a young fruit-and-vegetable seller named Mohamed Bouazizi set himself on fire in a desperate protest against bureaucratic indifference and police corruption in Tunisia. His gruesome death provoked a month of fierce anti-government protests, and on 14 January President Zine al-Abidine Ben Ali fled into exile, ending 23 years of dictatorial rule. Inspired by the Tunisian experience, mass demonstrations against the politically bankrupt regime of President Hosni Mubarak began soon after in Egypt. Within three weeks that popular revolt, focused around Cairo's Tahrir Square, succeeded in toppling Mubarak's thirty-year dictatorship. Sensing that a seismic shift in regional politics was now underway, protests erupted in Bahrain and Yemen. As popular movements for change radiated across the Middle East and North Africa, the question was not whether this 'Arab Spring' would continue but which repressive government would fall next.[3]

Qaddafi, who had ruled Libya since seizing power in a military coup in 1969, eyed these developments suspiciously. Despite his pretensions to creating a unique system of self-governing socialist people's committees, Libya remained under his firm, if eccentric, direction. In 1977 Qaddafi dramatically abolished the government and declared Libya to be a *jamahiriya* (state of the masses). Qaddafi continued only as the honorary, but unchallengeable, 'guide of the revolution'. Over the following four decades the ruling circle around Qaddafi remained tight and repressive, while the formation of opposition parties was outlawed under Law 71 of 1972 and punishable by death.[4]

Confrontations with a range of foreign powers made Libya a pariah by the mid-1980s, especially in the Western world. But in an extraordinary reversal of political fortunes, after giving up his weapons of mass destruction and restoring relations with several Western powers from December 2003 onwards, Qaddafi was actually courted as a North African buttress against al-Qaeda. During 2004, British prime minister Tony Blair and French president Jacques Chirac both visited Libya. Between October 2004 and the end of 2009 the European Union also granted €834.5 million worth of arms export licences to Libya.[5] Four decades after first taking power, Qaddafi still appeared in complete control of his country.

On Tuesday, 15 February 2011, just four days after Mubarak's resignation, protests began in Libya. An estimated 200 people gathered in front of police headquarters in Benghazi demanding the release of a well-known human rights lawyer, Fathi Terbil. People were injured as the demonstration was broken up by the security forces. When general protests against the government spread to other towns the following day, the security forces employed lethal force. Fourteen people were killed, and Libyan supporters of the Arab Spring, especially exiles overseas with better access to social media, issued the call for a 'Day of Rage' on 17 February. Despite text messages sent across the Libyan phone system warning that live ammunition would be used to disperse mobs, large demonstrations took place in at least four major cities, including Benghazi and Tripoli, on 17 February. Human Rights Watch estimated that 24 protesters were killed. The demonstrations then rapidly increased in scale and ferocity, evolving into a countrywide popular uprising.[6]

Although it was difficult to confirm all the terrifying and sensational reports coming out of Libya (Qaddafi had not allowed a free media in 40 years and was not about to now), people took to the streets in Benghazi, Bayda, Ajdabiya, Misrata and Zawiya. Some set fire to symbols of the regime, attacked police stations and stormed government buildings. Eyewitness accounts reported 'dozens' killed by security forces in Benghazi. It was credibly claimed that by 20 February, at least 173 people had been killed during four days of demonstrations across the country.[7]

About this time, the first shaky videos purportedly showing armed government supporters going door-to-door in Benghazi attacking suspected opponents of the Qaddafi regime were broadcast on international news networks. There were also stories of military aircraft flying low over mass protests in a menacing display of potential lethal violence. It was reported that three people had been killed in Tajoura, on the outskirts of Tripoli, when a fighter plane opened fire. Armed Qaddafi loyalists also patrolled Tripoli in pickup trucks, arresting or shooting at anyone suspected of public dissent.[8]

As the uprising spread, the Libyan police were forced out of Benghazi on 18 February and Misrata by 24 February. Towns across the east of the country began to slip completely from the government's control. Some protestors started arming themselves, and volunteer militias were formed across the east as the situation shifted inexorably from demonstration to armed insurrection.

On the night of Sunday, 20 February, Qaddafi's heir apparent, his son Saif al-Islam, appeared on television threatening that 'thousands' would die and 'rivers of blood' would flow if the rebellion did not stop. The next day two Libyan fighter jets landed in Malta, and their pilots alleged that they had been ordered to bomb Benghazi. Soon after, Qaddafi, speaking in Tripoli, called upon loyalists to 'get out of your houses' and attack all opponents of the regime. Invoking language that was reminiscent of the 1994 genocide in Rwanda, he described protesters as drug-crazed 'rats', 'cockroaches', 'cowards and traitors'. He left little doubt about his intentions, as he promised to 'cleanse Libya house by house' and ensure the country was 'purified' of rebels. Nor was an extensive knowledge of history required to understand Qaddafi's attempt to invoke Tiananmen Square as an example where national unity was revealed to be 'worth more than a small number of protesters'.[9]

Estimates of the number of civilians killed between 15 and 22 February vary. Residents of the Tajoura district east of Tripoli described bodies littering the streets. The International Commission of Inquiry that was mandated by the UN Human Rights Council received medical records regarding protesters shot dead in Tripoli, with doctors testifying that more than 200 bodies were brought into their morgues over 20–21 February alone. The International Criminal Court (ICC) in the Hague also later estimated that 500 to 700 civilians were killed during February, prior to the outbreak of civil war.[10]

Although a precise body count was impossible to obtain, by 22 February it was apparent that the Qaddafi regime, in its desperation to hold on to power, was determined to violently crush the uprising. Despite censorship, confusion, rumors and misinformation, the threat of mass atrocities was both imminent and real.

The UN Security Council responds

On 20 February the UN secretary-general, speaking to Qaddafi on the phone from New York, told him that the violence against civilians 'must stop immediately'. Unsurprisingly, Qaddafi did not heed Ban's counsel, but the diplomatic pressure on his regime intensified. In Geneva the UN High Commissioner for Human Rights, Navi Pillay, described the violence as possibly constituting 'crimes against humanity' and reminded members of the Human Rights Council – of which Libya, shamefully, was a member – of their responsibility to protect their people from atrocities. These sentiments were echoed in a joint statement by the UN special advisers on the prevention of genocide and the responsibility to protect. Meanwhile, the Arab League moved to ban Libya from attending its meetings, and the Organisation of the Islamic Conference condemned Qaddafi's actions. The African Union (AU) followed, with Jean Ping calling for an immediate end to the 'repression and violence'. Coordinated diplomatic action in New York and Geneva then resulted in Libya's suspension from the Human Rights Council.[11]

The main diplomatic battleground, however, was the UN Security Council. On the evening of Friday, 25 February, the UN secretary-general spoke to the Council. Hardeep Singh Puri, India's permanent representative and an elected member during 2011, has commented that by that stage, no one 'wanted to be heard or seen saying or doing anything that would give the appearance of defending' Qaddafi. The sentiment was reinforced when Libya's ambassador, Abdurrahman Mohamed Shalgham, also addressed the Council, invoking the ghosts of Pol Pot and Adolf Hitler before saying that Qaddafi intended to burn Libya to the ground if he could not rule it. Shalgham's public denunciation of Qaddafi made a powerful impression – not just because of the tears his emotional speech inspired amongst the Libyan diplomats sitting behind him, but because of who he was. Shalgham had been friends with Qaddafi since they were both young men and was one of the colonel's longest-surviving allies. Not long after Shalgham's speech, the entire Libyan diplomatic delegation to the UN defected.[12]

Resolution 1970, unanimously adopted by the UN Security Council on 26 February, the evening after Shalgham's speech, explicitly invoked the 'Libyan authorities' responsibility to protect its population'. The resolution included a comprehensive package of coercive measures – an arms embargo, asset freezes, travel bans and referral of the situation to the ICC – aimed at persuading the Qaddafi regime to stop killing its people. Puri has commented, 'the ICC referral was designed as a strong dose of medicine in the hope that more decisive action, in the form of use of force stipulated in Article 42, would not have to be invoked'.[13]

During the nineteen days between Resolution 1970 and the adoption of Resolution 1973 on 17 March, escalating violence prompted regional and international organisations to again urge Qaddafi to stop the killing and resolve the crisis through 'peaceful means and serious dialogue'. On 10 March the AU's Peace and Security Council established a High-Level Committee on Libya. On 12 March the Arab League called for a 'no-fly zone'.

But Qaddafi appeared not to be listening. By 16 March his forces were approaching the opposition stronghold of Benghazi and his son Saif al-Islam was quoted as saying the rebellion would 'be over in forty-eight hours'. Libyan television broadcast a message that the army was coming to Benghazi 'to cleanse your city from armed gangs'. Qaddafi senior also directly threatened the rebels on national radio and television, saying that the army was on its way and that it would 'show no mercy and no pity'.[14]

With Qaddafi's forces on the outskirts of Benghazi, the risk of a massacre seemed highly probable if the city fell. Urged on by the Arab League, ten UN Security Council members supported Resolution 1973 (Bosnia-Herzegovina, Colombia, France, Gabon, Lebanon, Nigeria, Portugal, South Africa, the United Kingdom and the United States) and five abstained (Brazil, China, Germany, India and Russia). All three African members of the UN Security Council voted in favor. Such a vote was entirely in keeping with Article 4(h) of the AU's Constitutive Act, which advocates a policy of 'non-indifference' rather than noninterference in the sovereign affairs of other states when crimes against humanity are involved.

In addition to deploring Libya's failure to comply with Resolution 1970, Resolution 1973 called for an immediate 'cease-fire and a complete end to violence and all attacks against, and abuses of, civilians'. It stressed the need 'to intensify efforts to find a solution to the crisis which responds to the legitimate demands of the Libyan people'. The text also authorised 'all necessary measures', including coercive military action but short of a 'foreign occupation force', in order to halt atrocities. Two scenarios were specifically identified: the protection of 'civilians and civilian populated areas under threat of attack' and the imposition of a 'ban on all flights in the airspace of the Libyan Arab Jamahiriya in order to help protect civilians'.[15]

It was notable that no member of the BRICS group – Brazil, Russia, India, China and South Africa – all of whom were on the Security Council at the time, opposed Resolution 1973. After the vote, Ambassador Vitaly Churkin emphasised that Russia 'was a consistent and firm advocate of the protection of the civilian population', and that for this reason Russia 'did not prevent the adoption of this resolution'. Ambassador Li Baodong similarly explained that while China had abstained, 'we support the Security Council's adoption of appropriate and necessary action to stabilize as soon as possible the situation in Libya and to halt acts of violence against civilians'. For at least one of those who voted, Ambassador Ivan Barbalić of Bosnia-Herzegovina, the UN's failure to stop past atrocities weighed heavily. He later commented that Benghazi could have potentially developed into 'a situation not unlike Srebrenica', had it been retaken by Qaddafi's forces.[16]

Those UN Security Council members who voted for Resolution 1973 understood that they were voting for air strikes to protect civilians. They did so because when protests began in Benghazi during February 2011, Qaddafi reverted to the things he knew best – inflammatory rhetoric mixed with deadly repression. Outside Libya, Qaddafi had no significant international allies who could pressure him to moderate his behavior. Inside Libya there were no restraints upon his decision-making. Although Libya was a country of six million people, one man had made a negotiated outcome to the deteriorating conflict next to impossible.

All necessary measures

Implementation of Resolution 1973 began on 19 March with a massive bombardment of Libyan air defenses and military hardware, with a particular focus on Qaddafi's forces outside Benghazi. Although the United States, United Kingdom and France initiated the operation, the NATO-led coalition assembled to enforce Resolution 1973 would eventually encompass eighteen states. Notably, four Arab countries – Qatar, Jordan, Morocco and the United Arab Emirates – made military contributions.[17]

In terms of the no-fly zone, Qaddafi did not have much of an air force to disable. He did, however, have tanks, heavy artillery and ground troops. Although estimates vary, the regular Libyan armed forces constituted approximately 100,000 personnel. Qaddafi, who had some personal experience of plotting a coup, deliberately kept the army weak. The exception was four well-resourced brigades directly linked to his tribe or to one of his sons, along with the internal security forces.[18]

Although Qaddafi's troops outside Benghazi were destroyed by NATO bombers, his remaining forces displayed considerable resilience. After retreating from Benghazi they were able to maintain control of most of the west of the country (with the notable exception of Misrata) and retake several towns that had recently ousted the security forces. Despite being targeted by NATO, Qaddafi's troops also continued to pose a threat to civilians. NATO claimed that on 20 April alone it destroyed twenty-five tanks belonging to pro-Qaddafi forces that were shelling civilian areas in Ajdabiya and Misrata.[19]

Military operations in Libya proceeded on the assumption that targeted air strikes would cause Qaddafi to abandon his 'cleansing' campaign. But Resolution 1973 also emphasised the need for a cease-fire and AU mediation. This was especially important to the South African and Indian delegations on the Security Council.[20] On 10 April, after air strikes had begun, an AU delegation that included the presidents of South Africa, Uganda, Congo-Brazzaville, Mali and Mauritania claimed to have secured Qaddafi's support for a 'road map' to end the conflict. The road map allegedly included a cease-fire and negotiations on political reform. However, the emerging political representatives of the rebellion in Benghazi, the self-styled National Transitional Council (NTC), rejected the initiative.

The NTC saw the African Union, whose secretariat received substantial funding from Libya, as protecting Qaddafi's interests. They were especially sceptical given that two members of the AU delegation – President Jacob Zuma of South Africa and President Yoweri Museveni of Uganda – had already publicly criticised the intervention. Museveni had written that while Qaddafi had made mistakes, he was a 'true nationalist', and that Museveni '[preferred] nationalists to puppets of foreign interests' – an inelegant stab at the opposition. Another delegate, President Mohamed Ould Abdel Aziz of Mauritania, came to power in a military coup in 2008 and had close ties to Qaddafi, who had cancelled Mauritania's $100 million debt. It was therefore hardly surprising that the NTC repeated its demand that Qaddafi and his family leave Libya as a precursor to peace talks.[21]

Although Qaddafi's gesture may have been empty, it should have been vigorously pursued. However, the concerns of the NTC were also valid. The fact that the AU delegation publicly referred to Qaddafi as 'Brother Leader' rankled, as did the fact that the most prominent member of the delegation, President Zuma, did not visit Benghazi, returning to South Africa after spending time with Qaddafi in Tripoli. It was later revealed that at Qaddafi's request Zuma also secretly took over $30 million (US) in cash home with him, illegally stashing it away in case Brother Leader needed funds for an ICC defense. Although this was not publicly known at the time, suspicions that Zuma was not a neutral mediator were clearly well founded.[22]

Most importantly, in Benghazi, the heart of the rebellion, the AU's criticism of 'regime change' did not sit comfortably with people whose lives were at risk if the regime survived. Allegations that Qaddafi was recruiting mercenaries from AU member states, especially Chad and Niger, also heightened suspicions. The AU delegation had been welcomed at Qaddafi's personal compound in Tripoli, but in Benghazi about a thousand protestors gathered outside their hotel. One woman was photographed with a placard that read, 'The people want to change the regime'.[23]

A diplomatic opportunity was possibly missed, but this was as much the AU's mistake as it was an error by those enforcing the UN's civilian protection mandate. While the AU delegation had announced Qaddafi's agreement to their road map, Qaddafi made no such public statement. His private commitment may have been genuine, but to the NTC it appeared to be a cynical delaying tactic. Crucially, despite the immediate cease-fire promised in the road map, even as the AU delegation checked into their hotel in Benghazi, Qaddafi's forces continued to shell the besieged city of Misrata.[24]

Over 8,000 sorties were eventually flown by the NATO-led alliance over Libya. NATO Secretary-General Anders Fogh Rasmussen later insisted, 'No comparable air campaign in history has been so accurate and so careful in avoiding harm to civilians'. But a later investigation by the UN's International Commission of Inquiry found that 60 civilians were accidentally killed in at least five aberrant NATO air strikes. While the commission declared, 'We are quite sure that NATO did not deliberately attack civilians', this was little solace for those who lost loved ones.[25]

The immediate objective of stopping Qaddafi's assault on Benghazi was easily achieved by the NATO-led alliance, and while the east of the country was under the control of rebels by the end of April, most of the west, including Tripoli, was still controlled by Qaddafi's forces. Meanwhile the Benghazi-based NTC was quickly transforming itself into an alternative government. Various civilian militias had slowly consolidated into a rebel army under the NTC's loose overall direction. Increasingly, any attempt by Qaddafi's forces to retake key towns and villages in the east was met by fearsome NATO air strikes in coordination with the defending rebels. By any measure, Libya was now in the midst of a full-blown civil war, in which the NATO-led alliance had clearly taken sides.

Atrocities continued. The UN's International Commission of Inquiry later concluded that 'crimes against humanity and war crimes' were committed by Qaddafi's forces, including acts of 'murder, enforced disappearance, and torture' that were 'perpetrated within the context of a widespread or systematic attack against a civilian population'.[26] In particular, the rebel-held western city of Misrata, home to half a million people, was subjected to a vicious siege by loyalist forces from mid-March until May.

Qaddafi's troops indiscriminately shelled Misrata with rockets, mortars and artillery. A hospital in the city was attacked and cluster munitions were fired into the el-Shawahda residential district. Loyalist snipers preyed upon civilians. In at least one case, Qaddafi's forces used civilians as a human shield to deter NATO attacks on their positions. There was a deliberate attempt to starve the civilian population and block humanitarian aid from reaching Misrata. There were also widespread allegations that loyalist forces were guilty of the 'murder, rape and sexual torture' of Misrata's residents. Doctors testified to 'military-sanctioned rape' of women and girls as young as fourteen. In all, more than 1,100 Misrata residents died as Qaddafi's forces besieged the city.[27]

Given the extensive nature of war crimes perpetrated in Misrata, it was clearly within the 'all necessary measures' mandate for NATO to attack Qaddafi's forces encircling the city. But as the duration of the Libya operation lengthened beyond all expectations, it became a battle of nerves between Qaddafi and NATO as much as between Qaddafi and the rebels. Military stalemate and de facto partition of Libya seemed like a distinct possibility. Meanwhile, international public support for the intervention withered.[28]

Far away from the front lines of Misrata, the battle to hold perpetrators of mass atrocity crimes legally responsible for their actions also continued. On 27 June an ICC arrest warrant was issued for Qaddafi, his son Saif al-Islam and the head of intelligence services, Abdullah al-Senussi, for alleged crimes against humanity committed since mid-February. Still, it was not until late May that the military momentum started to shift decisively in favor of the rebels, with NATO air support proving crucial. The rebels broke the siege of Misrata and started to advance on Tripoli. Intense fighting continued, but after six months the final collapse of Qaddafi's forces was rapid. On the night of 21 August, rebel forces were inside Tripoli.

Even as it became clear that all was lost, Qaddafi's forces continued to commit war crimes. On 23 August soldiers from the 32nd Brigade carried out a massacre of prisoners at a warehouse that had been used as a place of detention. More than 50 'civilians and combatants' were murdered by their guards in addition to an unknown number who had been tortured to death earlier. In the words of one investigative report, high-ranking military commanders were at the warehouse, ordered the massacre, and conspired to 'conceal and destroy evidence of their crimes'. Human Rights Watch documented similar atrocities in al-Qawalish, al-Khums and Bani Walid.[29]

Regime change

The fact that Resolution 1973 was adopted without a single negative vote on the Security Council reflected that even those with serious reservations about military intervention recognised that the world needed to act. Air strikes to halt the attacks of Qaddafi's forces on civilians in Benghazi, Misrata and elsewhere were therefore clearly justifiable under 'all necessary measures' in Resolution 1973. However, as the civil war became a war of attrition between Qaddafi's forces and armed rebels, other forms of military intervention appeared to violate the spirit of the UN Security Council mandate.

For example, despite an arms embargo under Resolution 1970, some countries provided sizeable quantities of weapons to the rebels. In June, France admitted to supplying assault rifles, rocket launchers and anti-tank missiles, arguing that such actions were both morally justifiable and within the parameters of Resolution 1973. Dwarfing the French contribution was that of Qatar, which allegedly supplied militias connected to the NTC with eighteen shipments amounting to 20,000 tons of weaponry.[30]

Other forms of support from key members of the NATO-led alliance included providing military advice during the final rebel offensive on Tripoli and Sirte. During August 2011 the *New York Times* reported that 'Britain, France and other nations deployed special forces on the ground inside Libya to help train and arm the rebels'.[31] Although not in direct violation of Resolution 1973, which only expressly forbade 'a foreign occupation force of any form on any part of Libyan territory', these countries were unquestionably intervening in Libya as partisans to the conflict. This was not in keeping with the spirit of the civilian protection mandate represented in Resolution 1973.

Although much of this support was only publicly admitted in late October, after the Qaddafi regime had collapsed, rumours and reports were circulating as early as June. Ambassador Puri of India commented that NATO's role had casually shifted from protecting civilians to enhancing the war-fighting capabilities of the rebels.[32] There was a growing perception that NATO was no longer acting as a defensive shield for populations at risk, but as the NTC's private air force.

Those who had advocated for Resolutions 1970 and 1973 faced growing criticisms that R2P had been co-opted by Western powers and a committed clique of armed rebels intent on overthrowing Qaddafi. The contrary argument was that while Qaddafi's forces had been engaged but not broken, they still constituted a grave threat to all civilians. But as the time lengthened and the focus of the intervention shifted, NATO members were left open to criticism regarding double standards and clandestine agendas. R2P was never intended to provide mood lighting for regime change.

US president Barack Obama was careful to stay on message, announcing on 21 March that, 'when it comes to our military action, we are doing so in support of United Nations Security Council Resolution 1973 that specifically talks about humanitarian efforts, and we are going to make sure that we stick to that mandate'.[33] But in a joint op-ed by President Obama, President Nicolas Sarkozy of France and Prime Minister David Cameron of the United Kingdom, published around the world on 15 April, these western leaders tried to have it both ways. After referring to the 'bloodbath' that had been prevented in Benghazi, the three leaders argued:

> Our duty and mandate under UN Security Council Resolution 1973 is to protect civilians, and we are doing that. It is not to remove Qaddafi by force. But it is impossible to imagine a future for Libya with Qaddafi in power. ... It is unthinkable that someone who has tried to massacre his own people can play a part in their future government. The brave citizens of those towns that have held out against forces that have been mercilessly targeting them would face a fearful vengeance if the world accepted such an arrangement. It would be an unconscionable betrayal.[34]

Where a government is the primary perpetrator of ongoing atrocities, regime change may sometimes be the only effective way to end the crimes. In this context, permanently disabling the capacity of the Qaddafi regime to harm its own people was seen by some as essential to discharging the mandate of civilian protection. Diplomatic motivations are always mixed, but the fact that the governments who concluded that Qaddafi had to be overthrown did not openly argue for this course of action was disingenuous. The result was a deep breach of trust between states leading the intervention and those who now saw the Libyan mission as having been hijacked and compromised.

Brazil and the responsibility while protecting

Following the fall of Tripoli, Libya's new leaders, having won a bitter civil war, faced enormous challenges. After forty-two years of dictatorship under Qaddafi, most public infrastructure had been damaged or destroyed, and whatever limited governmental bureaucracy that existed had collapsed. In addition, political divisions and regional interests conflicted with the NTC's stated desire to promote national reconciliation.

According to the NTC an estimated 12,000 Libyans, including soldiers from both the rebel and loyalist forces, were killed during the civil war.[35] One death, however, was especially notable. As Tripoli fell, Qaddafi and his entourage fled to Sirte. Qaddafi continued to denounce the rebels in messages broadcast via foreign media and retreated deeper into a fantasy world where he still believed he was the beloved leader of the Libyan people.[36] When rebels reached the center of Sirte on 20 October, Qaddafi made the fateful decision to flee in a convoy of vehicles. After being detected by NATO aircraft, his convoy was bombed, apparently without anyone realising Qaddafi was in one of the cars. Qaddafi survived but was wounded and disoriented. He then hid in a drainage pipe to avoid rebel soldiers. Upon discovery he was beaten and tortured before being executed. His corpse was then publicly displayed in Misrata as a trophy of war.

Although the UN, ICC and numerous human rights organisations would all call for an investigation into the execution of Qaddafi, within Libya there initially seemed to be little appetite for anything except rejoicing over his demise. Nevertheless, his treatment at the hands of his captors (recorded on smartphone and broadcast around the world) clearly constituted a war crime.[37]

While rebel forces had largely escaped critical scrutiny in the Western media during the civil war, international human rights organisations raised serious concerns about the conduct of some rebel units. Human Rights Watch reported, for example, on the situation in Tawergha, near Misrata, where rebels had taken reprisals against an entire town mainly comprised of black Africans who were collectively accused of siding with Qaddafi. The town of 30,000 people was depopulated and much of it put to flame.[38]

The UN's International Commission of Inquiry later concluded that anti-Qaddafi forces 'committed serious violations, including war crimes and breaches of international human rights law'. These crimes included 'unlawful killing, arbitrary arrest, torture, enforced disappearance, indiscriminate attacks and pillage'. A March 2012 report detailed ongoing attacks by anti-Qaddafi militias against former residents of Tawergha, but also noted that 'the significant difference between the past and the present is that those responsible for abuses now are committing them on an individual or unit level, and not as part of a system of brutality sanctioned by the central government'.[39]

The end of the civil war also led to a broader debate about the legitimacy of the intervention. Announcing the end of NATO's operation in late October, the alliance's secretary general, Anders Fogh Rasmussen, claimed that NATO-led forces had 'prevented a massacre and saved countless lives'. But Thabo Mbeki, former president of South Africa, argued that NATO members on the UN Security Council had actively 'blocked' the AU's attempts to peacefully resolve the conflict. The country's president, Jacob Zuma, went further, declaring in June that Resolution 1973 was 'being abused for regime change, political assassinations and foreign military occupation'. A softer, but more widely reported, critique came from former UN secretary-general Kofi Annan. Speaking at the University of Ottawa on 4 November, Annan expressed concern over the fact that 'regime change came up very quickly' in Libya.[40]

Like South Africa, Brazil was an elected member of the UN Security Council during 2011 and had voted for Resolution 1970. Unlike South Africa, it abstained on Resolution 1973. During November, Foreign Minister Antonio Patriota seized upon an opportunity to influence the post-Libya debate. Brazil published a short paper on the 'responsibility while protecting' (RwP) that was officially submitted to the UN secretary-general but was also quickly circulating amongst UN member states and nongovernmental organisations in New York.[41] In mid-December, Brazilian ambassador Maria Luiza Ribeiro Viotti convened a private luncheon for UN ambassadors to discuss a way forward. I was also invited, and I recall a particularly strident speech by Ambassador Puri insisting that RwP had enabled diplomats from the Global South to defend the concept of R2P from Western interventionists who now wanted to misuse it to promote armed rebellion and regime change.

The essence of RwP was that military force must be a last resort, that any response to atrocities must be proportional to the threat posed, that there needed to be increased Security Council accountability with regard to such operations and that no intervention should cause more harm than it seeks to prevent. As Brazilian academics Oliver Stuenkel and Marcos Tourinho argued, RwP was 'intended as an addendum (and not a substitute) to the concept of R2P', with its main champion being Patriota himself.[42]

One impact of Brazil's 'responsibility while protecting' was to resuscitate meaningful discussion at the UN around the need for prudential criteria for use-of-force mandates authorised by the Security Council. In various high-level reports, books and speeches, Gareth Evans, Australia's former foreign minister and a cochair of the international commission that developed R2P, had proposed five such criteria:

1. *Seriousness of harm.* Is the threat clear and extreme enough to justify military force?
2. *Proper purpose.* Is the central purpose to halt or avert the threat, despite 'whatever other purposes or motives may be involved?'
3. *Last resort.* Has every reasonable non-military option been explored?
4. *Proportional means.* Are the scale, duration and intensity of military action the minimum necessary?
5. *Balance of consequences.* Is there a reasonable chance of success in averting the threat without worsening the situation? Is action preferable to inaction?[43]

Over the course of 2012, Evans constantly argued that the Libya intervention had initially met all five criteria, but that as the civil war dragged on, the mission's proper purpose had been corrupted along with its proportional means. In short, in Libya the interveners slid from civilian protection into regime change by stealth.

Evans and Patriota both insisted (often quoting each other) that the principles inherent in the responsibility while protecting presented a means to reestablish diplomatic consensus around R2P and clarify the future parameters of any UN-sanctioned use of force to halt atrocities. Or as Evans put at it at a private seminar in Brazil that Patriota presided over:

> It is not a matter of satisfying a court of law about any of these guidelines. ... The courts in question are of rationality, public opinion, and peer group understanding – and if a strong, credible and articulate case cannot be publicly made and defended under all five of the headings I have mentioned, then scepticism and cynicism about the proposed use of force in any particular case is likely to be justified.[44]

RwP dominated diplomatic conversations during 2012 and refocussed the post-Libya debate around the centrality of prevention, rather than armed intervention, to R2P.

Amongst some supporters of R2P there was scepticism about Brazil's intentions. The Libya intervention began just as I was taking over as executive director of the Global Centre and moving to New York. I recall how excited I was to visit the White House executive offices for the first time and politically engage with Samantha Power and other staff from the National Security Council who were working on mass atrocity prevention and human rights. I admired Power, but I recall a passionate disagreement between her and Evans about whether Brazil's RwP critique was legitimate or just an attempt to discredit the Western powers that had led the Libyan intervention.[45]

Although Brazil would allow the RwP discussion to subside after Patriota resigned as foreign minister in August 2013, two Brazilian academics would later praise it as 'an innovative and constructive proposal to strengthen the Security Council and bridge the gap between an overly trigger-happy NATO and excessively resistant China and Russia'.[46]

The responsibility to rebuild

Six months after the civil war ended, Gallup conducted an opinion poll of Libyans' view of the intervention in their country. Not only did seventy-five percent of surveyed Libyans approve of the NATO-led intervention, seventy-seven percent hoped that 'Western societies' would soon send 'governance experts' to help rebuild their country.[47] However, ignoring the lessons of Timor-Leste and other states emerging from civil war, the biggest failure in Libya was not the UN Security Council's willingness to intervene but its determination to withdraw as quickly as possible. With rival militias enthusiastic to see the back of the UN, Libyans were left to sort out the post-Qaddafi mess amongst themselves. Political infighting, pervasive insecurity and warlordism were the result.

In New York, the UN Security Council continued to receive periodic updates on Libya's progress. During October 2011, March 2012 and March 2013 the Council reviewed the situation in the country and renewed the mandate of the small UN Support Mission in Libya (UNSMIL). It also adopted resolutions emphasising 'the Libyan authorities' primary responsibility for the protection of Libya's population'.[48] However, with a civil war now tearing Syria apart, a burgeoning Islamist insurgency in Mali (fueled in part by illicit arms from Libya) and other emerging crises, Libya became a marginal concern.

As the world focused its attention elsewhere, a deepening schism between former allies in the struggle against Qaddafi destroyed any chance of consolidating a stable government in Tripoli. In July 2012 Libya held its first parliamentary election in four decades, with a diverse array of political voices elected to the General National Congress (GNC). Although many foreign journalists were surprised by the fact that Islamist parties won only a quarter of the seats in the GNC, the parliament continued to be plagued by factionalism. Real power continued to lie with thousands of heavily armed former rebels from literally hundreds of rival militias competing for territory, influence and power.

This internecine struggle was increasingly perceived as a battle between allied Islamist forces (of which powerful militias from Misrata were the leading element) and 'moderate' forces (the Zintan militias and their allies). But Libyan politics was not only a struggle between shifting alliances of rival militias, it was overlaid with tribal affiliations and a multitude of personal, political and communal enmities. Growing lawlessness, banditry and an enhanced terrorist threat (including the deadly September 2012 attack on the United States diplomatic compound in Benghazi) contributed to the view of many foreign observers that post-Qaddafi Libya had become a lawless wasteland.

This is the context within which Operation Dignity was launched by a former Libyan military commander, Khalifa Haftar, in May 2014. His military campaign was initially directed against the conveniently vague target of 'terrorism' and the more specific control exerted by Islamist militias in Benghazi. Amidst renewed fighting, elections to the new House of Representatives, which would replace the GNC, were held on 25 June. Just two years earlier, approximately 1.7 million Libyans had participated in a historic election, but in 2014 only 630,000 registered voters exercised their franchise.[49]

Islamist parties fared even worse in the 2014 elections than they had in 2012. In the aftermath of the vote, several influential Islamist militias and their political allies refused to accept the new House of Representatives and the newly formed government. These militias then launched operation Libya Dawn during July to counter Haftar's Operation Dignity and take control of the country. According to the UN, by December there were at least 393,000 people internally displaced by renewed fighting, with an additional 100,000 taking refuge in neighboring countries. Rival armed groups indiscriminately shelled residential areas and attacked medical facilities and schools. Divisions that had been suppressed since the beginning of the anti-Qaddafi rebellion were now used to mobilise for war.[50]

Despite the new government's attempt to rule Libya from a run-down hotel in Tobruk, the country remained militarily and politically divided between east and west. To make matters worse, the conflict also became part of a broader struggle for influence across the Middle East and North Africa. Egypt and the United Arab Emirates supported the Tobruk-based government, while Sudan, Turkey and Qatar were allegedly backing the rump GNC in Tripoli. Attempts by UNSMIL to reconcile the warring parliaments, governments and militias remained inchoate until 2016, when a UN-backed Government of National Accord was finally established in Tripoli. A partial political reunion of the country was also made possible by the emergence of a new enemy – the so-called Islamic State of Iraq and the Levant (ISIL), which established outposts in Derna and Sirte.

Despite some political progress, Libya remained broken. On 4 April 2019, the country's preeminent warlord, Field Marshal Khalifa Haftar, ordered his self-proclaimed Libyan National Army to launch a military offensive against the UN-recognised Government of National Accord in Tripoli. As of mid-2020 the government remains intact, but the armed conflict continues.

Conclusion

In March 2011, for the first time in history, R2P was invoked by the UN Security Council in imposing coercive military measures against a UN member state without its consent. It is no surprise, therefore, that the nature and conduct of the Libya intervention continue to be subjected to forensic analysis. But neither the ferocity of the debate nor the misery caused by the ongoing crisis in post-Qaddafi Libya should distract us from the fact that Resolutions 1970 and 1973 constituted an appropriate and timely response to a situation where mass atrocities were occurring and the threat of further escalation was imminent. The problem was in the disputed implementation of the mandate. And while we should not cringe from debating the meaning of the 2011 Libya intervention and its unintended consequences, we should also not lose sight of how and why the Libyan intervention happened in the first place.

I recall speaking at an event in Thailand in 2012 alongside the then UN special adviser for R2P, Edward Luck. Afterwards someone in the crowd approached me. Jamal was working in Benghazi in March 2011 and was in a café when Qaddafi announced that the army would enter Benghazi that night and would 'show no mercy'.[51] He told me that as the message kept being broadcast again and again, fearful men stood around talking softly to one another, realising that this might be the last night of their lives. People were calm, Jamal said, but one by one his friends all said goodbye to one another, embraced and headed home to be with their families. People were resigned to the fact that the imminent arrival of Qaddafi's troops meant that many of them would possibly die. Qaddafi, they believed, would wreak a terrible vengeance upon Benghazi for its insubordination. Instead, the NATO intervention began early the next morning.

The real lesson of Libya is that we need timely and carefully calibrated reactions to all mass atrocity situations. Clarity of purpose, proportionality and precision remain essential. In this sense, perhaps the last word is best left to the then UN secretary-general, Ban Ki-moon, discussing Libya behind closed doors at a ministerial meeting in New York during September 2011. Facing a table of foreign ministers from around the world, including several who had voiced their skepticism regarding R2P in the aftermath of Libya, he argued, 'I would far prefer the growing pains of an idea whose time has come to sterile debates about principles that are never put into practice'.[52]

That same week, at the opening of the sixty-sixth UN General Assembly, Syria's foreign minister declared that in confronting mass protests and the 'blatant conspiracies' of foreigners, his own government had 'exercised its responsibility to protect its citizens'.[53] Ironically, in invoking the language of R2P he paid a backhanded compliment to the strength of the emerging norm, despite the political blowback from Libya. However, the UN Security Council's inability to adequately respond to atrocities in Syria proved to be an even greater crucible than the overthrow of Qaddafi, providing the UN with its greatest diplomatic failure since the genocides in Rwanda and Srebrenica.

Notes

1 This chapter draws upon earlier work originally published as Simon Adams, "Libya and the Responsibility to Protect," *GCR2P Occasional Paper*, no. 3 (October 2012), https://reliefweb.int/sites/reliefweb.int/files/resources/libyaandr2poccasionalpaper-1.pdf.

2 "Ban Strongly Condemns Qadhafi's Actions Against Protesters, Calls for Punishment," *UN News*, 23 February 2011, https://news.un.org/en/story/2011/02/367342-ban-strongly-condemns-qadhafis-actions-against-protesters-calls-punishment.

3 In Egypt, military rule was reinstalled in 2013. In Yemen the transition collapsed into a civil war, resulting in a Saudi Arabia–led military intervention in 2015. Only in Tunisia has the democratic revolution held together.

4 Matthew Weaver, "Muammar Gaddafi Condemns Tunisia Uprising," *The Guardian*, 16 January 2011; and Ronald Bruce St. John, *Libya: From Colony to Independence* (London: Oneworld Publications, 2008), 221–224.

5 Ibid, 241; "EU Arms Exports to Libya: Who Armed Gaddafi?," *The Guardian*, 2 March 2011; and Dirk Vandewalle, *A History of Modern Libya* (Cambridge, UK: Cambridge University Press, 2012), 114–116, 152–161, 186, 192.

6 Human Rights Watch, "Libya: Security Forces Fire on 'Day of Anger' Demonstrations," 17 February 2011, http://www.hrw.org/news/2011/02/17/libya-security-forces-fire-day-anger-demonstrations; and "'Day of Rage' Kicks Off in Libya," *Al Jazeera*, 17 February 2011, http://www.aljazeera.com/news/africa/2011/02/201121755057219793.html.

7 Nick Meo, "Libya Protests: 140 'Massacred' as Gaddafi Sends in Snipers to Crush Dissent," *The Telegraph (UK)*, 20 February 2011, http://www.telegraph.co.uk/news/worldnews/africaandindianocean/libya/8335934/Libya-protests-140-massacred-as-Gaddafi-sends-in-snipers-to-crush-dissent.html; Angelique Chrisafis, "Libya Protests: 'Now We've Seen the Blood Our Fears Have Gone,'" *The Guardian*, 21 February 2011; Human Rights Watch, "Security Forces Kill 84 Over Three Days," 18 February 2011, http://www.hrw.org/news/2011/02/18/libya-security-forces-kill-84-over-three-days; and Human Rights Watch, "Governments Should Demand End to Unlawful

Killings," 20 February 2011, http://www.hrw.org/news/2011/02/20/libya-governments-should-demand-end-unlawful-killings.

8 Meo, "Libya protests: 140 'massacred' as Gaddafi sends in snipers to crush dissent"; Chrisafis, "Libya protests: 'Now we've seen the blood our fears have gone'"; and "Libya protests spread and intensify," *Al Jazeera*, 21 February 2011, http://www.aljazeera.com/news/africa/2011/02/2011221133557377576.htmlal-Jazeera.

9 Vivienne Walt, "Gaddafi's Son: Last Gasp of Libya's Dying Regime?," *Time*, 21 February 2011, http://www.time.com/time/world/article/0,8599,2052842,00.html; "Moammar Gaddafi Clings to Power in Libya, Protests Continue," *Washington Post*, 22 February 2011; and "Libya Protests: Defiant Gaddafi Refuses to Quit," *BBC News*, 22 February 2011, http://www.bbc.co.uk/news/world-middle-east-12544624.

10 International Criminal Court – Office of the Prosecutor, First Report of the Prosecutor of the International Criminal Court to the UN Security Council Pursuant to UNSCR 1970 (2011), 4 May 2011; "Fresh Violence Rages in Libya," *Al Jazeera*, 22 February 2011, http://www.aljazeera.com/news/africa/2011/02/201122261251456133.html; "Libya Protests: Defiant Gaddafi Refuses to Quit," *BBC News*; James Downie, "When Numbers Lie: Why Isn't There an Accurate Death Toll in Libya?," *The New Republic*, 1 April 2011, http://www.tnr.com/article/world/86090/libya-death-toll-war-qadaffi.

11 UN General Assembly Resolution 65/265, A/RES/65/265, 1 March 2011, http://daccess-dds-ny.un.org/doc/UNDOC/GEN/N10/528/44/PDF/N1052844.pdf?OpenElement; and "UN Secretary-General's Special Adviser on the Prevention of Genocide, Francis Deng, and Special Adviser on the Responsibility to Protect, Edward Luck, on the Situation in Libya," *UN Press Release*, 22 February 2011, http://www.un.org/en/preventgenocide/adviser/pdf/OSAPG,%20Special%20Advisers%20Statement%20on%20Libya,%2022%20February%202011.pdf; "Libya: African Union Condemns Libya Crackdown," *Radio France International*, 24 February 2011, http://allafrica.com/stories/201102241041.html; Secretary-General's Remarks to United Nations Security Council Meeting on Peace and Security in Africa, New York, 25 February 2011, http://www.un.org/apps/news/infocus/sgspeeches/search_full.asp?statID=1095; Statement by Navi Pillay, United Nations High Commissioner for Human Rights, Human Rights Council, 15th Special Session, Geneva, 25 February 2011, http://www.ohchr.org/EN/NewsEvents/Pages/DisplayNews.aspx?NewsID=10760&LnglI.

12 Hardeep Singh Puri, *Perilous Interventions: The Security Council and the Politics of Chaos* (New York: HarperCollins, 2016), 62, 65–66, 68.

13 Ibid, 68–72, 78–93.

14 David Usborne, "'This Will Be All Over in 48 Hours:' Gaddafi's Son Vows to Crush Revolution," *The Independent (UK)*, 17 March 2011; "Gaddafi Tells Benghazi His Army Is Coming Tonight," *Al Arabiya News*, 17 March 2011, http://www.alarabiya.net/articles/2011/03/17/141999.html.

15 United Nations Security Council Resolution 1973, S/RES/1973, 17 March 2011, https://www.un.org/securitycouncil/s/res/1973-%282011%29.

16 The Barbalić quote is from an event hosted by the Global Centre for the Responsibility to Protect, New York, 28 November 2011. Quotes regarding China and Russia's position on Libya from Alex J. Bellamy, *The Responsibility to Protect: A Defense* (Oxford, UK: Oxford University Press, 2015), 97. A record of the various Security Council members' explanation of their vote on Resolution 1973 is also available at UN Doc. S/PV.6498, 17 March 2011, https://www.securitycouncilreport.org/atf/cf/%7B65BFCF9B-6D27-4E9C-8CD3-CF6E4FF96FF9%7D/Libya%20S%20PV%206498.pdf.

17 Ivo H. Daalder and James G. Stavridis, "NATO's Success in Libya," *New York Times*, 30 October 2011.

18 Report of the International Commission of Inquiry on Libya (Advance Unedited

Version), United Nations Human Rights Council, A/HRC/19/68, 8 March 2012, 46–49.

19 Kareem Fahim, "With Confidence and Skittishness, Libyan Rebels Renew Charge," *New York Times*, 20 March 2011; Harriet Sherwood and Chris McGreal, "Libya: Gaddafi Has Accepted Roadmap to Peace Says Zuma," *The Guardian*, 10 April 2011.

20 Puri, *Perilous Interventions*, 92.

21 "Libya: Gaddafi has accepted roadmap to peace says Zuma"; Simon Denyer and Leila Fadel, "Gaddafi Accepts African Union's Road Map for Peace," *Washington Post*, 10 April 2011; Jason Straziuso, "Uganda Says It Would Welcome Libya's Gadhafi," *Boston Herald*, 30 March 2011; and Simon Tisdall, "Gaddafi Figures Prominently on the Roadmap for Peace," *The Guardian*, 11 April 2011.

22 Max Du Plessis, "Gaddafi's Money and the Prospects of Accountability: Zuma Exposes Not Just Himself, but South Africa Too," *Daily Maverick*, 10 April 2019, https://www.dailymaverick.co.za/article/2019-04-10-gaddafis-money-and-the-prospects-of-accountability-zuma-exposes-not-just-himself-but-south-africa-too/; "Gaddafi's Stolen Loot May Have Been Hidden in Nkandla," *Business Insider SA*, 7 April 2019, https://www.businessinsider.co.za/gaddafi-money-in-south-africa-2019-4; "Parties Call for Probe into Claims Zuma Kept 'Gaddafi Millions' at Nkandla," *IOL News*, 8 April 2019, https://www.iol.co.za/news/politics/parties-call-for-probe-into-claims-zuma-kept-gaddafi-millions-at-nkandla-20784056.

23 Dan Murphy, "Why the African Union Road Map for Libya is Unlikely to Go Anywhere," *Christian Science Monitor*, 11 April 2011, http://www.csmonitor.com/World/Backchannels/2011/0411/Why-the-African-Union-road-map-for-Libya-is-unlikely-to-go-anywhere.

24 Ibid.

25 Report of the International Commission of Inquiry on Libya (Advance Unedited Version), United Nations Human Rights Council, A/HRC/19/68, 8 March 2012, 2, 20–21; Colum Lynch, "UN Report: Human Rights Abuses Continue in Libya," *Washington Post*, 2 March 2012; NATO, "Press Briefing on Libya," 21 June 2011, http://www.nato.int/cps/en/natolive/opinions_75652.htm; "Counting the Cost of NATO's Mission in Libya," *BBC News*, 31 October 2011, http://www.bbc.co.uk/news/world-africa-15528984; Ian Davis, "How Good Is NATO after Libya," *NATO Watch Briefing* Paper, no.20, 8 September 2011, http://www.natowatch.org/sites/default/files/Briefing_Paper_No.20_NATO_After_Libya.pdf; C.J. Chivers and Eric Schmitt, "In Strikes on Libya by NATO, an Unspoken Civilian Toll," *New York Times*, 17 December 2011.

26 Report of the International Commission of Inquiry on Libya (Advance Unedited Version), United Nations Human Rights Council, A/HRC/19/68, 8 March 2012, 1.

27 Ibid, 18–19, 160–163, 185, 186; Physicians for Human Rights, "Witness to War Crimes: Evidence from Misrata, Libya," August 2011, http://physiciansforhumanrights.org/library/reports/witness-to-war-crimes.html; Human Rights Watch, "Indiscriminate Attacks Kill Civilians," 17 April 2011, http://www.hrw.org/news/2011/04/17/libya-indiscriminate-attacks-kill-civilians; Tarik Kafala, "'Cleansed' Libyan Town Spills Its Terrible Secrets," *BBC News*, 12 December 2011, http://www.bbc.co.uk/news/magazine-16051349; Human Rights Watch, "Cluster Munitions Strike Misrata," 15 April 2011, http://www.hrw.org/en/news/2011/04/15/libya-cluster-munitions-strike-misrata.

28 In the United States in late March, the percentage of 'likely voters' who supported the intervention was forty-six percent; by August it was down to twenty-four percent. Andrew C. Miller and Paul B. Stares, "How New Atrocity-Prevention Steps Can Work," Expert Brief – Council on Foreign Relations, 15 August 2011, www.cfr.org/conflict-prevention/.

29 Physicians for Human Rights, "32nd Brigade Massacre: Evidence of war crimes and the

need to ensure justice and accountability in Libya," December 2011, http://physiciansforhumanrights.org/library/reports/32nd-brigade-massacre.html; Report of the International Commission of Inquiry on Libya (Advance Unedited Version), United Nations Human Rights Council, A/HRC/19/68, 8 March 2012, 9–11; Human Rights Watch, "Libya: Halt Exhumations of Mass Graves," 22 September 2011, http://www.hrw.org/news/2011/09/22/libya-halt-exhumations-mass-graves.

30 Louis Charbonneau and Hamuda Hassan, "France defends arms airlift to Libyan rebels," *Reuters*, 30 June 2011, http://in.reuters.com/article/2011/06/30/idININdia-58000920110630; "Update 1-NATO: not involved in French arms aid to Libya rebels," *Reuters*, 30 June 2011, http://af.reuters.com/article/libyaNews/idAFLDE75T0TD20110630; Sam Dagher, Charles Levinson, and Margaret Coker, "Tiny Kingdom's Huge Role in Libya Draws Concern," *The Wall Street Journal*, 21 October 2011.

31 Eric Schmitt and Steven Lee Myers, "Surveillance and Coordination With NATO Aided Rebels," *New York Times*, 21 August 2011; and "Qatar Admits It Had Boots on the Ground in Libya: NTC Seeks Further NATO Help," *Al Arabiya News*, 26 October 2011, http://www.alarabiya.net/articles/2011/10/26/173833.html.

32 Barbara Plett, "UN Security Council Middle Powers' Arab Spring Dilemma," *BBC News*, 7 November 2011, http://www.bbc.co.uk/news/world-middle-east-15628006.

33 Jesse Lee, "President Obama Answers Questions on Libya: 'A Testament to the Men and Women in Uniform,'" *The White House Blog*, 21 March 2011, https://obamawhitehouse.archives.gov/blog/2011/03/21/president-obama-answers-questions-libya-testament-men-and-women-uniform

34 "Joint op-ed by President Obama, Prime Minister Cameron and President Sarkozy: 'Libya's Pathway to Peace'," *White House Press Release*, 14 April 2011, http://www.whitehouse.gov/the-press-office/2011/04/14/joint-op-ed-president-obama-prime-minister-cameron-and-president-sarkozy.

35 Ian Black, "Libya Revolution Casualties Lower than Expected, Says New Government," *The Guardian*, 8 January 2013.

36 Kareem Fahim, "In His Last Days, Qaddafi Wearied of Fugitive's Life," *New York Times*, 22 October 2011.

37 "ICC Prosecutor: Concerns over Gaddafi's Death," *Al Jazeera*, 16 December 2011, http://www.aljazeera.com/news/africa/2011/12/2011121653911503123.html.

38 Human Rights Watch, "Libya: Militia's Terrorizing Residents of 'Loyalist' Town," 30 October 2011, http://www.hrw.org/news/2011/10/30/libya-militias-terrorizing-residents-loyalist-town; Amnesty International, "The Battle for Libya: Killings, Disappearances and Torture," 13 September 2011, http://www.amnesty.org/en/library/asset/MDE19/025/2011/en/8f2e1c49-8f43-46d3-917d-383c17d36377/mde190252011en.pdf; and Human Rights Watch, "Libya: Apparent Execution of 53 Gaddafi Supporters," 23 October 2011, http://www.hrw.org/news/2011/10/24/libya-apparent-execution-53-gaddafi-supporters.

39 Report of the International Commission of Inquiry on Libya (Advance Unedited Version), United Nations Human Rights Council, A/HRC/19/68, 8 March 2012, 1-2, 15–16, 44, 87, 128–136, 141, 148–149, 156.

40 "Nato Chief Rasmussen 'Proud' as Libya Mission Ends," *BBC News*, 31 October 2011, http://www.bbc.co.uk/news/mobile/world-africa-15516795; "Mbeki: We Should Learn from Libya's Experiences," *Mail & Guardian Online*, 5 November 2011, http://mg.co.za/article/2011-11-05-mbeki-we-should-learn-from-libyas-experiences/; Mike Blanchfield, "Don't Fear Islamic Resurgence from Arab Spring, Former UN Chief Tells Students," *The Globe and Mail*, 4 November 2011.

41 Letter dated 9 November 2011 from the Permanent Representative of Brazil to the United Nations addressed to the Secretary-General, A/66/551-S/2011/701, https://www.globalr2p.org/wp-content/uploads/2020/06/2011-RWP-Concept-Paper.pdf.

42 Oliver Stuenkel and Marcos Tourinho, "Regulating Intervention: Brazil and the Responsibility to Protect," *Conflict, Security & Development* 14, no. 4 (2014): 391.

43 For a more detailed explanation of the criteria, see Gareth Evans, *The Responsibility to Protect: Ending Mass Atrocity Crimes Once and For All* (Washington, DC: Brookings Institution Press, 2008), 139–147.

44 Gareth Evans, "R2P and RWP after Libya and Syria," *GCR2P/FGV/Stanley Foundation Workshop, Responsibility While Protecting: What's Next?*, Rio de Janeiro, 23 August 2012, http://www.gevans.org/speeches/speech485.html.

45 Power's most recent book provides an account of how the Obama administration debated how to respond to atrocities in Libya. Samantha Power, *The Education of An Idealist: A Memoir* (New York: Dey St, 2019), 289–311.

46 Stuenkel & Tourinho, "Regulating Intervention: Brazil and the Responsibility to Protect," 397.

47 Gallup Opinion Briefing: Libyans Eye New Relations With the West, 13 August 2012, https://news.gallup.com/poll/156539/opinion-briefing-libyans-eye-new-relations-west.aspx.

48 Global Centre for the Responsibility to Protect – UN Security Council Resolutions Referencing R2P, http://www.globalr2p.org/resources/335.

49 "Libyan Elections: Low Turnout Marks Bid to End Political Crisis," *BBC News*, 26 June 2014, https://www.bbc.com/news/world-africa-28005801.

50 UN Support Mission for Libya and Office of the High Commissioner for Human Rights, Update on Violations of International Human Rights and Humanitarian Law During the Ongoing Violence in Libya, 23 December 2014, https://www.ohchr.org/Documents/Countries/LY/UNSMIL_OHCHRJointly_report_Libya_23.12.14.pdf.

51 Name changed.

52 I was present at the meeting and took notes. See also, Remarks by UN Secretary-General Ban ki Moon at Breakfast Roundtable with Foreign Ministers on "The Responsibility to Protect: Responding to Imminent Threats of Mass Atrocities," 23 September 2011, https://www.un.org/sg/en/content/sg/speeches/2011-09-23/remarks-breakfast-roundtable-foreign-ministers-responsibility-protect.

53 "At UN, Syria Warns of 'Blatant Conspiracies' from Outsiders Against Its People," *UN News*, 26 September 2011, http://www.un.org/apps/news/story.asp?NewsID=39802&Cr=syria&Cr1.

3

MOMENTS ON THE MARGINS OF SYRIA'S CIVIL WAR

Contents

On the sidelines of the 2017 United Nations General Assembly in New York – that one week of the year when world leaders converge on the metropolis for a global festival of diplomacy and bloviation – I finally caught up with a Syrian friend whom I had never met before. I was originally introduced to Amir online.[1] At the time the forces of Syrian president Bashar al-Assad were intensifying their siege of eastern Aleppo, and my organisation was in touch with a few contacts who were still inside the city. We would use their information in our advocacy with the UN Security Council and to counter claims by the Syrian and Russian governments that they were simply killing terrorists, rather than conducting a merciless bombing campaign against besieged civilians in Syria's largest city.

Amir was a member of the Syria Civil Defence, a group commonly known as the 'White Helmets,' whose volunteers were spending their days pulling wounded civilians and mangled corpses from under the rubble of buildings destroyed by air strikes. The slogan of the White Helmets was a verse from the Quran: 'to save a life is to save all of humanity'. It was a slogan made all the more poignant by the fact that while the group had rescued thousands of Syrians, more than 150 White Helmets had been killed since 2013.

I was first introduced to some of the White Helmets, including Khaled Omar Harrah, at a meeting at the United Nations in 2014. It was Khaled Omar who had rescued the 'miracle baby' from an Aleppo building bombed by Syrian government forces a few months earlier. After working for a dozen hours to clear away rubble and dig towards an injured infant trapped between two collapsed concrete slabs, Khaled was able to free tiny Mahmoud, who was only ten days old. Khaled then lay on his back, cradling the crying baby in his arms. YouTube videos of that moment have been viewed millions of times by people around the world. It made Khaled and the White Helmets famous.

It was during 2016 that someone put me in contact with Amir. He was also from Aleppo, was in his early twenties and had been taking photographs of the work of his fellow White Helmets. On 23 September, Syrian government forces, backed by the Russian air force, launched a major offensive against rebel-held eastern Aleppo. The UN International Commission of Inquiry later reported that there were at least twenty-eight air strikes on Aleppo that day and that approximately '300 people – including 96 children – were killed in the first four days of the offensive alone'.[2] I texted Amir on 24 September and asked what the situation was like inside the besieged city. Amir responded in English: 'Thank you my friend. Aleppo go to death. If the aircrafts still targeting the city like yesterday all people in Aleppo will be killed.'

The next morning the UN Security Council held an emergency session to discuss Aleppo. It was 9:53 am in New York and early evening in Syria when I texted Amir again for an update. He texted back that there were 'a lot of airstrikes in Aleppo today' by 'both Assad and Russian helicopters and aircrafts'. According to Amir and others, there were more than sixty air strikes on 25 September, killing thirty civilians and wounding eighty people. Amir told me that the bombs dropped that day included cluster munitions, which are banned under international law.[3]

A day later, 26 September, the *New York Times* reported on Aleppo. The English grammar was more precise than Amir's, but the sense of catastrophe was similar:

> Undeterred and infuriated by Western accusations of war crimes and barbarity in the aerial assault on Aleppo, the Syrian government and its ally Russia intensively bombed the city in northern Syria on Monday for the fourth consecutive day. Residents and rescuers there described the bombardment as among the worst yet in the five-year war.[4]

Approximately a hundred civilians were being killed, mutilated or maimed every day in air strikes. The dead and wounded included many children, some of whom were filmed being carried into a local hospital covered in masonry dust. Adult victims lay nearby on a blood-smeared and dirty floor receiving rudimentary treatment.

That day at 2:16 pm I texted Amir again: 'I am being interviewed on French TV shortly to discuss Aleppo. Any update?' Forty minutes later, after not hearing anything, I texted once more: 'I'm praying you are ok.' Twenty-one minutes later Amir let me know he was alive and texted, 'thank you my friend'.

Not long after that I got my first message from Amir in Istanbul. He had not joined the 2.5 million Syrian refugees who had fled to Turkey, but was sent there by the White Helmets. Although this enabled him to escape Aleppo's death throes, he was far from safe. Working for the White Helmets, he would continue to cross the porous border between Syria and Turkey over the following months.

I continued to check in with Amir. We texted about air strikes and refugees, but also regarding a short documentary about the White Helmets winning an

Oscar. And then in September 2017 we finally got to meet in person when another extraordinary documentary about Syria's civil war was shown at an event hosted by the German government during the UN General Assembly. The film follows Khaled Omar during the months leading up to his death. Amir was due to speak at the event on behalf of the White Helmets. I was asked to speak on behalf of those who had failed to get the Security Council to uphold its responsibility to protect the people of Syria.

I watched *Last Men in Aleppo* knowing how it was going to end: Aleppo would fall, and after years of running towards danger, Khaled Omar would be killed in August 2016 while trying to rescue civilians from yet another air strike.

On the day of the UN event, Amir spotted me in the mingling crowd of diplomats, UN bureaucrats and human rights activists. I enthusiastically welcomed him to New York and we embraced. In an ugly armed conflict that had killed so many Syrians, I had invested an unreasonable amount of hope in his personal survival.

If the Second World War was the first armed conflict to be filmed and widely viewed by the general public via movie newsreels, and Vietnam was the first nightly televised war, then Syria is the first major war to be exhaustively documented on iPhones and watched by millions of people on YouTube, Facebook and Twitter. Amir was not only a witness to that war, he was a digital chronicler of his people's suffering. He had worked on *Last Men in Aleppo*, and by focussing on the everyday heroism of the White Helmets the film undermined attempts by the Russian and Syrian governments to portray the rescuers as terrorist fanatics.[5]

For me, *Last Men in Aleppo* also brought back that gut-wrenching feeling of the final days of the siege in 2016 and left me contemplating three dark moments that I experienced as a human rights advocate operating on the diplomatic periphery of Syria's war. Each of these moments represented an inflection point in a conflict that has now lasted more than nine years and killed more than half a million people. Each also provides insight into how the UN Security Council has fundamentally failed the people of Syria.

The corridors of power and the hallways of indifference (summer 2011)

Before despair there was hope. The Arab Spring arrived in Syria on 16 February 2011 when a group of teenagers in the southern city of Deraa spray-painted on the wall of their school, 'It's your turn, Doctor' – a provocative prediction that the mass protests that had toppled other Arab dictators would soon envelop Syria and the regime of the former ophthalmologist, now president, Bashar al-Assad. The boy who actually wrote the graffiti was fourteen-year-old Naief Abazid, who later claimed that he had no conception of the implications of his act of vandalism. He was just trying to impress the older boys who told him what to write. He later confessed to a journalist, 'I only realized it was serious when I got to prison'.[6]

The following day, the children were arrested by the Mukhabarat, the security police. Naeif was hung by his wrists from the ceiling of a jail cell, beaten and whipped with thick cables. A delegation of elders from the local community, working with the boys' parents, went to the police to beg for mercy. They met with Atef Najib, a cousin of President Assad who was in charge of security in Deraa. He apparently told the delegation, 'Forget about your children. Go have new kids. If you can't, send us your wives and we will get them pregnant for you'.[7]

For the parents of Deraa, subdued by years of dictatorship, this was too much. On 18 March, a month after the boys had been arrested, a protest was held outside the Omari mosque calling for the boys' release. This simple defiant gesture, and the resulting confrontation with the security forces, escalated into even larger protests against the Assad regime over the following days. Even as the security forces used gunfire to drive people off the streets, the protesters in Deraa were not cowed. The release of Naief and the other boys on 20 March did little to assuage people's anger. And while Naief 'just wanted to go home and see [his] mother', he and the other boys were overwhelmed by the hero's welcome bestowed upon them. One day later, protestors in Deraa set fire to the Baath Party's local office. Anti-government protests also grew in other cities, towns and villages across Syria from mid-March onwards. Syria's revolution had begun.[8]

Unable to organise freely, the opposition used the period after Friday prayers, when Muslims were leaving their mosques, as an opportunity to gather. Even as deadly repression intensified and literally thousands of protesters disappeared into detention, on Friday, 1 July 2011, possibly as many as three million Syrians participated in mass demonstrations across the country. Locals estimated that half a million people protested in Hama alone, with people chanting, 'Leave! Leave! The people want the fall of the regime!' Huge demonstrations were also held in Damascus, Homs, Latakia, Aleppo and Deir al-Zour. The foreign media said the numbers were 'impossible to verify' but confirmed that hundreds of thousands were in the streets. They also reported that government forces had shot fourteen people dead.[9]

It was clear that although the burgeoning protest movement was most popular amongst the country's Sunni majority (who constituted around seventy percent of the population), demonstrators came from all of Syria's diverse religious communities. In Darayya, a large suburb south of Damascus, some leaders of the protest movement rejected the violence of the state in peculiarly brave and idealistic ways. Ghiyath Matar, a local activist who became known as 'Little Gandhi', handed out flowers and water to the security forces when they came to disperse protests. Such gestures initially confused and immobilised the troops, who had been told that the movement was a foreign conspiracy. Eventually, however, Matar was arrested and tortured to death.[10]

Darayya did not submit. As in the rest of the country, however, the political centre of gravity slowly shifted from peaceful mass protests to armed resistance. After the government killed a number of demonstrators, armed rebels forced the security forces out of Darayya. Even though the government then put the area under siege, activists continued to experiment with democracy. In October 2012 they set up a local governing council, held elections and insisted that the local units of the rebel Free Syrian Army (FSA) submit to the council's authority – which they did. Armed extremists from al-Qaeda and the Islamic State of Iraq and the Levant (ISIL) were never able to gain significant influence inside Darayya. Even as Syria descended into a bloody civil war and the besieged residents lived without regular access to electricity, food, water and medicine, Darayya continued to embody 'the hopes of the many Syrians who reject extremists of all stripes'.[11]

The people of Darayya held out for three years against the government's 'kneel or starve' tactics. During the siege, literally thousands of barrel bombs were dropped on the area. As malnutrition and starvation increased, government forces turned their attention to the crops grown inside Daraya, bombing the fields and food that the besieged population relied upon for survival. Hospitals and other civilian infrastructure were also targeted. Nevertheless, people endured, even maintaining an underground library throughout the siege. When Darayya finally surrendered in August 2016, the remaining residents and FSA fighters were evacuated to the north. President Assad himself came on a triumphant tour after his forces retook the area.

Since 1970, the Assad dictatorship had ruled not just by repression alone but also by presenting itself as the protector of Syria's religious minorities (including Christians, Druze and Alawites) and the secular enemy of political Islam of the Muslim Brotherhood variety. In particular, the Alawite sect, to which the Assad family belongs, was disproportionately represented in the state's internal security and intelligence services. With dictators now falling across the Arab world, the Syrian government saw the protests in Deraa, Darayya and elsewhere as not only posing a threat to the Assad family's rule but endangering the survival of their state. Deeply fearful of the Sunni majority they had marginalised for so long, Assad and his allies were prepared to do almost anything to hold onto power. Despite President Assad's lifting of the forty-eight-year state of emergency that April, the government mobilised its security forces to systematically shoot down, imprison or disappear its political opponents. Approximately 850 Syrians were killed between March and May alone.

Around July 2011, as mass protests were still continuing in Syria, I ran into an Indian diplomat I knew in the lobby of One Dag Hammarskjöld Plaza on Second Avenue in New York, where a number of countries had their diplomatic missions to the United Nations. India was serving as an elected member of the UN Security Council at the time, and the diplomat and I chatted for a while before I raised the uncomfortable issue of the deteriorating situation in Syria. In strident tones, he informed me that although he was personally appalled by the violence, his country's willingness to support a proposed resolution on Syria was tempered by the alleged misuse of the R2P principle in Libya. I objected, arguing that we needed to fight for the consistent application of all human rights norms in all cases. To deliberately ignore the suffering of the people of Syria because of the alleged sins of Western diplomats regarding Libya seemed morally and politically dubious.

At the time, the fear of many human rights activists was that if the Security Council did not speak and act quickly to end the killing in Syria, then further deterioration was inevitable. Months had already passed without the Security Council adopting a single resolution. There was also growing concern that if the Syrian government succeeded in drowning the protest movement in blood, what was left of the opposition would inexorably move towards the politics of the gun.

In response to my hushed but emphatic diatribe, my Indian colleague reminded me that Russia was a traditional ally of the Syrian government and was instinctively hostile to the idea that the UN Security Council should sanction Assad. The Russians also possessed, according to this diplomat, considerable insight into the thinking of the ruling circle around President Assad. He informed me that in the opinion of the Russians, 'You human rights guys are naïve, because you think the choice is between Assad or democracy, but the alternative to secular Assad is a wasteland ruled by jihadis. That's what the Russians are telling us'. But in mid-2011 there was no widespread terrorism, no Jabhat al-Nusra, no so-called Islamic State, no beheadings, no sectarian warfare. This seemed more like a self-fulfilling prophecy than reasoned political analysis. I talked to the diplomat for a while longer until he bade me farewell.

The rest of that summer of 2011 was wasted in recriminations amongst the permanent members of the Security Council about what was occurring in Syria. In the hallways of the UN, the Russians continued to insist that the entire Arab Spring was nothing more than a Western plot to initiate regime change across the Middle East. I had no doubt that the United States and others were keen to see some of these Arab dictators fall, but to dismiss a movement made up of millions of ordinary people in such a way was astoundingly condescending.

Meanwhile, the opposition in Syria continued to hold mass protests, even as the number of armed groups also continued to grow. The process was aided in part by the fact that at the end of March, President Assad had given an amnesty to more than 250 political prisoners. As Charles Lister of the Middle East Institute later commented:

> It appears clear that the large majority of those [released prisoners] were Islamists of one kind or another. ... This may have been an attempt to appease the growing anti-government sentiment across the country; but it is more likely that it was yet another devious attempt by the Assad regime to manipulate its adversary, this time by unleashing those it could safely label as 'jihadist' or 'extremist' among its ranks.[12]

Assad was aware that his best chance of survival lay in portraying the struggle as being between his secular dictatorship and armed Sunni extremists. But as the political complexion of the opposition changed, so too did the international political debate over what to do.

In August, the United States, United Kingdom and France denounced the government's atrocities and called, essentially, for regime change in Damascus. For the Russians, this confirmed that human rights concerns were just a convenient smoke screen for the attempted overthrow of Assad. But the Russians' counterargument, that Assad was committed to political reform and just wanted to defend his country from terrorism, was palpably untrue. Meanwhile, India, which held the presidency of the Security Council during August, negotiated a strong presidential statement that expressed 'profound regret at the death of many hundreds of people' in Syria and condemned 'the widespread violations of human rights and the use of force against civilians by the Syrian authorities'.[13] Crucially, however, the presidential statement was not binding on the Syrian government. That required a resolution.

Two months later, after extensive and bitter negotiations, on 4 October 2011 Russia and China vetoed a draft UN Security Council resolution that would have condemned 'grave and systematic human rights violations' in Syria. Nine members of the Council voted for the resolution and four abstained. The defeated resolution would have demanded an immediate end to the violence, denounced extremism and insisted that the Syrian authorities allow for freedom of expression and assembly. While the draft text raised the option of sanctions if the government did not comply, it did not threaten military intervention.

Four months later, in February 2012, Russia and China vetoed a second draft UN Security Council resolution aimed at holding the Syrian government accountable for crimes against humanity. Watching the discussion in the chamber after the vote, the depth of emotion was palpable.[14] Although the resolution had been supported by thirteen of the fifteen members of the Council, diplomats and human rights advocates were deeply despondent.

What became clear in the aftermath of the February 2012 veto was that Security Council inaction emboldened those inside Syria who were most committed to a military victory. The killing rate in Syria increased from approximately 1,000 per month to approximately 5,000 per month during 2012 as the civil war metastasised. Between February and November 2012, the overall death toll soared from 5,000 to over 50,000.[15]

Patterns of violence also changed. With each veto and each failure of the Security Council to hold the Syrian government accountable, President Assad's forces deployed more extreme armed force. For example, the Syrian government did not widely utilise helicopters to attack their opponents until after the second veto in February 2012. Even then, the government exercised some restraint, conducting fewer than twenty documented strikes using helicopters during April and May. Following a third double veto at the UN Security Council on 19 July, however, the number of helicopter attacks increased to almost seventy by the end of the month. Moreover, on 24 July, just five days after the vote, fixed-wing aircraft were used against civilian areas for the first time. During August the regime conducted more than 110 air strikes against opposition targets, including more than sixty using fixed-wing aircraft.[16]

From then on, government aircraft were routinely deployed against residential neighbourhoods. Adopting a policy of collective punishment, government helicopters and fighter jets bombed opposition-controlled cities, focussing on places where civilians congregated and were most exposed, including bakeries, schools and health clinics.[17] This in turn strengthened the most extreme elements within the armed opposition, especially those with external sources of support.

Years later, I still think about that 'jihadi wasteland' conversation with the Indian diplomat. I stood in the corridors of power staring into the face of courteous indifference. And while he was right to argue that the situation in Syria was complicated and dangerous, that was precisely why coordinated diplomatic action was so desperately necessary that first summer of the conflict. Such action could have potentially constrained Assad and contained the conflict. Instead, political inertia helped turn Syria into the world's worst situation of ongoing atrocities, civilian displacement and humanitarian catastrophe. Hundreds of thousands of people would die as the government and armed opposition now battled to the death for control of the country.

That Sarajevo market moment (autumn 2013)

Throughout 2012 the civil war in Syria became more brutal and desperate. Deaths and mass defections reduced the estimated size of President Assad's army by half. Whole swathes of the country were lost to the government. The core of the security establishment, however, remained loyal. Led mainly by Alawites, these were people who saw the Assads (both father Hafez and son Bashar) as the secular defenders of Syria's religious diversity. With some notable exceptions, Alawites (roughly eleven percent of the population), Druze (three percent) and Christians (eight percent) did not break with the dictatorship. They may have been deeply uneasy about what was happening, but with the end of the mass protest movement the alternative now seemed infinitely worse for them and their people. The rise of armed extremist groups enabled pro-government forces to plausibly present the choice as being between Assad and a sectarian apocalypse.

In the summer of 2013, I was sitting on a plush leather couch in the office of a senior French diplomat. I was there to discuss a number of conflicts that were on the Security Council's agenda, and the conversation eventually turned to Syria. By that time Russia and China had vetoed three draft resolutions and blocked attempts to impose international sanctions on those responsible for atrocities in Syria. I was trying to ascertain whether there was a plan to push for another resolution and whether there was a diplomatic approach that could get the Russians to abstain from vetoing. There was a pause in the conversation and then the French diplomat said to me, 'I don't think things will change regarding Syria until there is a Sarajevo market moment. Something more horrible than anything we have seen so far'.

He was referring to August 1995, when Bosnian Serb forces besieging Sarajevo deliberately shelled the market, killing and severely wounding dozens of civilians. Coming just one month after the genocide of over 8,000 Bosniak men and boys at Srebrenica, television images of the Sarajevo market massacre outraged global public opinion and led to NATO air strikes against the forces who perpetrated the atrocity. No one at the UN was seriously advocating for air strikes on Syria, but perhaps awareness of an especially hideous atrocity, the French diplomat argued, might galvanise global opinion and help end Russian and Chinese obstruction at the Security Council.

It is therefore somehow sickeningly fitting that after two years of diplomatic failure it was a chemical weapons attack on Syrian civilians that provided a brief moment of political hope during 2013. A subsequent UN investigation proved beyond reasonable doubt that on 21 August, rockets containing weaponised sarin were fired into two residential areas on the outskirts of Damascus. The poison gas quickly killed approximately 1,400 civilians, including a large number of children. Despite the Syrian government's attempt to blame armed rebels for the attack, an independent UN report and other credible investigations pointed to the most likely source of the rockets being a nearby base of the Republican Guard. Evidence of Syrian government culpability was overwhelming.[18]

Global revulsion at this war crime, combined with the credible threat of military strikes by the United States and France, led to a diplomatic breakthrough at the Security Council. After two and a half years of paralysis, the Council adopted a resolution supporting a Russia–United States deal for Syria to surrender its chemical weapons. Just a few weeks prior, the Syrian government had still denied that it possessed chemical weapons. But on 14 September Syria quickly acceded to the Convention on the Prohibition of the Development, Production, Stockpiling and Use of Chemical Weapons and on their Destruction and provided details of its extensive stockpiles.[19]

Some advocates pointed out that although the chemical weapons attack was horrific, the estimated 1,400 people who were killed only amounted to about one percent of the total fatalities of the conflict. What, they asked, made this atrocity so special? Such arguments neglected the unique threat posed by chemical weapons. Although approximately 5,000 people were being killed every month in Syria during 2013, the chemical weapons attack murdered more than a thousand civilians in two neighborhoods in just a few hours.[20]

Chemical weapons are inherently indiscriminate, inhuman and immoral. They have been illegal since the Hague Convention of 1899. Prompted by horror at the ghastly consequences of mustard and chlorine gas during World War One, the Geneva Protocol of 1925 reinforced an international prohibition on the use of chemical weapons. Despite Mussolini's troops' use of mustard gas in Ethiopia, the norm was established. Although Adolf Hitler, himself a survivor of a World War One gas attack, used Zyklon B as a tool of genocide at Auschwitz, chemical weapons were not openly deployed on a major battlefield again until the Iran–Iraq War of 1980–1988.

In August 2012, President Obama had been widely quoted as saying that the use of chemical weapons by Assad's forces in Syria would cross a 'red line'. While Obama didn't specify that he was talking about punitive military action, that is how it was universally interpreted. And in the immediate aftermath of the 21 August 2013 chemical weapons attack, air strikes against Syrian military targets by the United States and France appeared imminent. Targets were selected, and the US and French militaries began their preparations. However, as the days passed, the anticipated air strikes did not materialise, and in an unusual development, President Vladimir Putin of Russia wrote an op-ed in the *New York Times* pleading for restraint. Putin argued that if 'we can avoid force against Syria, this will improve the atmosphere' in international politics and open 'the door to cooperation on other critical issues'.[21]

By the start of September, it was clear that Obama had backed himself into a corner. His 'red line' comments were a threat he was compelled to act upon. But he had also declared that he wanted congressional approval for any air strikes on Syria, and in the days after 21 August it became clear that majority support would not be forthcoming. If Obama did not carry out air strikes, he would show the world that his red line did not exist; if he did strike, he would have to defy Congress. This explains why, to the discomfort of Samantha Power and some other senior officials, Obama seized upon an unexpected Russian initiative for Assad to peacefully surrender his chemical weapons.[22]

The diplomatic compromise that was then brokered by Russia and the United States over Syria's chemical weapons, although prompted by the threat of military action outside of international law, was significant. Crucially, the Security Council took a unanimous decision regarding Syria: Resolution 2118 of 27 September 2013. Teams from the Organisation for the Prohibition of Chemical Weapons (OPCW) eventually visited 21 Syrian government sites to confirm that they had dismantled or destroyed equipment for the manufacture of chemical weapons. The OPCW also oversaw the removal of 1,300 tons of the government's declared stockpile of chemical weapons.[23]

Although Resolution 2118 did nothing to prevent the commission of atrocities in Syria as long as conventional weapons were used, it did enable the Security Council to test Putin's proposition that the compromise would foster further diplomatic collaboration. Promisingly, after torturous negotiations the Security Council then unanimously adopted Resolution 2139 on 22 February 2014, calling on all sides in Syria to permit humanitarian access to displaced or besieged civilians. The resolution also demanded that 'all parties take all appropriate steps to protect civilians, including members of ethnic, religious and confessional communities', and stressed that 'in this regard, the primary responsibility to protect its population lies with the Syrian authorities'.[24]

The displeasure of Syria's ambassador to the UN was clear as Ambassador Churkin of Russia raised his hand to vote with the rest of the Council. The real test, however, would be in implementation. Government obstruction (and that of some armed opposition groups) ensured that the humanitarian situation continued to deteriorate throughout 2014, despite the UN's best efforts to bring aid to starving, sick and displaced Syrians.

It was ISIL's rise and rapid advance across Iraq and Syria during 2014 that altered the dynamic of the entire Syrian conflict once again. With the Iraqi government requesting urgent military support in June, President Obama also increased assistance to select Syrian rebel groups and launched an international military coalition to 'degrade and destroy' ISIL. Western publics reacted tentatively, but approvingly, to air strikes to protect vulnerable civilians in Iraq, as well as to the punishing bombardment of ISIL combatants in Syria. Beyond the issue of defeating ISIL, however, there remained no international agreement on how to protect civilians, halt atrocities and end Syria's war.

President Putin's response to ISIL was to increase Russia's direct support for Assad. On 28 September 2015, Putin addressed the UN General Assembly in New York and said that the Western powers were making 'an enormous mistake' by refusing 'to cooperate with the Syrian government and its armed forces, who are valiantly fighting terrorism face to face'.[25] Two days later, Russia directly militarily intervened in Syria. With large numbers of Iranian and Hezbollah forces already supporting Syrian government troops on the ground, and Russian fighter jets now carrying out air strikes, the military balance of power shifted decisively in favour of Assad.

Despite its promises, the Syrian government also continued using chemical weapons. In October 2018 the British Broadcasting Corporation published a major investigation alleging that at least 106 chemical weapons attacks had taken place in Syria since the government acceded to the Chemical Weapons Convention in September 2013. These included government attacks on Aleppo during the final battle for the city, as well as the notorious assault on Khan Sheikhoun in April 2017. The UN International Commission of Inquiry on Syria also reported on thirty-seven documented instances of chemical weapons use between March 2013 and March 2019, including thirty-two attacks perpetrated by Syrian government forces.[26]

I am no enthusiast for military intervention, and R2P does not allow for such action outside of international law. However, given that Russia had systematically obstructed and repeatedly vetoed any diplomatic action at the UN Security Council, I think the United States and France should have conducted sustained air strikes that week in August 2013, destroying Assad's air force and chemical weapons infrastructure. While such air strikes would not have been strictly legal, they certainly would have been legitimate. They could have removed the threat of further chemical warfare and deprived Assad of mastery of the skies. This, in turn, might have forced some of the generals around him to rethink the calculus of victory and defeat, potentially opening up the possibility of a negotiated solution *sans* Assad. It is also extremely unlikely that Russia would have militarily intervened in September 2015 if not for the fact that by then President Putin was convinced that Washington and Paris were not going to do so.

The most disturbing result from the failure to strike in the autumn of 2013 was that it was now clear that there was no 'red line'. Even though he had to hand over most of his chemical weapons stockpile, Assad was emboldened. The effect this had on Syria's moderate political opposition, who were pleading for intervention and civilian protection, was devastating. Numerous fighters deserted the Free Syrian Army and similar secular groups for more extremist armed factions. From then on, the three Western permanent members of the UN Security Council – the

United Kingdom, France and the United States – were palpably unable to influence the course of the conflict or restrain those who were waging it. Assad had exposed their utter debility.

Since Syria's potential 'Sarajevo market moment' in 2013, the death toll has reached more than half a million people, and the conflict has continued to inspire perpetrators on all sides to commit new and appalling atrocities. Caught between the crimes of the government and those of armed extremist groups, villages and towns that have existed for centuries as part of the unique Levantine amalgam of cultures and faiths have now been broken apart by sectarianism and war. No city represented this tragedy more than Aleppo.

No one left to text (winter 2016)

Strategically located between Mesopotamia and the Mediterranean, Aleppo is one of the oldest inhabited cities on earth. When mass protests began in Syria in 2011, Aleppo had a population of around three million people. It was Syria's largest city but initially remained free from the violence that split communities apart in places like Hama or Homs. Aleppo was often described in the international press as Syria's 'commercial hub', and the city's economic elite generally supported the government. The security forces also closely monitored anywhere where young people came together. And so it was not until mid-2012 that the war truly arrived in Aleppo.

Armed opposition groups took control of eastern Aleppo in July 2012, effectively dividing the city in half. Over the following four years the front lines between the government-held west of the city and the opposition-held east hardly moved. Life carried on in divided Aleppo as the battle for the country continued between Assad's forces and a cornucopia of armed opposition groups now vying for power, influence and territory. However, while 'opposition forces' across Syria grew ever more fractured, radical and desperate, the intervention of the Syrian government's Iranian and Hezbollah allies started to make a significant difference on the battlefield. Then Russia militarily intervened in September 2015, claiming to be targeting ISIL fighters, but bombing all opposition-held territory and allowing the government to maintain its control of the skies.

By 2016 it became clear that the battle for Aleppo would be decisive. The opposition-held portion of the city had already endured years of bombardment, with government helicopters dropping 'barrel bombs' on residents. Tens of thousands of civilians moved to the government-held west of the city, sought sanctuary in rebel-held territory elsewhere in Syria or fled across the border into refugee camps. The UN estimated that by early 2016 the population of east Aleppo, which once numbered more than a million people, had fallen to only 320,000. Other reports put the number of noncombatants living in east Aleppo through the final phase of the siege from September until December 2016 somewhere between 110,000 and 200,000 people. There were also between 5,000 and 8,000 opposition fighters.[27]

In June 2016 the government launched a major offensive to retake the Castello Road in the north of Aleppo and sever the main supply route into the opposition-held east of the city. After several weeks of intense fighting, by 27 July the road was in government hands and eastern Aleppo was encircled. Although a counteroffensive by opposition forces briefly managed to open another supply route, this was quickly retaken from them. By 4 September, east Aleppo was surrounded and cut off from the outside world.

Efforts by the United States to negotiate with the Russians and secure a cease-fire in Aleppo exposed just how weak Washington's bargaining position had become. On 12 September, Russia agreed to facilitate a temporary cease-fire, but seven days later Russian and Syrian government helicopters and warplanes bombed a UN and Syrian Red Crescent convoy as it attempted to carry out its preapproved mission to deliver humanitarian supplies to Aleppo. During the attack, which lasted half an hour, seventeen aid trucks were incinerated and more than a dozen humanitarian workers killed.[28] The Russian and Syrian governments denied responsibility for the bombing – which was a war crime – but the cease-fire was finished.

From 19 September until around 18 October, Russian and Syrian government aircraft then relentlessly bombed east Aleppo. On 8 October, for the fifth time since the Syrian conflict began, Russia also vetoed a UN Security Council resolution demanding a cease-fire and an end to the obliteration of east Aleppo.[29] There was a lull in air strikes between 18 October and mid-November as Syrian government troops and their allied militias prepared for a final ground assault. The air strikes resumed on 17 November, and just over a week later pro-government troops finally broke through the opposition front line in the suburb of Hanano. By the end of November, they had split east Aleppo into two shrinking enclaves.

On 5 December the UN Security Council met in New York to vote on another draft resolution calling for an urgent cease-fire in Aleppo. Russia vetoed the resolution and the killing continued. As one suburb of eastern Aleppo after another now quickly fell to government forces, there were widespread reports of extrajudicial killings and the detention of any man or boy considered capable of holding a weapon or harboring an anti-government thought. Those civilians and militants left in east Aleppo were forced into a shrinking pocket of territory. On 14 December Russia negotiated a deal for the remaining opposition fighters to evacuate to elsewhere in the country, and the fall of Aleppo was complete. The government officially declared victory on 22 December.

It is beyond my capacity to list all the atrocities that were committed in Aleppo during the siege, but it is worth keeping in mind that the siege itself was a war crime – violating Article 23 of the Fourth Geneva Convention, which prohibits the blockage of medical supplies and food to civilian noncombatants.[30] Civilians trapped inside Aleppo also faced unrelenting attack. Incendiary weapons, illegal cluster munitions and improvised barrel bombs (often filled with scrap metal) were used to break down east Aleppo's buildings and murder and maim its residents. Many people went underground, sheltering in improvised bunkers and emerging only to hunt for food. Meanwhile, government aircraft targeted water supplies and bombed bakeries and vegetable markets, denying civilians the ability to feed themselves. One resident described how the heavy bombing made 'the ground beneath our feet shake. It [felt] like the end of the world'.[31]

Our colleagues at the Syrian Network for Human Rights calculated that 4,045 barrel bombs were dropped on east Aleppo during 2016 alone, killing 506 civilians, including 140 children.[32] While the barrel bombs were indiscriminate, there were also seventy-three targeted attacks on medical personnel, emergency clinics and hospitals between June and December. A number of hospitals were bombed multiple times, with the hospital known as M2, in the al-Maadi district, sustaining serious damage from twelve different attacks between June and December. According to the UN, by the end of the year 'all hospitals were bombed out of service' in east Aleppo. These attacks killed both patients and staff, constituting war crimes and crimes against humanity under international law.[33]

In the final stages of the siege the government also deployed chemical weapons against east Aleppo. There were credible reports that chlorine gas was being dropped from helicopters, with incidents reported on 2 August, 10 August and 6 September. More than 200 victims were treated for exposure to chemical agents, and several children died. At least ten more chlorine attacks were reported in Aleppo between October and mid-December as government forces prepared for their final assault.[34]

On the last day, as Aleppo fell to Assad's conquering army, I was sitting in Al Jazeera's studio at UN headquarters with a TV camera pointing at me. I had been asked to do an interview about the end of the siege and what that meant for human rights, for R2P and for the future of the United Nations. I sat in the studio with a shot of the UN on the screen behind me, waiting for the producer to tell me when we were going live.

Throughout the siege there had been numerous Syrian nongovernmental organisations operating in east Aleppo. Over the years I had been in sporadic contact with a number of individuals from these different groups, including the White Helmets. While I was waiting to be interviewed, as I had done so many times over the previous years, I reached for my iPhone to text colleagues, contacts and friends inside Syria and check what updated info they had. That was when I realised that literally every person I knew in Aleppo was now displaced, missing or dead. Presidents Assad and Putin had conquered Aleppo. Russian vetoes had ensured that the bitterly divided UN Security Council failed to protect anyone. And now there was no one left to text.

Conclusion

Four years later, Aleppo remains a ruin and the war has entered its end phase. Naief Abazid, the fourteen-year-old schoolboy who spray-painted the wall in Deraa and helped ignite Syria's revolution, is now a refugee in Europe. Speaking to a journalist, he recalled the first months of the uprising in his home town:

'We had this hope, that this week or next week Assad would be gone. After a year, the hope disappeared.'[35] In July 2018, Syrian government forces recaptured Deraa, where the uprising began.

Since 2011, thirteen million Syrians have been displaced from their homes. Over six million have become refugees. Almost ten years after the conflict first began, only portions of Idlib Governorate in the northwest remain beyond the control of Damascus. And in areas previously held by opposition armed groups, President Assad has used a new decree, Law 10, to confiscate abandoned housing and seize land for redevelopment, allowing loyalists and property developers to benefit from Syria's ruination. But for most ordinary people the war has delivered nothing but misery. According to one report from a 'typical' pro-government village, with a population of around 3,000 people, eighty men had been killed and 130 wounded fighting for Assad. This amounted to roughly one third of the male population between the ages of 18 and 50.[36]

In June 2018 a reporter from the *Economist* painted a bleak picture of what a drive through Assad's Syria now looked like:

> On the highway from Damascus to Aleppo, towns and villages lie desolate. A new stratum of dead cities has joined the ones from Roman times. The regime has neither the money nor the manpower to rebuild. Before the war Syria's economic growth approached double digits and annual GDP was $60bn. Now the economy is shrinking; GDP was $12bn last year. Estimates of the cost of reconstruction run to $250bn.[37]

Since 2011 the UN secretary-general, high commissioner for human rights and various world leaders have all called for atrocities committed in Syria to be referred to the International Criminal Court for investigation. Since 2013 the UN Security Council has passed more than two dozen resolutions on humanitarian access, peace talks and chemical weapons in Syria. Several of these refer to the government's responsibility to protect. None have been fully implemented. Meanwhile, Russia and China have jointly vetoed ten draft resolutions, and Russia has independently vetoed a further six, systematically obstructing efforts to hold perpetrators of atrocities in Syria accountable for their crimes.

The misuse of the veto to protect perpetrators of atrocities in Syria has led to a growing movement to change the way the UN Security Council reacts – and votes – in mass atrocity situations. More than 115 of the 193 member states of the United Nations have signed a 'Code of Conduct regarding Security Council action against genocide, crimes against humanity and war crimes', vowing not to vote against any credible resolution aimed at preventing or halting atrocities. During 2015 France and Mexico also launched a related initiative which has been signed by 96 states and calls upon the five permanent members to voluntarily refrain from using their veto in atrocity situations.

Since the conflict first began in 2011, I have had the honour of appearing on public platforms with numerous young Syrians whose lives have been shattered by the war. Some, like Noura Al-Jizawi, have become heroes of mine. Noura helped lead the 2011 mass protests in Homs and survived seven months of detention and torture by Assad's security services. She now lives in exile with her husband and their young daughter. We both spoke at an event at the European Union in May 2019. In a private conversation afterwards, she shared her passion for the rich archaeological heritage of her ancient home city of Homs. We also talked about her work helping Syrian women who are survivors of torture and sexual violence. For Noura and other young Syrians like her to retain their vitality, decency and empathy in the midst of such cruelty and horror is extraordinary. They are inspiring examples of what Syria was, and what it still could be.

Having spent years on the margins of Syria's war, I have watched as the international diplomatic community oscillated between impotent rage and muted accommodation. Assad may have 'won the war', but we should not rest until there is comprehensive accountability for the atrocities that have been committed. Regardless of their position or affiliation, and despite how much time may pass, those responsible for war crimes and crimes against humanity should face international justice. Not for revenge, but because it is only by upholding universal human rights that the international community can redeem itself from beneath Aleppo's rubble.

While that path to justice is likely to be painfully slow, during April 2020 two of President Assad's former security officers were put on trial in Germany for crimes against humanity. One of the accused, Anwar Raslan, is a former colonel who worked at Branch 251 of Syria's military intelligence service, where it is claimed he oversaw the torture of 4,000 prisoners between April 2011 and September 2012, before he defected. Both men had come to Germany as asylum seekers, and the local authorities initiated their arrest under the legal principle of universal jurisdiction, which allows for the prosecution of crimes in one country even if they happened elsewhere. A Syrian torture survivor, watching the opening of the trial in Koblenz, commented, 'When we were being interrogated, we were blindfolded and handcuffed. We were powerless. Now, we want the truth to be told, we want to reveal what is still happening to our friends in Syria today and we want that to be told through a fair trial'.[38]

The trial of the two security officers constitutes small blow to the impunity that has characterised Syria's bloody war. It will not be the last.

Notes

1 Name changed.
2 Report of the Independent International Commission of Inquiry on the Syrian Arab Republic, 2 February 2017, A/HRC/34/64: 6, 8. https://documents-dds-ny.un.org/doc/UNDOC/GEN/G17/026/63/PDF/G1702663.pdf?OpenElement.
3 Neither Russia nor Syria was a signatory to the 2008 Convention on Cluster Munitions.
4 Rick Gladstone and Somini Sengupta, "Unrelenting Assault on Aleppo is Called Worst Yet in Syria's Civil War," *New York Times*, 26 September 2016.

5 Bellingcat Investigation Team, "Chemical Weapons and Absurdity: The Disinformation Campaign Against the White Helmets," 18 December 2018, https://www.bellingcat.com/news/mena/2018/12/18/chemical-weapons-and-absurdity-the-disinformation-campaign-against-the-white-helmets/.

6 Mark MacKinnon, "The Graffiti Kids Who Sparked the Syrian War," *The Globe and Mail*, 2 December 2016.

7 Ibid.

8 Avi Asher-Schapiro, "The Young Men Who Started Syria's Revolution Speak About Deraa, Where It All Began," *Vice News*, 15 March 2016, https://news.vice.com/article/the-young-men-who-started-syrias-revolution-speak-about-daraa-where-it-all-began; and MacKinnon, "The Graffiti Kids Who Sparked the Syrian War."

9 "Syria: 'Hundreds of Thousands' Join Anti-Assad Protests," *BBC News*, 2 July 2011, https://www.bbc.com/news/world-middle-east-13988701.

10 Liz Sly, "Syrian Activist Ghiyath Matar's Death Spurs Grief, Debate," *Washington Post*, 14 September 2011.

11 Christian Caryl, "Mourning the Syria that Might Have Been," *Foreign Policy*, 16 September 2016, https://foreignpolicy.com/2016/09/16/mourning-the-syria-that-might-have-been/.

12 Kathy Gilsinan, "How Syria's Uprising Spawned a Jihad," *The Atlantic*, 15 March 2016, https://www.theatlantic.com/international/archive/2016/03/syria-civil-war-five-years/474006/.

13 Statement by the President of the Security Council, 3 August 2011, S/PRST/2011/16, https://undocs.org/S/PRST/2011/16.

14 United States Mission to the United Nations, "Explanation of vote by Ambassador Susan E. Rice, U.S. Permanent Representative to the United Nations, at a Security Council session on Syria, February 4, 2012," http://usun.state.gov/briefing/statements/183334.htm.

15 United Nations Office of the High Commissioner for Human Rights, "Data Analysis suggests over 60,000 People killed in Syria Conflict: Pillay," 2 January 2013, http://www.ohchr.org/EN/NewsEvents/Pages/DisplayNews.aspx?NewsID=12912&LangID=E.

16 Elizabeth O'Bagy, Christopher Harmer, Jonathan Dupree and Liam Durfee, "Syrian Air Force and Air Defense Capabilities," *Institute for the Study of War*, May 2013, http://www.understandingwar.org/sites/default/files/Updated%20Syrian%20Air%20Force%20and%20Air%20Defense%20Capabilities%20Brief_8May.pdf; Human Rights Watch, "Death from the Skies: Deliberate and indiscriminate Air Strikes on Civilians," 10 April 2013, https://www.hrw.org/report/2013/04/10/death-skies/deliberate-and-indiscriminate-air-strikes-civilians.

17 Human Rights Watch, "Death from the Skies: Deliberate and indiscriminate Air Strikes on Civilians."

18 Report of the United Nations Mission to Investigate Allegations of the Use of Chemical Weapons in the Syrian Arab Republic on the alleged use of chemical weapons in the Ghouta area of Damascus on 21 August 2013, A/67/997-S/2013/553, 16 September 2013, http://www.securitycouncilreport.org/atf/cf/%7B65BFCF9B-6D27-4E9C-8CD3-CF6E4FF96FF9%7D/s_2013_553.pdf; Eliot Higgins, "Sy Hersh's Chemical Misfire: What the Legendary Reporter Gets Wrong about Syria's Sarin attacks," *Foreign Policy*, 9 December 2013; Muhammed Idrees Ahmad, "A Dangerous Method: Syria, Sy Hersh, and the Art of Mass-Crime Revisionism," *Los Angeles Review of Books*, 1 June 2014; Human Rights Watch, "Syria: Government likely Culprit in Chemical Attack," 10 September 2013, http://www.hrw.org/news/2013/09/10/syria-government-likely-culprit-chemical-attack; Yasmin Naqvi, "Crossing the Red Line: The Use of Chemical Weapons in Syria and What Should Happen Now," *International Review of the Red Cross*, 99, no. 3 (2017), 959–993.

19 Anne Barnard, "In Shift, Syrian Official Admits Government Has Chemical Arms," *New York Times*, 10 September 2013; Naqvi, "Crossing the Red Line," 959–993.

20 Ken Roth, "Syria: What Chance to Stop the Slaughter?," *New York Review of Books*, 21 November 2013.

21 James Ball, "Obama Issues Syria a 'Red Line' Warning on Chemical Weapons," *Washington Post*, 20 August 2012; and Vladimir V. Putin, "A Plea for Caution from Russia," *New York Times*, 11 September 2013.

22 Samantha Power, *The Education of An Idealist: A Memoir* (New York: Dey St, 2019).

23 Naqvi, "Crossing the Red Line."; and Scott Shane, "Weren't Syria's Chemical Weapons Destroyed? It's Complicated," *New York Times*, 7 April 2017.

24 United Nations Security Council Resolution 2139, S/RES/2139, 22 February 2014, http://www.un.org/en/ga/search/view_doc.asp?symbol=S/RES/2139(2014).

25 Speech by President V. Putin at 70th Session of the UN General Assembly, 28 September 2015, http://en.kremlin.ru/events/president/news/50385.

26 Nawal al-Maghafi, "How Chemical Weapons Have Helped Bring Assad Close to Victory," *BBC News*, 15 October 2018, https://www.bbc.com/news/world-middle-east-45586903; UN Commission of Inquiry on Syria, 12 March 2019, https://twitter.com/uncoisyria/status/1105408408830820355?s=21; Human Rights Watch, "Syria: A Year On, Chemical Weapons Attacks Persist," 4 April 2018, https://www.hrw.org/news/2018/04/04/syria-year-chemical-weapons-attacks-persist; and Naqvi, "Crossing the Red Line," 970–972.

27 Maksymilian Czuperski, Faisal Itami, Ben Nimmo, Eliot Higgins and Emma Beals, "Breaking Aleppo," *Atlantic Council*, February 2017, 7–9, http://www.publications.atlanticcouncil.org/breakingaleppo/wp-content/uploads/2017/02/BreakingAleppo.pdf.

28 Ibid, 18; Report of the Independent International Commission of Inquiry on the Syrian Arab Republic, A/HRC/34/64A, 2 February 2017, 17–18, 20. https://documents-dds-ny.un.org/doc/UNDOC/GEN/G17/026/63/PDF/G1702663.pdf?OpenElement.

29 China abstained on the draft resolution, forcing Russia to veto alone.

30 By mid-2016 it was estimated that there were thirty-nine communities, with a combined population of almost a million people, living under siege. The government was responsible for thirty-six of these sieges, including east Aleppo. Czuperski, Itami, Nimmo, Higgins, Beals, "Breaking Aleppo," 13.

31 "The Agony of Aleppo," *The Economist*, 1 October 2016. On the range of weapons used against Aleppo's residents, and bombing of food supplies, see Report of the Independent International Commission of Inquiry on the Syrian Arab Republic, A/HRC/34/64, 2 February 2017, 5–6, 10–11, 11–16.

32 Czuperski, Itami, Nimmo, Higgins, Beals, "Breaking Aleppo," 19, 32, 37–40.

33 Ibid, 21–23; Report of the Independent International Commission of Inquiry on the Syrian Arab Republic, A/HRC/34/64, 2 February 2017, 8–10, 19.

34 Ibid, 42–45; Ibid, 12, 20. While chlorine has many legitimate uses, it is still illegal to utilise it as a weapon.

35 MacKinnon, "The Graffiti Kids Who Sparked the Syrian War."

36 "Picking Up the Pieces: How Syrian Society Has Changed," *Synapse Network*, 6 August 2018, http://www.synaps.network/picking-up-the-pieces; Hasan Arfeh, "The Institutionalization of Demographic Change in Syria," *Atlantic Council*, 4 April 2019, https://www.atlanticcouncil.org/blogs/syriasource/the-institutionalization-of-demographic-change-in-syria.

37 "The Future of Syria: Smaller, in Ruins and More Sectarian," *The Economist*, 30 June 2018. Also, Krishnadev Calamur, "No One Wants to Help Bashar al-Assad Rebuild Syria," *The Atlantic*, 15 March 2019, https://www.theatlantic.com/international/archive/2019/03/where-will-money-rebuild-syria-come/584935/.

38 Cathrin Schaer, "Landmark Trial Against Alleged Syrian War Criminals: What Next?," *Al Jazeera*, 30 April 2020, https://www.aljazeera.com/news/2020/04/landmark-trial-alleged-syrian-war-criminals-200430084719264.html; and "Syrians Held in Germany for Suspected Crimes Against Humanity," *BBC News*, 13 February 2019, https://www.bbc.com/news/world-middle-east-47226974.

4

TERRORISM, GENOCIDE AND THE ISLAMIC STATE

Contents

At the first Friday prayers during the holy month of Ramadan, Abu Bakr al-Baghdadi rose to give a sermon in the Great Mosque of al-Nuri in Mosul. It was 4 July 2014, and just a few weeks earlier the armed group that he commanded, the Islamic State of Iraq and the Levant (variously abbreviated as ISIL, ISIS, IS or Da'esh), had swept across the Nineveh Plain in northern Iraq, vanquishing the Iraqi army and Kurdish Peshmerga and seizing towns and villages. Mosul, Iraq's second-largest city and home to almost two million people, unexpectedly fell to ISIL on 10 June after panic set in amongst the security forces, who suddenly surrendered or fled. Although Raqqa, in neighbouring Syria, would be the so-called Islamic State's official capital, Mosul represented its greatest conquest. With Mosul under its control, ISIL no longer considered itself to be an armed movement. It declared the lands it occupied to now constitute a caliphate under the spiritual guidance of Baghdadi.

Unusually, Baghdadi allowed his sermon that day to be filmed. He was dressed in black robes and a turban, with a long greying beard. The significance of the moment – Baghdadi's first public speech as caliph – would not have been lost on anyone in the audience. Because the role of 'commander of the faithful' was a 'burden' that ISIL had now officially proclaimed and Baghdadi had accepted, they believed that he was entitled to the loyalty of all Muslims everywhere. Or as Baghdadi put it, 'I am the leader who presides over you', and all Muslims should 'obey me as long as I obey God'.[1] Someone who was not present in the Great Mosque of al-Nuri that day to listen to Baghdadi was the mosque's imam, Mohammed al-Mansouri. When ISIL fighters overran Mosul a few weeks earlier, Mansouri refused to swear allegiance and was executed.[2]

The Great Mosque of al-Nuri was more than 850 years old and was known across the Middle East for its iconic leaning minaret. Baghdadi, on the other hand, was something of a mystery. Born Ibrahim Awwad al-Badri al-Samarrai, he was forty-three years old and a former inmate of a US detention center in Iraq, having been arrested in 2004 because of his affiliation with armed extremist groups. Abu Bakr al-Baghdadi was his *nom de guerre*, and after his release he rejoined those trying to supplant Osama bin Laden's al-Qaeda in Iraq. ISIL was created in April 2013 under Baghdadi's leadership.[3] Through effective propaganda and merciless violence the group steadily spread its influence during the following year, establishing bases in Syria and eventually seizing the Iraqi town of Fallujah and the Syrian city of Raqqa during January 2014. This was followed soon after by the conquest of huge swathes of Iraq, including Mosul. Even the Iraqi capital of Baghdad appeared under threat. And although the path that had led Baghdadi to the Great Mosque was convoluted and bloody, he was now about to commit genocide and had the attention of the entire world.

Terrorism versus atrocities

The so-called Islamic State emerged because of the corruption and sectarianism of Iraq under Prime Minister Nouri al-Maliki and the bloodbath created by President Bashar al-Assad in neighbouring Syria. Those two failed rulers and Syria's sectarian civil war did more to recruit for ISIL than any religious exhortation by Baghdadi. In particular, the Arab Spring brought into stark relief the composition and conduct of the ruling elite in a range of Middle Eastern countries. It also exposed the clash between the region's major rivals – Saudi Arabia and Iran – as well as cleavages between Sunni and Shia, between urban and rural communities, between traditional tribal affiliations and modern identities and between the generations.[4]

These factors were compounded by the fact that anyone with even the slightest sense of history realised that the borders between Iraq and Syria were more a product of European colonialism than geographic logic. As a result, nationalism, pan-Arabism, ethnicity and faith have always been contested notions in the region. Poverty and conflict deepened the alienation that many people felt, especially the young, making them susceptible to the transborder extremist theology of ISIL.

The Sunni communities in Iraq where ISIL built its initial support had been beset by a decade of deadly conflict – most notably the disastrous and illegal 2003 United States–led invasion and occupation of Iraq, followed by an al-Qaeda-influenced insurgency and a bloody sectarian civil war that did not end until around 2011. A protest movement that started in December 2012 against the sectarianism of the Maliki government was violently suppressed by the Iraqi security forces (ISF). In particular, armed clashes in April 2013 around the Sunni-majority town of Hawijah left several hundred people dead. ISIL exploited widespread Sunni disaffection with the Iraqi government to build alliances with various local tribes. In a world of insecurity and unemployment, ISIL offered certainty and the promise of a better world both on earth and in the afterlife.

Meanwhile, as the civil war in Syria intensified from 2012 onwards, sectarian divisions became more bitter and bloody. ISIL moved fighters across the border from Iraq and was able to recruit fresh adherents by establishing itself as the most theologically extreme and lethal armed group fighting the Syrian government.

Following the seizure of Mosul, ISIL enhanced its global notoriety through expert manipulation of social media, including online videos of the beheading of foreign journalists and humanitarian workers. This was followed by the gruesome February 2015 burning alive of a captured Jordanian pilot imprisoned in a steel cage. Spectacular terrorist attacks in Europe also added to the deadly mystique surrounding the group, including the major November 2015 attack on a nightclub and other sites in Paris that killed 130 people. Such attacks made ISIL the focus of intense fear in the Western world, but the media frenzy surrounding these attacks distracted from ISIL's real objective.

ISIL's beheading of helpless captives and spraying of bullets at the patrons of a Paris rock venue were propaganda of the cruelest kind, with the focus on recruiting sympathisers and striking fear into the hearts of enemies. Celebrating those terrorist attacks on social media was an important part of what passed for ISIL's foreign policy, but what the so-called Islamic State truly desired was the ongoing acquisition of territory, material resources and power across Syria, Iraq and the Middle East. This was reflected in ISIL's main slogan, '*baqiya wa tatamadad*' – 'enduring and expanding'.

Between 2014 and 2017, ISIL had tanks, heavy weaponry and an army of more than 30,000 fighters at its disposal on a territory that was, at its peak, larger than England. As a result, ISIL's war of expansion in Syria and Iraq was mainly fought on a conventional battlefield, albeit with none of the constraints of the Geneva Conventions. Although it started out as an extremist insurgency, at its apex the so-called Islamic State governed over ten million people. It had its own currency and tax system, and managed its own social services. ISIL beheaded so-called infidels and crucified dissidents, but it also employed teachers, ran hospitals and organised the collection of garbage. It controlled significant oil fields and ruled over Iraq's second largest city, Mosul, as well as Ramadi, Fullujah, Tikrit, Sinjar and, in Syria, Raqqa.[5]

This meant that organisationally ISIL was both an occupying power and an inchoate statelet, whether the UN Security Council cared to recognise it as such or not. ISIL certainly had the resources of a small state, with an estimated annual GDP of between $4 billion and $8 billion at the peak of its power. Economically this placed 'the caliphate' somewhere between Liberia and Monaco. One report estimated that ISIL's income in 2015 amounted to about $2.4 billion, with around twenty-five percent of funds coming from the sale of oil from more than twenty oil fields it controlled. ISIL also controlled forty percent of Iraq's wheat crop, several hydroelectric dams and phosphate mines and other major economic infrastructure.[6]

Although the so-called Islamic State controlled expansive territory and considerable resources, it totally rejected the international political system. It not only dismantled the physical border between eastern Syria and northwestern Iraq, it considered all national borders to be an affront to God's supreme authority. ISIL wanted to eradicate the Westphalian system of sovereign states and replace it with the singular adherence to the word of God as personally interpreted by Baghdadi and his followers.

Between 2014 and 2017 ISIL was responsible for the systematic perpetration of mass atrocity crimes. Indeed, committing these crimes was immeasurably more important to ISIL's strategy for 'enduring and expanding' across Iraq and Syria than was its penchant for killing Westerners in faraway places. To acknowledge this is not to ignore ISIL's willingness to engage in horrific terrorist attacks. Rather, it means that the group's surviving senior officials should be held accountable under international law for atrocity crimes committed in areas previously under their command and control. We should have held its self-declared caliph and his closest aides to a higher level of international criminal responsibility, not a lower one.

The evidence is overwhelming. The UN Assistance Mission for Iraq (UNAMI) and the Office of the High Commissioner for Human Rights (OHCHR) reported that the deliberate nature, scale and impact of ISIL's executions, enslavement, forced conversions and other exactions in Iraq 'may amount to war crimes, crimes against humanity and possibly genocide'.[7] Their January 2016 report outlined numerous killings by ISIL, including gruesome public executions by beheading, burning people alive or driving a bulldozer over them. The report also detailed targeted attacks against religious minority communities, sectarian massacres of Shia captives, murder of religious leaders, destruction of civilian objects and cultural artifacts, mass abduction of children and use of child soldiers and summary execution of former police, soldiers and government officials. UNAMI and OHCHR also alleged that on several occasions ISIL deployed chlorine gas in attacks on Kurdish military positions in northern Iraq.[8]

Similar carnage was inflicted in Syria, where comprehensively documenting ISIL's atrocities was extraordinarily difficult. Nevertheless, the Syrian Observatory for Human Rights reported that between June 2014 and December 2015 alone, ISIL was responsible for the execution of 3,700 people in Syria, at least 2,000 of whom were civilians.[9] As in Iraq, this included prisoners of war and alleged enemy collaborators, as well as those whom ISIL considered to be violating its interpretation of sharia law. ISIL actively promoted these atrocities via propaganda circulated on the internet. For example, in one seven-minute video, sixteen men accused of informing for the Iraqi government were murdered by rocket-propelled grenade, by drowning or by being decapitated. Videos of men 'guilty' of homosexuality being thrown from tall buildings by ISIL militants also made their way to the internet. Perhaps most notorious of all, however, was ISIL's video of the massacre of approximately 1,700 captured Shia Iraqi military cadets at Camp Speicher, following the fall of the Iraqi city of Tikrit in June 2014.[10]

As a result, while ISIL was primarily perceived as a terrorist menace in the Western world, what made the armed extremist group truly unique was, as one expert argued, that 'their state rejects peace as a matter of principle' and 'hungers for genocide'.[11]

Hungry for genocide

The so-called Islamic State wanted to use its armed might to scrub away unique cultures that have developed over millennia and repaint the map of the Middle East black. ISIL believed that it was a duty for its members to kill unbelievers and apostates. The state that ISIL aspired to build could only be fully achieved, therefore, by the extirpation of the diverse ethnic, cultural and religious foundations of Iraq and Syria. There was no room for Turkmen, Alawites, Kurds, Christians and others within the caliphate. ISIL also declared war on more than fifteen million people in Iraq – the majority of the population – who were Shia and whom it considered to be irredeemable heretics.

Prior to June 2014, the Nineveh Governorate was one of the most diverse parts of Iraq, with significant millennia-old minority communities. The predominately Turkmen city of Tal Afar fell to ISIL on 16 June. The largest Christian city in Iraq, Qaraqosh, was also overrun at the start of August. Both were purged of what ISIL considered to be un-Islamic buildings and practices. In Mosul, meanwhile, Christian houses were reportedly marked with an *N* for 'Nazarene'. Mosul's Christians were ordered to convert or pay a protection tax (jizya), acknowledging their submission. Those not complying with this order were given until 19 July to abandon the city. Once home to tens of thousands of Christians, by the end of July Mosul was declared to be Christian free. Having successfully subjugated Iraq's largest and most vibrant Christian communities, Abu Muhammad al-Adnani, ISL's menacing spokesman, threatened their coreligionists abroad: 'We will conquer your Rome, break your crosses, and enslave your women.' If this could not be achieved in his own lifetime, then he promised that ISIL's children and grandchildren would 'sell your sons as slaves at the slave market'.[12]

While ISIL carried out sectarian attacks against the Shia population and targeted vulnerable Christian communities, the threat they posed to the Yazidi minority was existential. Christians, Jews and Muslims share an entwined monotheistic tradition that means that even for the extremists of ISIL, Christians were still regarded as 'people of the book' and were provided very limited protection under their distorted interpretation of sharia law. The Yazidis enjoyed no such indulgence.

A small ethno-religious group encompassing approximately 400,000 people and concentrated mainly in communities around Mount Sinjar in northern Iraq, the Yazidis were considered to be polytheists by ISIL. The group referred to the Yazidis as *mushrikin*, or 'those who commit the sin of idolatry/paganism'.[13] Yazidi religious traditions predate Christianity and Islam, and although Yazidis are considered by some to be ethnic Kurds, to be a Yazidi you must be born of Yazidi parents and cannot convert. The occluded nature of many Yazidi communities has led to them being marginalised and persecuted throughout history, including under the Ottoman Empire. However, when ISIL overran the Sinjar region on 3 August 2014, the Yazidis became the focus of atrocities intended to permanently eradicate their existence.

In the village of Kocho, for example, ISIL captured almost the entire population of around 1,170 Yazidis, who were unable to flee north to the safety of Mount Sinjar. On 15 August ISIL ordered everyone to report to the local school. As families arrived, Yazidi men and boys who appeared to be over the age of twelve (meaning boys who were inspected by ISIL fighters and had visible underarm hair) were separated from the women and other children and transported to a nearby location where at least 250 were lined up and shot. Women and the remaining children were then driven to nearby villages and placed in temporary holding facilities. The fate of women beyong childbearing age – deemed unfit for enslavement – remains unclear, although many were separated from the group and subjected to mass execution. That left only the young boys, girls and women of childbearing age from Kocho. The boys were destined for training camps where they would be forced to convert to Islam and sent to fight for ISIL. The women and girls would become slaves.[14]

Across northern Iraq, ISIL enslaved at least 3,500 Yazidi women and girls. While mothers were permitted to keep their youngest children with them, girls above the age of nine were traded or sold. In *Dabiq*, ISIL's propaganda magazine, the group theologically justified this and said that Yazidi female captives should be divided amongst ISIL fighters who participated in the Sinjar offensive. ISIL formally established a department of 'war spoils' to regulate enslavement and issued religious rulings regarding permitted sexual relations between ISIL fighters and their slaves. As a result, even young girls of around eleven years of age were raped by the ISIL men they 'belonged' to. One young girl abused by an ISIL fighter later remarked on how he prayed beforehand, considering the sexual assault to be a pious act. Hundreds of Yazidi women and girls were also sold at slave markets in Syria for between $200 and $2,000 (US). Indeed, UNAMI and OHCHR claimed that enslavement became so pervasive that in June 2015 ISIL even offered slaves as a prize to the winners of a Quran memorisation competition in Mosul.[15]

During December 2015 the UN Security Council held its first debate on the issue of modern slavery. The Council heard heartbreaking testimony from Nadia Murad, a young Yazidi woman from Kocho who had been enslaved by ISIL. Nadia detailed how ISIL preyed upon women and girls from the minority Yazidi community in Iraq, using them 'as spoils of war, as objects to be sold' or as gifts for its fighters.[16] Nadia eventually escaped from ISIL and made her way to a refugee camp in Kurdistan before being granted asylum in Germany.

ISIL's targeting of Yazidi women was about not just the sexual gratification of its fighters but the destruction of the Yazidis as a people. Across the Sinjar region, the Yazidis were subjected to targeted killings, forced religious conversion and the transfer of children (as slaves, converts or child soldiers) to persons outside of the Yazidi community. Such acts, carried out as a deliberate policy by ISIL, constituted genocide. As a UN International Commission of Inquiry report later put it – drawing directly from Article II of the Genocide Convention – ISIL 'intended to destroy the Yazidis of Sinjar, composing the majority of the world's Yazidi population, in whole or in part'.[17]

ISIL also sought to destroy the economic way of life that sustains Yazidi society in northern Iraq. Even as they were eventually forced out of the Sinjar area, ISIL fighters poisoned wells, burned down orchards and broke essential electrical infrastructure. For example, in the small Yazidi town of Sinune, north of Mount Sinjar, ISIL stole almost all the livestock and 'destroyed, stole or burned' approximately eighty-five percent of the agricultural machinery and vehicles. Around 400 of 450 irrigation wells in the Sinune subdistrict were also rendered unusable. As a result, as one Yazidi farmer who did later return to his small village put it, 'we have come back to a dead land'.[18] As part of this genocidal strategy, ISIL also wanted to 'cleanse' Iraq of its unique cultural heritage.

Cultural cleansing

Raphael Lemkin, who was personally responsible for the creation of the term *genocide*, believed that humanity's cultural heritage was 'a product of the contributions of all nations'. As a Polish Jewish refugee during the Second World War, Lemkin was painfully aware of how the Nazis demolished the cultural underpinnings of Jewish life in occupied Europe. For Lemkin the killing of a people 'in a spiritual and cultural sense' was linked to their destruction in a physical sense. Lemkin's conception of genocide included 'desecration and destruction of cultural symbols, destruction of cultural leadership, destruction of cultural centers, prohibition of cultural activities' and forced conversion to an alien religion or way of life. The intentional eradication of a people's 'traditions, monuments, archives, libraries, and churches' amounted to the destruction of 'the shrines of a nation's soul'. Regrettably, opposition from some members of the United Nations saw Lemkin's ideas regarding culture diluted in the final version of the Genocide Convention that was adopted in December 1948.[19]

This is not to say that the connection between culture, conflict, persecution and atrocities was completely ignored. The 1954 Convention for the Protection of Cultural Property in the Event of Armed Conflict highlights that 'damage to cultural property belonging to any people whatsoever means damage to the cultural heritage of all' humankind. Cultural heritage is protected under the convention and is part of customary international humanitarian law (Rules 38–41). Jurisprudence was further advanced at various international criminal tribunals and via the International Criminal Court (ICC), which has jurisdiction over genocide, crimes against humanity and war crimes. According to Article 8 of the 2002 Rome Statute, war crimes may include 'intentionally directing attacks against buildings dedicated to religion, education, art, science or charitable purposes, historic monuments' and other civilian objects.[20]

ISIL's 'caliphate' included several thousand major archaeological sites from some of humanity's earliest civilisations, and between 2014 and 2017 the armed group systematically pursued the destruction of what it considered to be deviant aspects of Iraq and Syria's cultural heritage. In the Mosul Museum they used sledgehammers and power tools to deface, topple and destroy ancient statues from pre-Islamic Mesopotamia. At Nimrud, ISIL militants blew up and bulldozed the ruins of an ancient Assyrian city. At Palmyra in Syria ISIL partly destroyed a Roman theatre that was listed as a UNESCO World Heritage site and beheaded Khaled al-Asaad, the archaeologist who had spent his career protecting the ruins. They burned books from Mosul's historic library and illegally trafficked Roman and Assyrian antiquities for profit.[21]

Meanwhile, in the Sinjar region of northern Iraq, where ISIL committed genocide against the Yazidi population, they also systematically destroyed at least sixty-eight Yazidi temples and shrines. In the twin villages of Bashiqa and Bahzani, all thirty-eight significant Yazidi shrines and temples – including two shrines that were at least 700 years old – were systematically destroyed by ISIL fighters using explosives and bulldozers, and tombstones dating back to the thirteenth century were desecrated. At the shrine of Sheikh Mand, near Mount Sinjar, ISIL executed fourteen elderly villagers inside the shrine before blowing it up. Ceremonies and rituals performed at all these religious sites, with elders transmitting traditions from one generation to the next, are essential to the survival of the Yazidi faith. ISIL's motivation, in the words of one Yazidi survivor, was 'to erase everything that connected us to our culture and heritage'.[22]

While these acts may seem to pale in comparison to some of ISIL's other atrocities, it is important to realise that ISIL's attacks on Yazidi temples and Christian churches, as well as on Roman ruins, Assyrian statues and other artefacts, represented a systematic attempt to scrub away the history and memory of entire peoples. Moreover, unlike other physical infrastructure such as bridges or schools, what was broken and destroyed cannot be easily rebuilt. It is lost.[23]

Far from hiding these acts of armed vandalism, ISIL celebrated them. The destruction of Nimrud was filmed and released online. The partial demolition of Palmyra was featured in a major article in ISIL's magazine, *Dabiq*. A video filmed at the Mosul Museum featured an ISIL militant celebrating the toppling 'of idols of peoples of previous centuries, which were worshipped instead of Allah'. The video declared that ISIL did not care what people outside the caliphate thought of this destruction, or that the statues 'are worth billions of dollars'. According to another ISIL publication, it was unbelievers who had uncovered many of Iraq's ancient ruins and presented them 'as part of a cultural heritage and identity that the Muslims of Iraq should embrace and be proud of'. According to ISIL this was an affront to God.[24]

When the head of the UN Educational, Scientific and Cultural Organization (UNESCO), Irina Bokova, described ISIL's vandalism as a policy of 'cultural cleansing' that constituted possible war crimes, ISIL could not contain its outrage. In a choreographed video of the destruction of reliefs at the ancient Parthian and Arab Kingdom site of Hatra during early 2015, ISIL declared: 'Some of the infidel organizations say the destruction of these alleged artefacts is a war crime. We will destroy your artefacts and idols anywhere and Islamic State will rule your lands'.[25]

Bokova's comments were grounded in international law. In February 2015, UN Security Council Resolution 2199 condemned the 'targeted destruction' of cultural heritage in Syria and Iraq, including religious sites and objects, by ISIL and other armed extremist groups. The Council also imposed international sanctions. Then in September 2016, Ahmad al-Faqi al-Mahdi, a member of an armed extremist group in Mali, was found guilty at the ICC of a war crime for his role in the deliberate destruction of the UNESCO World Heritage site at Timbuktu. During March 2017 the UN Security Council adopted Resolution 2347, deploring the destruction of humanity's cultural heritage and noting that the ICC verdict 'for the first time convicted a defendant for the war crimes of intentionally directing attacks against religious buildings and historic monuments and buildings'. The historic resolution stressed that states 'have the primary responsibility in protecting their cultural heritage' in conformity with international law.[26]

But were states prepared to act accordingly? A few months later, the Global Centre for the Responsibility to Protect cohosted an event with the governments of France and Italy on the margins of the UN General Assembly regarding how to protect cultural heritage from terrorism and mass atrocities. The speakers included the foreign minister of Italy, Angelino Alfano; the high representative for foreign affairs and security policy of the European Union, Federica Mogherini; the head of UNESCO, Irina Bokova; and the chief prosecutor of the ICC, Fatou Bensouda. All the speakers emphasised that defending cultural heritage was not just about preserving stones and statues but about protecting vulnerable populations. Particular attention was drawn to the ongoing threat posed by ISIL in Syria and Iraq.

According to the United Nations, sectarian bomb attacks on Shia communities and the deliberate destruction of 'houses belonging to Christian families' revealed the systematic nature of ISIL's attacks on religious minorities in Iraq. But the UN also noted that ISIL 'continued to deliberately and wantonly loot and destroy places of religious and cultural significance', including 'ancient sites, as well as churches, mosques, shrines, tombs, and graves', that it considered un-Islamic. Yazidi and Christian places of worship were specifically targeted, with ISIL militants continuing to systematically loot and destroy these sites with explosives and bulldozers. In such cases there was an ongoing and disturbing convergence between ISIL's acts of cultural vandalism and its desire to exterminate entire peoples. As Bokova of UNESCO argued, in 'today's new conflicts, those two dimensions cannot be separated'. As a result, 'there is no need to choose between saving lives and preserving cultural heritage: the two are inseparable'.[27]

Overthrowing the caliphate

ISIL's capture of the towns and villages around Mount Sinjar on 3 August 2014 resulted in the mass execution of hundreds of Yazidi men and the enslavement of captured women and girls. Most of those who escaped ISIL's initial onslaught fled to Mount Sinjar. The Iraqi government, still in shock following the fall of Mosul, pleaded for emergency military assistance from the United States. On 9 August 2014 the US Air Force launched air strikes on ISIL fighters who were besieging

Yazidi civilians trapped on the mountain, protecting them from what US president Barack Obama described as a 'potential act of genocide'.[28]

Meanwhile, Syrian Kurdish militias – the People's Protection Units (YPG) – battled ISIL on the ground, and by 10 August they were able to open a corridor from Mount Sinjar, allowing thousands of Yazidis to escape along the rocky mountain paths into Syria. However, the air strikes did not come quickly enough and the protected corridor could not help people in the besieged village of Kocho, who phoned relatives in the United States pleading for their lives. Murad Ismael, one of the founders of the Yazidi human rights group Yazda, shouted down the phone to his contact in the White House: 'They are saying just to bomb the whole village'. Facing slavery, forced conversion or execution, 'they would rather they all die'. With more diplomatic nuance, Rita Izsák, the UN special rapporteur on minority issues, continued to call for 'all possible measures' to be taken 'urgently to avoid a mass atrocity and potential genocide within days or hours'.[29]

Nevertheless, the air strikes to protect besieged Yazidis on Mount Sinjar saved thousands of people from slavery or death at the hands of ISIL. Soon after, President Obama expanded the air strikes and promised to 'degrade and ultimately destroy' ISIL in both Iraq and Syria. The skies over Iraq then became congested with foreign fighter planes and armed drones as Australia, Belgium, Denmark, France, Jordan, the Netherlands and the United Kingdom all joined the United States in conducting extensive air strikes.[30]

The air strikes revealed that ISIL's greatest appeal was also its principal weakness – its physical control over territory in eastern Syria and western Iraq. Because ISIL was not a formal part of the international political or economic system, it was less susceptible to measures that did not involve the use of force, like sanctions or an arms embargo, than a normal state. However, ISIL did trade on the illicit fringes of the regional economy, relying on sources of income such as the black-market trade in oil and antiquities. Denying ISIL the opportunity to economically prosper was therefore an essential part of the strategy of constraining it. Sanctions aimed at choking ISIL's sources of income cut off seventy-five percent of its estimated revenue by early 2015.[31] But above all else, the struggle against ISIL was a military one.

What proved to be decisive was not just air strikes to prevent a genocide on Mount Sinjar but the efforts across Syria and Iraq of local ground forces with the capacity and fortitude to take territory from ISIL and hold it. This was demonstrated during the fierce battle for the Syrian border town of Kobane between September 2014 and January 2015. The battle was won mainly by Kurdish YPG fighters, who coordinated their tenacious defense with coalition air strikes and dealt ISIL its first major defeat. An estimated 1,000 ISIL fighters were killed in their failed attempt to take the town.[32] Western allies, especially the United States, also threw their support behind the Syrian Democratic Forces, an alliance of Arab and Kurdish armed groups (mainly the YPG) battling ISIL for control of eastern Syria. Meanwhile, in Iraq the struggle against ISIL relied on the Kurdish

Peshmerga, a reinvigorated ISF and allied Shia militias organised in the Popular Mobilization Forces.

ISIL's slogan of 'enduring and expanding' reflected its fighters' belief that their self-declared caliphate was divinely inspired. But ISIL was not only pushed back from Kobane; sustained attacks by a plethora of enemies arrayed against it reduced ISIL's territory by an estimated fourteen percent during 2015. The following year the caliphate shrank by another twenty-five percent, or 18,000 square kilometres (6,900 square miles). By October 2017 both Raqqa and Mosul had been retaken, and the amount of land held by ISIL was just one quarter of its January 2015 peak of around 90,800 square kilometres (56,400 square miles). ISIL was in full retreat.[33]

Constricting the territory controlled by ISIL had a corrosive effect on the morale of its adherents, especially those who had moved to the 'caliphate' from beyond the Levant. Unlike al-Qaeda or other small conspiratorial terrorist groups, ISIL's appeal was its physical control of contiguous cities, towns and villages. Beset by enemies on all sides, ISIL by 2016 was absorbing unsustainable losses. According to senior US military figures, possibly as many as 60,000 ISIL fighters (both local recruits and foreigners) may have been killed in the battle to overthrow the caliphate.[34]

At the peak of its power, ISIL released an estimated 15,000 pieces of propaganda in a single year, 'including 800 videos and some 20 magazines translated into 11 languages, including Mandarin'. However, one report noted that following the recapture of Mosul in July 2017, the output of ISIL propaganda decreased by more than two thirds. A few months later, around the time of the fall of Raqqa, 'it ended entirely'.[35] Without expansive territory and millions of subjects, ISIL resorted to hiding in remote pockets of territory in the deserts of Iraq and Syria, relying on deadly hit-and-run raids and sporadic terrorist attacks.

Despite having inflicted a series of devastating defeats upon ISIL, some of the forces engaged in the battle to defeat the extremist group continued to manipulate religious identities and communal loyalties. The ISF reportedly carried out extrajudicial killings, as well as the illegal detention and torture of people suspected of supporting ISIL. Similarly, UNAMI and OHCHR reported that some Shia militias affiliated with the Iraqi government regularly violated the rules of war and carried out violent reprisals against Sunni civilians.[36]

On 4 December 2015, OHCHR also expressed concern over forced evictions, looting and extrajudicial killings committed by the ISF and Kurdish security forces 'against Sunni Arab communities in parts of Iraq that have been reclaimed from ISIL'.[37] Amnesty International similarly reported in January 2016 that Kurdish Peshmerga forces had 'bulldozed, blown up, and burned down' thousands of Sunni Arab homes across thirteen towns and villages in northern Iraq. These actions were allegedly undertaken with the purpose of collectively punishing Sunni Arabs for alleged sympathy with ISIL and incorporating disputed territory into the Kurdish region.[38]

Civilians also faced death from above as foreign armies continued to bomb ISIL-controlled territory. In May 2019 the US-led international anti-ISIL coalition admitted that according to its investigations, in addition to killing ISIL fighters it had accidentally killed at least 1,302 civilians in Iraq and Syria in 34,502 air strikes carried out between August 2014 and April 2019. Meanwhile, according to the Syrian Network for Human Rights (SNHR), Russia's air strikes in Syria (supposedly directed against ISIL, but actually targeting all areas not held by the government and its allies) killed 6,686 civilians between September 2015 and September 2019. Every reckless air strike that killed innocent civilians in Iraq and Syria made the job of permanently defeating ISIL more difficult.[39]

The situation on the ground also remained politically complicated. The role of Kurdish forces in major anti-ISIL operations aggravated the region's other major power, Turkey. Ankara was implacably hostile to any expansion of power or territory by the Kurdish YPG along its borders, and in 2018 Turkey militarily intervened in northern Syria, displacing thousands of civilians and sowing the seeds for future conflict.

The so-called Islamic State did not simply collapse under the weight of its own contradictions and crimes. It was necessary to overthrow 'the caliphate' by force, with much blood shed in the process. With the fall of the Syrian village of Baghuz in March 2019, ISIL lost its last remaining pocket of territory.[40] But in the long term, truly defeating ISIL will require a coordinated strategy to counter the lingering appeal of the extremist group to some embittered and marginalised Iraqis and Syrians. This will require local governments to greatly improve their ability to deliver basic services, end corruption and halt human rights abuses. ISIL perpetrators also need to be held legally accountable for atrocities they have committed.

Justice and accountability

At a divisive May 2014 meeting of the UN Security Council in New York, Russia and China vetoed a draft resolution that would have referred all mass atrocities committed in Syria to the International Criminal Court for investigation. The resolution had been put forward by sixty-five states and was supported by the rest of the Council. Outside the chamber, human rights organisations widely criticised the double veto, arguing that justice and accountability for atrocity crimes was an essential part of demonstrating to ordinary Syrians that no one was beyond the reach of international law and that their suffering would not be ignored. Although the unstated intention of the Russian and Chinese veto was to protect the Syrian government from scrutiny, an ICC referral would have also enabled the court to prosecute any captured ISIL members accused of war crimes, crimes against humanity or genocide.

Then in early 2016 the UN secretary-general, Ban Ki-moon, presented a 'Plan of Action to Prevent Violent Extremism'. Central to the secretary-general's approach was the idea that policies for 'preventing extremism and promoting human rights' needed to be pursued in tandem:

> All too often, national counter-terrorism strategies have lacked basic elements of due process and respect for the rule of law. Sweeping definitions

of terrorism or violent extremism are often used to criminalize the legitimate actions of opposition groups, civil society organizations and human rights defenders. Governments should not use these types of sweeping definitions as a pretext to attack or silence one's critics.[41]

The real challenge, especially in countries lacking strong democratic traditions, is managing diversity and ensuring that human rights are equally protected, while also pursuing targeted measures against groups like ISIL or Boko Haram. Torture, arbitrary detention and mass hangings are a poor antidote. But in divided societies where the sort of structural reforms necessary to overcome discrimination and counter extremism are expensive and time consuming, states often opt for fierce repression and armed reprisals instead.

With ISIL broken on the battlefield, it also became possible to better assess the scale of the horror it had inflicted upon Iraq and Syria. Between 2014 and the end of 2017, ISIL was responsible for approximately 30,000 civilian deaths in Iraq alone. In November 2018, UNAMI and OHCHR released a joint report detailing the discovery of 202 mass graves in Iraq that contained the bodies of between 6,000 and 12,000 of ISIL's victims. The graves included 'women, children, elderly and persons with disabilities, members and former members of the Iraqi armed forces and police, and some foreign workers'. The sites included the 'Khasfa sinkhole' south of Mosul, where it is believed the bodies of up to 4,000 victims were dumped after execution by ISIL fighters.[42]

Another key site was Camp Speicher, where ISIL massacred approximately 1,700 army cadets and members of the Iraqi security forces on 12 June 2014. This was possibly the largest mass killing perpetrated by ISIL in either Iraq or Syria, and at least 15 mass graves were later discovered containing the remains of hundreds of the victims. According to the UNAMI/OHCHR report:

> The Government of Iraq has devoted a considerable amount of human and financial resources to the excavation and exhumation of the mass graves at Camp Speicher and to the identification of the victims. Information gathered at these sites formed the basis for the investigation, prosecution and conviction of a large number of defendants in 2016 and 2017, resulting in at least 91 death sentences and 35 executions carried out. More trials are expected to take place in relation to the Camp Speicher massacres.[43]

Utilising anti-terrorism laws, Iraqi trials of former ISIL members were flawed and perfunctory affairs, with scant evidence or witness corroboration and often relying on confessions obtained under extreme duress or torture. Death sentences were handed out after trials lasting only a few minutes. But no one was held legally accountable for war crimes, crimes against humanity or genocide.[44]

In September 2017 the UN Security Council finally adopted Resolution 2379, creating the UN Investigative Team to Promote Accountability for Crimes Committed by Da'esh/ISIL (UNITAD). Since then, UNITAD has been working to exhume mass graves and preserve evidence of atrocities committed by ISIL in Iraq. In March 2019, at the same time that UNITAD was exhuming mass graves around the village of Kocho, a number of Yazidi women and children were also being liberated from their ISIL captors following the final fall of Baghuz in Syria. But the fact remains that more than six years after their offensive on the Nineveh Plain began, not a single ISIL member has been held accountable in an Iraqi court of law for the genocide against the Yazidi.

UNESCO did, however, launch a campaign to rebuild the cultural heritage of northern Iraq and 'revive the spirit of Mosul'. Initial funding came from the United Arab Emirates and other significant donors. Hungary's right-wing government, meanwhile, offered to rebuild some Christian churches on the Nineveh Plain. And in Sinjar, an Iranian-backed Shia militia, the Imam Ali Brigades, rebuilt the Sayyida Zaynab shrine. Surveying these developments during 2019, a local Yazidi activist, Falah Hasan Issa, complained that no destroyed Yazidi shrines in Sinjar had been rebuilt. By contrast, 'there was only one Shia shrine, and they reconstructed it'. The respected head of the Yazidi faith, Khurto Hajji Ismail, or Baba Sheikh insisted that 'if they do not rebuild the shrines which were destroyed' by ISIL, 'the existence of the Yazidis in these areas will be forgotten'.[45] Despite the defeat of ISIL and the recent reconstruction of some Yazidi temples and shrines, culture remains a battlefield across northern Iraq.

Conclusion

In June 2017, with their enemies closing in on their last strongholds inside the Old City district of Mosul, a group of ISIL fighters blew up the Great Mosque of al-Nuri. They had packed the building with explosives, and as Iraqi government forces fought their way to within a hundred metres of the mosque, the ISIL fighters detonated a massive bomb, killing themselves and reducing the mosque and its famous leaning minaret to rubble. Denouncing the deliberate destruction of yet another of piece of Iraq's irreplaceable cultural heritage, the country's prime minister, Haider al-Abadi, described this as 'an official declaration of defeat' by ISIL in Mosul.[46] What was not mentioned was that the spot where Baghdadi had last been seen in public, and where he had given his first and only recorded public speech as caliph, was now buried under broken bricks and masonry dust. The Islamic State's black flag, which had flown from the minaret since June 2014, was buried along with the corpses of the last defenders of Baghdadi's vanishing caliphate.

Notes

1 "ISIS-Declared 'Caliph' al-Baghdadi Makes Video Appearance," *Deutsche Welle*, 6 July 2014, https://www.dw.com/en/isis-declared-caliph-al-baghdadi-makes-video-appearance/a-17761390; and Hannah Strange, "Islamic State Leader Abu Bakr al-Baghdadi Addresses Muslims in Mosul," *The Telegraph*, 5 July 2014, https://www.telegraph.co.uk/news/worldnews/middleeast/iraq/10948480/Islamic-State-leader-Abu-Bakr-al-Baghdadi-addresses-Muslims-in-Mosul.html.

2 "Why Mosul's Great Mosque of al-Nuri Mattered," *BBC News*, 21 June 2017, https://www.bbc.com/news/world-middle-east-39339373.

3 Graeme Wood, "What ISIS Really Wants," *The Atlantic*, March 2015, https://www.theatlantic.com/magazine/archive/2015/03/what-isis-really-wants/384980/.

4 Candace Karp, "You Can't Fight What You Don't Understand," *Foreign Policy*, 1 June 2015, http://foreignpolicy.com/2015/06/01/you-cant-fight-what-you-dont-understand-violent-extremism-islamic-state/.

5 Willem T. Oosterveld and Willem Bloem, "The Rise and Fall of ISIS: From Evitability to Inevitability," *Hague Centre for Strategic Studies*, 2017; Jason Burke, "Rise and Fall of ISIS: Its Dream of a Caliphate Is Over, So What Now?," *The Guardian*, 21 October 2017, https://www.theguardian.com/world/2017/oct/21/isis-caliphate-islamic-state-raqqa-iraq-islamist; and Seth G. Jones et al., "Rolling Back the Islamic State," *Rand Corporation*, 2017.

6 Stephen M. Walt, "ISIS as Revolutionary State," *Foreign Affairs*, 94, no. 6 (November/December 2015): 47; "ISIS Financing," *Center for the Analysis of Terrorism*, May 2016, 7, 9–11, https://cat-int.org/wp-content/uploads/2016/06/ISIS-Financing-2015-Report.pdf; and Burke, "Rise and Fall of ISIS: Its Dream of a Caliphate Is Over, so What Now?".

7 UNAMI & OHCHR, Report on the Protection of Civilians in the Armed Conflict in Iraq, 1 May to 31 October 2015, http://www.uniraq.org/images/humanrights/UNAMI-OHCHR_%20POC%20Report_FINAL_01%20May-31%20October%202015_FINAL_11Jan2016.pdf.

8 Ibid.

9 Ralph Ellis, "ISIS executed 2,114 civilians, human rights group says," *CNN*, 29 January 2016, http://www.cnn.com/2016/01/29/middleeast/syria-isis-executions/.

10 UNAMI & OHCHR, Report on the Protection of Civilians in the Armed Conflict in Iraq, 1 May to 31 October 2015, 16–17; and "The Caliphate Strikes Back," *The Economist*, 23 May 2015.

11 Wood, "What ISIS Really Wants."

12 Ibid; "And then There Were None," *The Economist*, 2 January 2016.

13 UNAMI/OHCHR, "Unearthing Atrocities: Mass Graves in Territory Formerly Controlled by ISIL," 6 November 2018, 8, https://www.ohchr.org/Documents/Countries/IQ/UNAMI_Report_on_Mass_Graves4Nov2018_EN.pdf.

14 Working with locals, the Yazidi Victims Demographic Documentation Project has tried to identity every victim of the attack on Kocho. According to their data, among the 1,170 Yazidis who fell into ISIL's hands were 287 men over the age of twenty who were killed or are still missing – ninety percent of the male population of Kocho in this age group. Valeria Cetorelli and Sareta Ashraph, "A Demographic Documentation of ISIS's Attack on the Yazidi Village of Kocho," *London School of Economics' Middle East Centre Report*, June 2019, http://eprints.lse.ac.uk/101098/1/Cetorelli_Demographic_documentation_ISIS_attack.pdf. See also, Independent International Commission of Inquiry on the Syrian Arab Republic, A/HRC/32/CRP.2: "They came to destroy": ISIS Crimes Against the Yazidis, 15 June 2016, 8–9, https://www.ohchr.org/Documents/HRBodies/HRCouncil/CoISyria/A_HRC_32_CRP.2_en.pdf; Simon-Skjodt Center for the Prevention of Genocide, "Our Generation is Gone": The Islamic State's Targeting of Iraqi Minorities in Ninewa, US Holocaust Memorial Museum, November 2015, https://www.ushmm.org/m/pdfs/Iraq-Bearing-Witness-Report-111215.pdf.

15 UNAMI & OHCHR, Report on the Protection of Civilians in the Armed Conflict in Iraq, 1 May to 31 October 2015, 17–18, http://www.uniraq.org/images/humanrights/UNAMI-OHCHR_%20POC%20Report_FINAL_01%20May-31%20October%202015_FINAL_11Jan2016.pdf; Independent International Commission of Inquiry on the Syrian Arab Republic, "They came to destroy": ISIS Crimes Against the Yazidis, 9–17, 29; David Zucchino, "Islamic State publication seeks to justify slavery and sexual

abuse," *Los Angeles Times*, 13 October 2014; Wood, "What ISIS Really Wants"; Jonathan Landay, Warren Strobel, Phil Stewart, "Exclusive – Islamic State ruling aims to settle who can have sex with female slaves," *Reuters*, 29 December 2015, http://www.reuters.com/article/us-usa-islamic-state-documents-group-exc-idUSKBN0UB0AW20151229; Rukmini Callimachi, "ISIS Enshrines a Theology of Rape," *New York Times*, 13 August 2015.

16 Statement by Nadia Murad Basee Taha to the UN Security Council, 18 December 2015, http://freedomfund.org/blog/5380/.

17 Independent International Commission of Inquiry on the Syrian Arab Republic, "They came to destroy": ISIS Crimes Against the Yazidis, 1, 20–31.

18 Amnesty International, Dead Land: Islamic State's Deliberate Destruction of Iraq's Farmland, December 2018, https://www.amnesty.org/en/documents/mde14/9510/2018/en/.

19 Donald Bloxham and A. Dirk Moses (eds), *The Oxford Handbook of Genocide Studies* (New York: Oxford University Press, 2010), 305; Donna-Lee Frieze, ed., *Totally Unofficial: The Autobiography of Raphael Lemkin*, (New Haven: Yale University Press, 2013), 172; Edward C. Luck, "Cultural Genocide and the Protection of Cultural Heritage," *The J. Paul Getty Trust Occasional Papers in Cultural Heritage Policy*, no. 2 (2018): 17–26.

20 Polina L. Mahnad, "Protecting Cultural Property in Syria: New Opportunities for States to Enhance Compliance with International Law?," *International Review of the Red Cross*, 99, no. 3 (2017), 1037–1074.

21 Marius Bosch and Maher Chmaytelli, "Islamic State Blows Up Historic Mosul Mosque Where It Declared 'Caliphate'," *Reuters*, 21 June 2017, https://www.reuters.com/article/us-mideast-crisis-iraq-mosul-mosque-idUSKBN19C2Q1; Benjamin Isakhan and Jose A. Gonzalez Zarandona, "Erasing History: Why Islamic State is Blowing Up Ancient Artifacts," *The Conversation*, 4 June 2017, http://theconversation.com/erasing-history-why-islamic-state-is-blowing-up-ancient-artefacts-78667; and "ISIS Financing," 19–20.

22 Rashid International, Endangered Archaeology in the Middle East and North Africa (Eamena) and Yazda, Destroying the Soul of the Yazidis: Cultural Heritage Destruction During the Islamic State's Genocide Against the Yazidis, 20 (2019), 34–35, 53; Benjamin Isakhan and Sofya Shahab, "The Islamic State's Destruction of Yezidi Heritage: Responses, Resilience and Reconstruction After Genocide," *Journal of Social Archaeology*, 20, no. 1 (2020), 12–14.

23 ISIL's destruction did not spare Islamic sites. ISIL blew up the historic tomb of the prophet Jonah in Mosul and ordered the removal of all decorative elements from mosques that they considered to deviate from Islamic law.

24 Isakhan and Gonzalez Zarandona, "Erasing history: why Islamic State is blowing up ancient artifacts."

25 Luck, "Cultural Genocide and the Protection of Cultural Heritage," 13; Isakhan and Gonzalez Zarandona, "Erasing history: why Islamic State is blowing up ancient artifacts."

26 UN Security Council Resolution 2199, S/RES/2199, 12 February 2015; and UN Security Council Resolution 2347, S/RES/2347, 24 March 2017.

27 UNAMI & OHCHR, "Report on the Protection of Civilians in the Armed Conflict in Iraq, 1 May to 31 October 2015, 8–9, 14, 16; Independent International Commission of Inquiry on the Syrian Arab Republic, A/HRC/32/CRP.2: "They came to destroy": ISIS Crimes Against the Yazidis, 19; Luck, "Cultural Genocide and the Protection of Cultural Heritage," 13.

28 White House Press Secretary, "Statement by the President," 7 August 2014, https://www.whitehouse.gov/the-press-office/2014/08/07/statement-president.

29 Jenna Krajeski, "The Daring Plan to Save a Religious Minority from ISIS," *The New Yorker*, 26 February 2018; and "Northern Iraq: UN Rights Experts Urge Action to

Avoid Mass Atrocity, Potential Genocide," *UN News*, 12 August 2014, https://news.un.org/en/story/2014/08/474982-northern-iraq-un-rights-experts-urge-action-avoid-mass-atrocity-potential.

30 Between August 2014 and March 2018, the US-led coalition conducted more than 13,300 air strikes on ISIL targets. "Islamic State and the crisis in Iraq and Syria in maps," *BBC News*, 28 March 2018, https://www.bbc.com/news/world-middle-east-27838034.

31 "The Caliphate Cracks," *The Economist*, 21 March 2015.

32 "The Pushback," *The Economist*, 21 March 2015.

33 All territory calculations are approximations. Columb Strack, "Islamic State in Decline," *IHS Markit*, 10 October 2017, https://ihsmarkit.com/research-analysis/islamic-state-in-decline.html; "Islamic State group 'lost quarter of territory' in 2016," *BBC News*, 19 January 2017; "Islamic State territory shrinks in Iraq and Syria: US-led coalition," *Reuters*, 5 January 2016, http://www.reuters.com/article/us-mideast-crisis-islamicstate-idUSKBN0UJ17F20160105; and Jones et al., "Rolling Back the Islamic State."

34 Jason Burke, "Rise and Fall of ISIS: Its Dream of a Caliphate Is Over, so What Now?," *The Guardian*, 21 October 2017.

35 Burke, "Rise and fall of ISIS"; "ISIS Financing," 22.

36 Daniel Byman, "Beyond Counterterrorism," *Foreign Affairs*, 94, no. 6 (November/December 2015): 15; and Anne Barnard, "Iraqi Forces and Militias Said to Loot Sunni Towns," *New York Times*, 18 March 2015.

37 OHCHR Press Briefing: Iraq/discrimination and violence, 4 December 2015, http://www.ohchr.org/EN/NewsEvents/Pages/DisplayNews.aspx?NewsID=16840&LangID=E.

38 Amnesty International, Iraq: Banished and Dispossessed: Forced Displacement and Deliberate Destruction in Northern Iraq, 20 January 2016, https://www.amnesty.org/en/documents/mde14/3229/2016/en/.

39 The Syrian Observatory for Human Rights claimed the actual number of civilians killed by coalition air strikes in Syria was more than 3,800 people. On casualties, see SNHR, "Russian Forces Killed 6,686 Civilians, including 1,928 Children, Since the Start of Their Military Intervention in Syria," 30 September 2019, http://sn4hr.org/wp-content/pdf/english/Russian_forces_have_killed_6686_civilians_including_1928_children_since_their_military_intervention_in_Syria_en.pdf; "US-led Forces killed 1300 Civilians in IS Airstrikes," *Deutsche Welle*, 31 May 2019, https://www.dw.com/en/us-led-forces-killed-1300-civilians-in-is-airstrikes/a-48995555; Diana Al Rifai, "US Coalition Airstrikes in Syria 'killed 250 Civilians'," *Al Jazeera*, 25 November 2015, http://www.aljazeera.com/news/2015/11/coalition-strikes-syria-killed-250-civilians-151124075241069.html.

40 Hassan Hassan, "ISIS Is Ready for a Resurgence," *The Atlantic*, 26 August 2018.

41 UN Secretary-General's Remarks at General Assembly Presentation of the Plan of Action to Prevent Violent Extremism, 15 January 2016, http://www.un.org/sg/statements/index.asp?nid=9388.

42 UNAMI/OHCHR, "Unearthing Atrocities: Mass Graves in Territory Formerly Controlled by ISIL," 6 November 2018, 1–2, 7. https://www.ohchr.org/Documents/Countries/IQ/UNAMI_Report_on_Mass_Graves4Nov2018_EN.pdf.

43 Ibid, 9.

44 Ibid, 4; Belkis Wille, "Executions in Iraq Not Real Justice for Speicher Massacre," *Human Rights Watch*, 23 August 2016, https://www.hrw.org/news/2016/08/23/executions-iraq-not-real-justice-speicher-massacre; Ben Taub, "Iraq's Post-ISIS Campaign of Revenge," *The New Yorker*, 24 & 31 December 2018.

45 Lizzie Porter, "Why an Iran-backed Paramilitary Group Has Rebuilt a Shrine in a Ruined Iraqi City," *Atlantic Council*, 19 August 2019, https://www.atlanticcouncil.org/blogs/iransource/why-an-iran-backed-paramilitary-group-has-rebuilt-a-shrine-in-a-

ruined-iraqi-city/; Lauren Green, "Hungary Leading the Way in Helping Persecuted Christians," *FoxNews*, 27 February 2020, https://www.foxnews.com/faith-values/hungary-leading-way-helping-persecuted-christians; UNESCO, Revive the Spirit of Mosul, https://en.unesco.org/fieldoffice/baghdad/revivemosul; and Rashid, Eamena and Yazda, Destroying the Soul of the Yazidis, 19.

46 "Battle for Mosul: IS 'Blows Up' al-Nuri Mosque," *BBC News*, 22 June 2017, https://www.bbc.com/news/world-middle-east-40361857; and "Why Mosul's Great Mosque of al-Nuri Mattered," *BBC News*, 21 June 2017, https://www.bbc.com/news/world-middle-east-39339373.

5

CLIMATE CHANGE AND MASS ATROCITIES

Contents

In early 2020 a massive plague of locusts invaded East Africa. The plague was the product of an unusually intense cyclone season the previous year that resulted in drenching rains across the Horn of Africa and the Arabian Peninsula. Many scientists blamed climate change and pointed to the Indian Ocean Dipole – where a high variance in sea-surface temperature between opposite sides of the ocean disrupts normal weather patterns. In 2018 there were two major cyclones in the Indian Ocean. In 2019 there were eight.

The plague of locusts, which originated in a remote region of Oman and Yemen, rapidly multiplied in size and destructive potential. During the early phase of the crisis, weak state structures and endemic conflict in Yemen and Somalia inhibited the ability of the UN Food and Agriculture Organization to systematically spray the swarm and contain it. As a result, the locust plague reproduced exponentially and eventually split into several massive swarms that descended upon crops in at least five countries across the region. By February, according to the *Economist,* one swarm over northern Kenya contained nearly 200 billion locusts and occupied 'a space in the sky three times the size of New York City'. The locusts also caused billions of dollars of damage and devoured all crops in their path, plunging local farmers into penury.[1]

The plague eventually reached Egypt, reminding anyone familiar with the Bible that locusts were among the plagues God inflicted upon the ancient Egyptians because they would not let the children of Israel go free. Exodus 10:15 says: 'For they covered the face of the whole earth, so that the land was darkened; and they did eat every herb of the land, and all the fruit of the trees which the hail had left: and there remained not any green thing in the trees, or in the herbs of the field, through all the land of Egypt.' Formidable.

Despite living with the calamity of locust plagues for millennia, it was not until the 1920s that scientists discovered that the locust and the grasshopper are actually the same insect.[2] Notwithstanding a general similarity of appearance, locusts and grasshoppers were previously thought to be two separate species. This was not just due to differences in coloration but because the grasshopper and locust could not be more dissimilar in behaviour. Grasshoppers are green, shy and antisocial. They actively avoid contact with other grasshoppers and normally live a solitary and docile life. By contrast, the locust is brown, bigger, stronger and 'gregarious', which is a scientific way of saying not only that it seeks out other locusts but that its social existence is defined by its participation in a swarm. Crucially, a grasshopper only transforms into a locust due to environmental catastrophe.

In drier climates, a period of plentiful rain results in a significant growth of grass and can cause a massive increase in a grasshopper population. But as the weather changes and grass becomes scarcer, the grasshoppers retreat to diminishing pastures. In arid regions that are prone to drought – like the Horn of Africa or the Arabian Peninsula – this then becomes a crisis of survival. For a solitary insect like the grasshopper, such an increase in population density is stressful in the extreme. Pushed up against one another, the grasshoppers release increased serotonin to the thoracic region of their nervous system, and in just a few short hours the humble grasshopper becomes the monstrous locust, literally changing color and shape and switching to apocalypse mode.

Only about eight of the more than 8,000 species of grasshoppers can undergo the metamorphosis from harmless grasshopper into pernicious locust. But those that can do so live on about twenty percent of the world's land surface. Scientist Steve Rogers of Cambridge University was part of the research team that discovered the link between grasshoppers, locusts and serotonin. In 2009 he commented that the transformation from grasshopper to locust 'is a strategy born of desperation and driven by hunger, and swarming is a response to find pastures new'.[3] Although humans and grasshoppers don't have a whole lot else in common, environmental stress and social crisis caused by climate change is something that humans are also having to come to terms with.

Climate change

Climate change poses an existential threat to life on this planet. That is the conclusion presented in numerous reports published by the Intergovernmental Panel on Climate Change (IPCC), the preeminent body established by the United Nations with a mandate to collate scientific evidence regarding the impact of human activity on the earth's environment. The IPCC was established in 1988 and publishes reports in support of the UN Framework Convention on Climate Change and the 2015 Paris Agreement. The IPCC's reports not only draw together the work of thousands of research scientists; their findings are scrutinised by all participating governments and published by consensus.[4]

The prognosis is negative. The IPCC's November 2014 Synthesis Report not only found overwhelming evidence that human activity and industrialisation were responsible for climate change, it detailed the widespread impacts that these changes had already had 'on natural and human systems on all continents and across the oceans'. This has taken many forms – oceans have warmed and risen, snow and ice are retreating at the earth's poles and each 'of the last three decades has been successively warmer at the Earth's surface than any preceding decade since 1850'. Meanwhile, 'atmospheric concentrations of carbon dioxide, methane and nitrous oxide' are at levels 'unprecedented in at least the last 800,000 years'. Extreme weather patterns (droughts, storm surges, extreme precipitation, coastal flooding, wildfires, water scarcity) are all becoming more common. Crop yields and plant life have been negatively affected, influencing food security. Finally, a growing number of species are now potentially facing extinction, as entire ecosystems are under stress. In short, our planet is in grave peril.[5]

Examining the 'future risks and impacts caused by a changing climate', the IPCC's conclusion was that only a radical and unprecedented alteration of the global economy – relying on intense multilateral collaboration and including a decisive shift away from fossil fuels – can save us. Even then, the effects of existing changes to the climate will last for decades or possibly centuries. In the medium term, the IPCC argued, climate change 'is projected to increase the displacement of people', especially in developing countries where vulnerable populations 'lack the resources for planned migration'. Climate change therefore 'can indirectly increase risks of violent conflicts by amplifying well-documented drivers of these conflicts such as poverty and economic shocks'.[6] In other words, while everyone on this planet will continue to suffer the adverse effects of accelerating climate change, the impact and consequences will not be borne equally.

This is why climate change matters more than any other crisis currently facing humanity. But as Joshua Busby argued in *Foreign Affairs* magazine in 2018:

> Making climate change all the more frightening are its effects on geopolitics. New weather patterns will trigger social and economic upheaval. Rising seas, dying farmlands, and ever more powerful storms and floods will render some countries uninhabitable. These changes will test the international system in new and unpredictable ways.[7]

How will the international community respond, for example, if and when a number of small island states in the Pacific become uninhabitable because of rising sea levels, causing entire peoples to become climate refugees? During 2018, population growth and severe drought caused Cape Town to become the first major city in the world to almost completely run out of water, before intensive conservation efforts ensured that the city of four million people did not run completely dry. But what if in the future such a crisis were to simultaneously affect a number of major cities and economies across Southern Africa, Western Europe or the Americas? Or if climate change starts to have a drastic impact upon the global production of staple crops – including corn, cassava, rice and wheat – that the bulk of humanity depends upon for sustenance? And in what ways will climate change intensify other threats facing humanity?

War, famine and cassava in Mozambique

In 1981, Julie Cliff, a young Australian doctor living in newly independent Mozambique, received a disturbing message from the far north of the country regarding the outbreak of a mystery disease that was paralysing people. Just six years earlier, in June 1975, Mozambique's Frente de Libertação de Moçambique (FRELIMO) liberation movement had come to power, ending four centuries of colonial rule. As the Portuguese soldiers and administrators retreated from the country, almost the entire white population of more than 200,000 people followed them, extracting their wealth and expertise from Mozambique at the moment when it was needed most. Those hastily departing included almost every medical doctor and health official in the country.

Cliff was one of the supporters of Mozambique's independence struggle who came to replace them. Called *cooperantes* by the locals, these dedicated foreigners were usually politically committed young professionals who wanted to help build a new Mozambique. After arriving in Maputo in 1976, Cliff joined the staff of the Central Hospital as head of the infectious-diseases unit. There were only around eighty doctors in the entire country at the time, serving a population of ten million people. But Cliff, who was in her early thirties, remembers that Maputo was 'exciting and optimistic' and that there was 'a very great spirit, a sense of people doing things together'.[8] Then in 1977, civil war broke out.

Although FRELIMO had identified as a national liberation movement during its long guerrilla war against Portuguese colonialism, at its February 1977 congress it redefined itself as a Marxist-Leninist party and set about constructing a one-party state. Under President Samora Machel, the new government proclaimed its socialist agenda and focused on the rapid expansion of health care and education as its main priorities. The percentage of the national budget dedicated to health rose from 4.6 to 11.9 percent by 1981. By the 1980s, approximately 1,200 new rural health clinics had been constructed, and thousands of new nurses, midwives and village-level health workers had been trained. Some of the most impressive gains happened within the first few years of independence. For example, by the early 1980s, for the first time in Mozambique's long history, the majority of children had been vaccinated against measles, polio and smallpox.[9]

Whatever potential existed for radical change was drained by the 1977–1992 civil war. Armed rebels from the Resistência Nacional Moçambicana (RENAMO) – created and backed initially by the intelligence services of white-ruled Rhodesia and then apartheid South Africa – waged a devastating fifteen-year campaign against the government. Although RENAMO promoted itself internationally as an anti-communist rebel movement, it failed to articulate a coherent political programme, and its fighters were responsible for countless atrocities. Besides attacks on government soldiers, RENAMO extorted, pillaged, mutilated and massacred civilians, forcibly recruited fighters (including children) and destroyed bridges, schools, health clinics and other infrastructure in order to render the country ungovernable.[10]

Mozambican government forces also committed war crimes as the armed conflict with RENAMO expanded and intensified. Facing a ruthless insurgency, FRELIMO turned inwards and the government became increasingly authoritarian. The radical and idealistic vision of 1975 withered as Mozambique became ever more broken, bankrupt and hungry.

In all, a million Mozambicans died, while 5.7 million were internally displaced or became refugees. The civil war also had a devastating impact on the environment. For example, the massive Gorongosa National Park in the centre of the country became a war zone. It lost ninety percent of its large wildlife, with the hippopotamus population falling from 3,500 to just 100, elephants, from 2,000 to around 200 and lions, zebras and buffaloes almost entirely wiped out.[11]

Julie Cliff had already moved from the Central Hospital to the Ministry of Health when a telex arrived on her desk on 13 August 1981: 'Polio outbreak, Memba District. 38 cases, Hyperreflexia.' But the last part of the communication, regarding the reflex symptoms, did not fit for a polio diagnosis. And so she went with a team of doctors to Nampula Province in the north of the country to investigate, later describing it as 'the most overwhelming thing I have ever done in my life'. The medical team, working closely with provincial and district health workers, found over a thousand cases of debilitating paralysis amongst the rural population. According to Cliff, 'Some people couldn't walk at all, some had lost the use of their arms as well as their legs'. Others were blinded or could not hear. Most of the victims were women or children. No one knew the cause of the baffling disease, nor could they provide a cure for people's suffering.[12]

Northern Mozambique was in the midst of a devastating drought in 1981. After excluding polio as the cause and conducting a range of blood, urine and spinal fluid tests, all of which failed to identify the malady, the medical team started looking at dietary causes rather than a viral pathogen. Almost as a last resort, they also 'decided to test cyanide levels, and they came back as the highest levels ever recorded in people'. Some of the victims had cyanide levels in their bodies twenty times higher than normal. And that was when Cliff and the medical team realised that these rural villagers – the most impoverished section of the population in one of the world's poorest countries – were being paralysed by the very crop that they depended upon for survival.[13]

Cassava originated in the Amazon and made its way to Africa via the Portuguese during the sixteenth century. Called manioc or yuca in Latin America, cassava is a woody shrub that can grow to about 1–3 metres in height, is perennial and flourishes in even the driest, sandiest and most marginal soils. It is resistant to drought, parasites and locusts and is a highly productive crop for farmers, requiring very little tending. The root, which is the most edible part, provides a good source of carbohydrates and some vitamins. According to Cliff, it therefore 'fills you up, and probably stops you dying in a really severe famine'.[14]

Like apples and almonds, cassava also contains cyanide, which is naturally broken down and not dangerous when ingested as part of a diverse diet. But what Julie Cliff discovered in 1981 was that because of drought in northern

Mozambique, local farming communities in parts of Nampula Province had be-come increasingly (and in many cases exclusively) dependent upon cassava for survival. The lengthy process of preparing the cassava for consumption by drying it in the sun for several weeks before storing it, which dissipated the cyanide, had also been dramatically shortened as other food sources became scarce. This in-tensified the toxicity of the cassava at the same time that people's natural dietary defence was being undermined by the lack of other foods. Moreover, water stress increases the amount of cyanide present in cassava, compounding the threat to those who were consuming it. As a result, the cyanide levels in the bodies of locals rose to dangerous levels, leading to an epidemic of an obscure disease known as *konzo*.[15]

Konzo is characterised by the abrupt onset of irreversible motor neuron damage and spastic paralysis. Some of those afflicted would eat cassava for weeks without acute symptoms before going to bed one evening and being unable to walk when they woke up. In all, the medical team identified 1,102 cases across five districts of Nampula Province in 1981. And although the existence of *konzo* was first diag-nosed by an Italian physician working in the Belgian Congo in 1938, its causes were completely unknown until the Mozambican medical team scientifically es-tablished the connection with cassava consumption.[16]

The return of strong seasonal rains to northern Mozambique in 1982 broke the drought and helped prevent a recurrence of the *konzo* epidemic. But a decade later, in early 1993, Julie Cliff became aware of another *konzo* outbreak in the same province. This time the cause was war.

Four months before the fall of the Berlin Wall, in July 1989, FRELIMO's fifth congress abandoned the party's commitment to Marxism-Leninism and endorsed a mixed economy. The following year, a new constitution was adopted and there was a tentative attempt to initiate peace talks with RENAMO. Following painful and lengthy negotiations, the government and RENAMO signed a peace accord in October 1992, agreeing to end their armed conflict and hold multiparty elections. But even as their delegations were negotiating in Rome, there was intense fighting in Mogincual District of Nampula Province, with both sides trying to control the greatest amount of territory possible before any formal ces-sation of hostilities. The district capital, Liupo, was the scene of a ferocious battle just one month before the final peace agreement was signed. All the major buildings in the town were destroyed, and the district remained divided between RENAMO and government forces.

In July 1993, Julie Cliff went with another medical team to Liupo – which she described as 'a ghost town' – to investigate reports of *konzo* in the district. Navigating the contours of the civil war, Cliff visited both government- and RENAMO-controlled areas.[17] Examining a group of patients, she and the team found that:

> ...fifty-four of the 72 patients had returned home after being displaced by war. Thirty-one patients became ill in their place of refuge and 23 after their

return home. All 72 had eaten bitter cassava at the time of the disease onset.[18]

Again, the main victims were women and children. The medical team concluded that intense fighting during the final stage of the war had caused locals to flee from rural areas, disrupting farming. Even those who stayed 'could not spend long in their fields and monkeys gained the upper hand'. Local farmers became dependent upon bitter cassava (the more resilient variant that is also higher in cyanide), as 'it was more productive, had a short reproductive cycle, and was resistant to predation by monkeys and wild pigs'. As Mozambique's civil war entered its end phase in Mogincual District, families were therefore forced to rely on insufficiently processed cassava for survival.[19] Indeed, the 600 people poisoned by cassava and disabled by *konzo* may have been among the war's last victims.

In the decades that have passed since the end of Mozambique's civil war, climate change has greatly increased the appeal of cassava. It is now the staple crop for about one billion people, the majority of whom live in Africa. In particular, in the Democratic Republic of the Congo and Tanzania and across northern Mozambique, cassava is now 'the most important crop for the largest proportion of farming households'. For rural communities that lack an awareness of *konzo* but have been decimated by HIV/AIDS, the fact that cassava requires comparatively little field labour compared to other crops also greatly increases its attractiveness.[20]

In terms of global production, cassava is now the sixth most important crop in the world – behind sugarcane, maize, rice, wheat and potatoes. As temperatures increase and droughts become more intense, cassava endures as a resilient staple for poor rural populations. And although the cultivation of cassava has expanded significantly across Africa, a research team led by Ros Gleadow and Tim Cavagnaro from Monash University, working with Julie Cliff, proved that drought, a global rise in temperature and an increase in carbon dioxide levels can result in a dramatic increase in the amount of cyanide present in cassava and the likelihood of it causing *konzo*. Although another Australian scientist, the late Howard Bradbury, devised a simple method for enhancing the process of leaching poisonous cyanide out of cassava before consumption, many rural African communities are still unaware of this method of preparation.[21]

Julie Cliff still lives in Maputo and continues to campaign against *konzo*. But in a world of 'too many competing priorities', *konzo* does not receive the international attention it deserves. Cliff suspects that because it only affects poor rural African communities, *konzo* cases have been historically underreported. For example, in 2000 the Ministry of Health in the Democratic Republic of the Congo estimated that there had possibly been as many as 100,000 *konzo* cases in that country. But unlike Ebola, a contagious pathogen that can spread beyond the rural areas where it originates, the presence of *konzo* in the Congo, Cameroon, the Central African Republic and Tanzania was barely reported internationally. According to Cliff, 'poverty in association with agricultural crises provoked by drought and war was a constant feature' in all major *konzo* outbreaks, with local people still facing a choice of being poisoned by their only food source or starving.[22] All these countries also face a growing threat of climate change. How they respond remains a matter of life or death.

Threat multiplier

Thousands of kilometres from tropical Mozambique, in the winter of 2006, Syria experienced the beginning of a crippling drought. By 2009 key crops had declined by more than half, plunging a million people into food insecurity. In the northeast of the country, farmers lost eighty-five percent of their livestock as wells dried up and animals died. About ten percent of the population saw their livelihoods wiped out. Crops failed, food prices increased and in 2008 the Syrian government had to import wheat for the first time in almost two decades. As the drought continued, one study from 2009 found that more than 150 villages in the northeast of the country had been depopulated. By 2010 more than 1.5 million Syrians had fled their farms, migrating to Aleppo, Damascus, Homs and other crowded urban centres.[23]

Rising temperatures and declining rainfall afflicted the entire Fertile Crescent, where agriculture was first born about 11,000 years ago, but fell particularly severely upon Syria. The ruling Assad family didn't create the drought, but decades of dictatorship and dysfunctional policies around water management and agriculture exacerbated its consequences. Facing poverty and water scarcity, resentments accumulated on the periphery of Syria's cities and in the countryside. Then came the Arab Spring, a popular uprising and eventually the civil war.

The confluence of these events has caused some to draw a causal link between them. In the words of former US secretary of state John Kerry, 'It's not a coincidence that immediately prior to the civil war in Syria, the country experienced its worst drought on record'. Environmental disaster intensified the 'political unrest that was just beginning to roil and boil in the region', adding stress on cities plagued by crumbling infrastructure, overcrowding and corruption.[24] In this scenario, climate change helped ignite the bitterest and bloodiest civil war of our times, providing a potentially disturbing portent of our collective future.

Kerry was not alone in detecting a general connection between climate change and deadly conflict. Former UN secretary-general Kofi Annan argued in his Millennium Report that climate change 'may increase social and political tensions in unpredictable and potentially dangerous ways'. In 2014 the US Department of Defense also famously described climate change as a 'threat multiplier', noting that a rise in global temperatures could 'intensify the challenges of global instability, hunger, poverty, and conflict', posing a special threat to already fractured societies. In such situations, climate stress could aggravate underlying social and political tensions or ignite fresh disputes. This was also recognised by the African Union's Peace and Security Council (PSC) at its May 2018 meeting. The PSC not only 'underscored' the 'linkage between climate change and peace and security in Africa', they noted that 'climate change is a threat to global peace and security'.[25]

The UN Security Council has also started to contemplate climate-related security risks. During a July 2018 debate, the UN deputy secretary-general, Amina Mohammed, reiterated that 'climate change acts as a threat multiplier'. Although elected member Bolivia, as well as permanent members China and Russia, argued that climate change was outside the Council's mandate, other states were frustrated by the fact that while the Council had previously recognised the risks presented by drought, water scarcity and food security in resolutions concerning the Lake Chad basin (March 2017), West Africa and the Sahel (January 2018) and Somalia (March 2018), the Council had not formally discussed the connection between conflict and climate in seven years. A UN Security Council debate on 'addressing the impacts of climate-related disasters on international peace and security' was finally held in January 2019. While the majority of the Council emphasised the importance of the issue, the United States (which under President Donald Trump had withdrawn from the Paris Agreement) strangely avoided using the words 'climate change' at all during their intervention.[26]

If nothing else, the effect of a global rise in temperature – resulting in desertification, drought and reduced access to clean water – could clearly be catastrophic for the two billion people who live in sub-Saharan Africa and Asia and depend upon an estimated 500 million smallholder farms to produce eighty percent of the food they consume. These findings were amplified in a 2017 report by the Environmental Justice Foundation, a London think tank, who claim that tens of millions of people may be displaced by climate change over the next decade, potentially creating the most catastrophic refugee crisis in human history. The impact of climate change 'will be felt most profoundly in regions and countries where exposure is greatest and where there is the lowest capacity to adapt'.[27]

Or in other words, climate change is not just about penguins and polar bears. The challenges may also increase the possibility of mass atrocity crimes – genocide, war crimes, ethnic cleansing and crimes against humanity. Although the UN's Framework of Analysis for Atrocity Crimes does not specifically address global warming, there are two risk factors that are directly relevant: motives or incentives and triggering factors. Triggering factors could include environmental changes that drastically affect entire societies, including severe drought or natural disaster. Motives or incentives could potentially include a dramatic widening of inequality because of climate change, environmental degradation and the political manipulation of access to depleted natural resources. But does the existing evidence support this grim prognosis?

In 2007, the then UN secretary-general, Ban Ki-moon, linked environmental stress to the outbreak of violent conflict in Darfur, Sudan, arguing that amid 'the diverse social and political causes, the Darfur conflict began as an ecological crisis, arising at least in part from climate change'. According to Ban, a harsh drought had resulted in armed hostilities between settled farmers and nomadic herders, helping to create 'the full-fledged tragedy we witness today'.[28]

In 2012, deadly intercommunal clashes between Orma and Pokomo communities in Kenya's Tana River Delta were perceived as being driven by tribal animosities and political rivalries. However, the two ethnic communities were mainly battling over water access, scarce grazing land and tensions arising from land development. Similar patterns of violence were also evident in the run-up to the 2017 election, with conflict between seminomadic pastoralists, settled farmers and conservationists in the central region of Laikipia, near Mount Kenya. Historical disputes over landownership in Laikipia county, dating back to colonial times, were exacerbated by drought in the neighbouring counties of Isiolo, Samburu and Baringo. As struggling pastoralists moved their herds of cattle into Laikipia in search of grazing lands, they sometimes seized control of local ranches or invaded protected conservation areas. At least twenty-five people (including ten police) were killed in the resulting clashes, and some local politicians were accused of using the issue to incite ethnic violence and mobilise political support ahead of the election.[29]

Fighting between seminomadic herders and settled farmers has also occurred in Ethiopia and the Central African Republic, sometimes escalating to the level of mass atrocity crimes. Arms proliferation and extended dry seasons caused by climate change may be having a similar effect on ethnic conflict in South Sudan, where traditions of cattle raiding between competing communities of ethnic Nuer, Murle and Dinka have increased in deadly intensity over the last decade.

Meanwhile, according to the UN Office for West Africa and the Sahel, during the first six months of 2018 conflict between nomadic herders and settled farming communities increased 'in frequency, intensity, complexity and geographic scope' across the entire Sahel region, but especially in Nigeria. Rising temperatures, drought and desertification in Nigeria have caused ethnic Fulani herders to migrate farther south than ever before. In doing so, they have often clashed with local farmers. The fact that the Fulani herders are mainly Muslim and the farming communities they are battling are predominately Christian has deepened inter-communal animosities in a country that has already had considerable experience of deadly conflict. While it was Boko Haram's atrocities that attracted international headlines, Amnesty International reported that 3,641 people were killed in clashes between nomadic herders and settled farmers between January 2016 and October 2018.[30]

At least ninety-five people were killed in Nigeria's Benue and Taraba states in the two-week period between 31 December 2017 and 15 January 2018 alone as a result of this intensifying pattern of intercommunal violence. According to the Benue State Emergency Management Agency, 80,000 people were also displaced. In an attempt to end a deadly cycle of raids and reprisal killings, the federal and state governments implemented cattle-grazing bans. The Nigerian government is also under pressure to intensify efforts to mitigate the effects of climate change by participating in regional initiatives to restore environments affected by drought and desertification in the Lake Chad basin.

When the UN Security Council visited the Lake Chad region in March 2017, the president of Niger, Mahamadou Issoufou, told the assembled ambassadors that the armed extremist group Boko Haram would not have 'taken root' in the region if not for the fact that Lake Chad had lost ninety percent of its surface area over the preceding half century – shrinking from approximately 25,000 square kilometres to around 2,500. As Lake Chad dried up, so did the local economy. A number of fishing communities, for example, are now marooned many kilometres from the shores of a lake that sustained their ancestors for generations. As Lake Chad shrank, Boko Haram grew.[31]

Where governance is weak, the threat posed by global warming looms largest. Accelerating climate change will also increase global hunger and the regularity of catastrophic environmental events. The resulting pressures may limit the capacity of some governments in the developing world to fulfil their basic functions. We have already seen this in relation to the 2014–2015 Ebola epidemic in West Africa. Understandably, the governments of Liberia, Guinea and Sierra Leone prioritised the health emergency over programmes dealing with past conflicts and strengthening human rights institutions. Similar re-prioritisation may occur in the face of expanded environmental crises.

Some years ago, the Robert Strauss Center for International Security and Law released a study of African governments' institutional resilience to potential challenges presented by climate change. Of the fifty-three African states studied, the ten most fragile were Côte d'Ivoire, Guinea-Bissau, Burundi, Zimbabwe, the Comoros, Chad, the Central African Republic, Sudan, the Democratic Republic of the Congo and Somalia.[32] Seven of these have already endured mass atrocities in their recent history or are experiencing them now. This is the context in which climate change could reignite old conflicts or create conditions for a new type of predatory politics.

War and water in Yemen

The more vulnerable the environment, the more readily it can be weaponised. In Iraq, for example, ISIL exploited the environment to pursue their genocidal programme against the Yazidis. In the summer of 2014, ISIL seized Yazidi villages, towns and farmland and displaced about 400,000 people. However, as ISIL was eventually forced to retreat from the Sinjar region, they imposed a 'scorched earth' policy. ISIL fighters systematically burned orchards, and around 400 out of 450 irrigation wells in the Sinune subdistrict alone were blocked, poisoned or sabotaged. Yazidi farmers who tried to return after ISIL's retreat found that their farms, and the rural economy upon which their entire way of life depended, had been turned into 'a dead land'.[33]

Meanwhile Yemen – on the southern tip of the Arabian Peninsula – is possibly the poorest and driest country in the Arab world. As one climate scholar has pointed out, in 'a region with little precipitation to begin with, small changes can have big impacts', and the UN predicts that Yemen's main cities may soon run out of water entirely.[34] Yemen's population has more than doubled from twelve million to twenty-nine million over the past 30 years, with most of that growth being absorbed into large urban areas with poor infrastructure. As the population and agriculture have expanded, the country's water needs have become greater than what seasonal rain, deep groundwater aquifers and a changing environment can provide.

Mismanagement of Yemen's depleted water resources and the overdependence of the local economy on the agricultural production of qat (or khat) – an addictive herbal stimulant – have turned a crisis into a catastrophe. According to some estimates, prior to 2011 approximately half of the country's water supply was being used to cultivate qat, which is chewed by a majority of Yemenis. Although the production and commerce of qat constituted a significant portion of GDP, the drug contributed very little in terms of Yemen's overall development.[35] It did, however, contribute to a precipitous decline in Yemen's water table over a period of just two decades.

After more than thirty years in power, Yemen's president, Ali Abdullah Saleh, was overthrown during 2011 following a wave of popular protests in the midst of the Arab Spring. Although Saleh was the fourth Arab dictator to fall, the revolution that toppled him did not result in a democratic blossoming. In the midst of a UN-facilitated political transition, the Houthis – an armed Shia movement from northeast Yemen – and military units still loyal to Saleh took control of most of the country during 2014. Then, after armed hostilities intensified between pro-Houthi/Saleh forces and Yemen's internationally recognised government, during March 2015 Saudi Arabia and a coalition of nine other countries responded to an emergency request for military intervention and began an air war against the Houthis.

Since March 2017, the United Nations has designated Yemen the largest humanitarian crisis in the world. By mid-2018, out of a population of 29.3 million, 22.2 million Yemenis needed humanitarian assistance, and more than 2.9 million civilians had been forcibly displaced from their homes. The UN also estimated that from March 2015 until June 2018, 'there were at least 16,706 civilian casualties, with 6,475 killed and 10,231 injured in the conflict'. The UN noted, however, that 'the real figure is likely to be significantly higher'. Meanwhile, the UN secretary-general's annual report on children and armed conflict documented the deaths of 502 children in Yemen during 2016, noting that the Saudi-led coalition was responsible for killing or wounding at least 683 children, while the Houthis were responsible for 414 casualties. The coalition was also responsible for attacks (mainly air strikes) on twenty-eight schools and ten hospitals. For the first time in the history of the notorious 'list of shame', the secretary-general named the Saudi-led coalition as being responsible for possible war crimes committed against children.[36]

While Yemen's water crisis antedates the current conflict, it has had a direct impact on the way the war has been conducted. In February 2016 it was reported that Saudi fighter jets bombed a reservoir upon which an estimated 30,000 Yemenis were dependent for drinking water. In 2016 and again in 2017, a desalination plant in the northern port of al-Makha (Mocha) was also bombed and damaged. Meanwhile, Houthi forces around the city of Taiz blocked shipments of fresh water to civilians living in areas that were not under their control. In short, throughout the conflict, armed forces on both sides have targeted civilian infrastructure and exploited water scarcity for military advantage – a potential war crime.[37]

At least fifteen million Yemenis have been left without adequate access to clean water and sanitation because of the war, with predictably catastrophic consequences. In October 2017 the World Health Organization reported that Yemen was experiencing the largest cholera outbreak in modern history, with more than one million cases and at least 2,000 deaths. Attacks on civilian and humanitarian infrastructure continued throughout 2018, with UNICEF's executive director, Henrietta Fore, reporting that 'on 27 July, the water station in al-Mina District, which provides Hodeida with most of its water', was hit by an air strike. According to Fore, such attacks were directly linked to the cholera epidemic.[38]

In short, nothing about Yemen's humanitarian disaster is natural. People are not suffering because of a plague of locusts or a hurricane or earthquake. Climate change and water scarcity may not have caused the war in Yemen, but they were successfully weaponised to intensify people's misery.

Conclusion

In its 2011 Human Development Report, the UN argued that an 'estimated 40 percent of civil wars over the past 60 years are associated with natural resources'.[39] But while this may be true, it is important not to conflate climate change, conflict and the risk of mass atrocities. At least one study has used data regarding temperature variation in Africa to argue that 'a 1°C increase in temperature' leads to 'a 4.5% increase in civil war'. According to the study, climate change could therefore dramatically increase the number of armed conflicts across sub-Saharan Africa, leading to an estimated 393,000 additional battle deaths by 2030.[40] Such predictive modelling runs the risk of being misleadingly deterministic. There is certainly no evidence that a two-degree increase in global temperatures will automatically increase the statistical likelihood of genocide in Africa or anywhere else.

I come from a 'sunburnt country', Australia, and in addition to locust plagues, I have personally experienced severe drought. While access to water was used as a weapon against Australia's Aboriginal peoples during colonial times, water scarcity in contemporary Australia has not resulted in civil war nor a refugee exodus. Similarly, no one is trying to bomb Southern California's depleted water reservoirs like they are in Yemen. And herders are not migrating south from Silicon Valley to kill people and secure access to the fertile orchards of Orange County. This should remind us of the indispensable role played by political history and economic development in mitigating climate-based risks.

Mass atrocities are the result of a convergence of vulnerabilities, of which climate change is just one. In the future, ethnic warlords, authoritarian rulers and aspiring demagogues will undoubtedly use the consequences of climate change to mobilise support – but to quote Vesselin Popovski of United Nations University, 'what will drive their fight is not the rain, the temperature, or the sea level'.[41] The primary causes of conflict will continue to be politics, economics and the pursuit of power. Because ultimately, humans are neither locusts nor grasshoppers. Unique amongst all the creatures who inhabit this planet, we alone can overcome the existential threat of global warming, but in order to do so we must better harness our politics.

Notes

1 "Locusts in Africa: Severe Swarms," *The Economist*, 1 February 2020, 42; Nita Bhalla, "Climate Change Linked to African Locust invasion," *Reuters*, 29 January 2020, https://news.trust.org/item/20200129162104-dctmm/; "Locusts: UN Calls for International Help in East Africa," *BBC News*, 20 January 2020, https://www.bbc.com/news/world-africa-51234135.
2 K. Harmon, "When Grasshoppers Go Biblical: Serotonin Causes Locusts to Swarm," *Scientific American*, 30 January 2009, https://www.scientificamerican.com/article/when-grasshoppers-go-bibl/: "A Brain Chemical Changes Locusts from Harmless Grasshoppers to Swarming Pests," *University of Cambridge – Research News*, 30 January 2009, http://www.cam.ac.uk/research/news/a-brain-chemical-changes-locusts-from-harmless-grasshoppers-to-swarming-pests; and Steve Connor, "Solved: the Mystery of why Locusts swarm," *The Independent* (UK), 30 January 2009.
3 Michael Kahn, "Study Shows What Makes Locusts swarm," *Reuters*, 29 January 2009, https://www.reuters.com/article/us-locusts-swarm/study-shows-what-makes-locusts-swarm-idUSTRE50T04620090130; and "A Brain Chemical changes Locusts from harmless Grasshoppers to swarming pests."
4 Intergovernmental Panel on Climate Change (IPCC), https://www.ipcc.ch.
5 IPCC, Climate Change 2014: Synthesis Report. Contribution of Working Groups I, II and III to the Fifth Assessment Report of the Intergovernmental Panel on Climate Change, IPCC, Geneva, Switzerland, 2–16.
6 Ibid, 16. See also, Alex Alvarez, *Unstable Ground: Climate Change, Conflict, and Genocide* (New York: Rowman & Littlefield, 2017).
7 Joshua Busby, "Warming World: Why Climate Change Matters More Than Anything Else," *Foreign Affairs*, July/August 2018, 49.
8 Julie Cliff, "An Orphan Disease," in Daniel Perlman and Ananya Roy (eds), *The Practice of International Health* (New York: Oxford University Press, 2009), 70–87; Jo Chandler, "Helping Heal Africa," *Sydney Morning Herald*, 13 December 2008; and Email from J. Cliff to S. Adams, 2 April 2019.
9 Stephen Gloyd, James Pfeiffer, and Wendy Johnson, "Cooperantes, Solidarity, and the Fight for Health in Mozambique," in Anne-Emanuelle Bird and Theodore M. Brown (eds), *Comrades in Health: U.S. Health Internationalists, Abroad and at Home* (New Brunswick, NJ: Rutgers University Press, 2013), 185.
10 Margaret Hall, "The Mozambican National Resistance Movement (RENAMO): A Study in the Destruction of an African Country," *Africa: Journal of the International African Institute*, 60, no.1 (1990): 39–68 and Stephen A. Emerson, *The Battle for Mozambique: The Frelimo-Renamo Struggle, 1977–1992* (Pinetown, South Africa: Helion & Company Ltd, 2014), 164–171.
11 International Committee of the Red Cross, "Natural Environment: Neglected Victim of Armed Conflict," 5 June 2019, https://www.icrc.org/en/document/natural-environment-neglected-victim-armed-conflict; Marc E. Stalmans, Tara J. Massad, Mike J. S. Peel, Corina E. Tarnita, and Robert M. Pringle, "War-induced Collapse and Asymmetric Recovery of Large Mammal Populations in Gorongosa National Park, Mozambique," *PLOS One*, 14, no. 3 (March 2019), https://journals.plos.org/plosone/article?id=10.1371/journal.pone.0212864.

12 Cátia L. A. Taibo, Julie Cliff, Hans Rosling, Casey D. Hall, Meeyoung M. Park, and Joseph A. Frimpong, "African Case Studies in Public Health: An Epidemic of Spastic Paraparesis of Unknown Aetiology in Northern Mozambique," *The Pan African Medical Journal*, May 2017; Chandler, "Helping Heal Africa,"; and Email from J. Cliff to S. Adams, 2 April 2019.

13 Chandler, "Helping Heal Africa."

14 Ibid; Anna Burns, Roslyn Gleadow, Julie Cliff, Anabela Zacarias, and Timothy Cavagnaro, "Cassava: The Drought, War and Famine Crop in a Changing World," *Sustainability*, 2, no. 11 (2010): 3573–3575; and Hipólito Nzwalo and Julie Cliff, "Konzo: From Poverty, Cassava, and Cyanogen Intake to Toxico-Nutritional Neurological Disease," *PLoS Neglected Tropical Diseases*, 5, no. 6 (June 2011).

15 Burns et al. "Cassava: The Drought, War and Famine Crop in a Changing World," 3580–3583.

16 Ibid, 3580–3583; Nzwalo, Cliff, "Konzo: From Poverty, Cassava, and Cyanogen Intake to Toxico-Nutritional Neurological Disease,"; Taibo et al., "African Case Studies in Public Health: An Epidemic of Spastic Paraparesis of Unknown Aetiology in Northern Mozambique."

17 Cliff, "An Orphan Disease," 81; Julie Cliff et al., "Konzo associated with war in Mozambique," *Tropical Medicine and International Health*, 2, no. 11 (1997), 1068–1074; and Email from J. Cliff to S. Adams, 2 April 2019.

18 Cliff et al., "Konzo Associated with War in Mozambique," 1070.

19 Ibid, 1071.

20 Nzwalo, Cliff, "Konzo: From Poverty, Cassava, and Cyanogen Intake to Toxico-Nutritional Neurological Disease."

21 Ibid; Burns et al., "Cassava: The Drought, War and Famine Crop in a Changing World," 3572–3607; "Cassava: Achieving food security and safety in the face of climate change," *Lens: Monash Magazine*, 19 December 2017, https://lens.monash.edu/@monash-magazine/2017/12/18/1229914/the-poisoned-plate-of-climate-change.

22 Nzwalo, Cliff, "Konzo: From Poverty, Cassava, and Cyanogen Intake to Toxico-Nutritional Neurological Disease,"; Burns et al., "Cassava: The Drought, War and Famine Crop in a Changing World," 3581; Dayna Kerecman Myers, "Julie Cliff on Konzo, the Orphan Disease," *Global Health Now*, 13 November 2016, https://www.globalhealthnow.org/2016-11/julie-cliff-konzo-orphan-disease; Amy Maxmen, "Bitter Harvest: Cassava and Konzo, the Crippling Disease, Part III," *Global Health Now*, 10 October 2016, https://www.globalhealthnow.org/2016-10/bitter-harvest-cassava-and-konzo-crippling-disease-part-iii.

23 Environmental Justice Foundation, "Beyond Borders: Our Changing Climate – Its Role in Conflict and Displacement," 2017, 32–37, https://ejfoundation.org/reports/beyond-borders; Colin P. Kelley et al., "Climate Change in the Fertile Crescent and Implications of the Recent Syrian Drought," *Proceedings of the National Academy of Sciences of the United States of America*, 112, no. 11 (January 2015), 3241–3246.

24 Jason Box and Naomi Klein, "Why a Climate Deal Is the Best Hope for Peace," *The New Yorker*, 18 November 2015. For the contrary view, see Jan Selby, Omar S. Dahi, Christiane Frohlich, and Mike Hulme, "Climate Change and the Syrian Civil War Revisited," *Political Geography*, 60 (2017), 232–244.

25 African Union Peace and Security Council, Press Statement from 774th Meeting, 21 May 2018, http://www.peaceau.org/uploads/psc.774.press.statement.link.climate.change.conflicts.africa.21.05.2018.pdf; Caitlin E. Werrell and Francesco Femia, "Climate Change and Security," *Crisis Response Journal*, 12, no. 3 (April 2017), 44–47; and Kofi Annan, *We the Peoples: The Role of the United Nations in the Twenty-first Century* (New York: United Nations, 2000).

26 "Climate-related Security Risks Debate," *What's In Blue*, 10 July 2018, https://www.whatsinblue.org/2018/07/climate-related-security-risks-debate.php; "Open Debate: 'Addressing the Impacts of Climate-related Disasters on International Peace and

Security,'" *What's In Blue*, 24 January 2019, https://www.whatsinblue.org/2019/01/open-debate-addressing-the-impacts-of-climate-related-disasters-on-international-peace-and-security.php.

27 Environmental Justice Foundation, "Beyond Borders: Our changing Climate – Its Role in Conflict and Displacement," 4, 20, 22, 40.

28 Ban Ki Moon, "A Climate Culprit in Darfur," *Washington Post*, 16 June 2007.

29 M. Mutiga, "Violence, Land and the Upcoming Vote in Kenya's Laikipia Region," International Crisis Group, 25 July 2017, https://www.crisisgroup.org/africa/horn-africa/kenya/violence-land-and-upcoming-vote-kenyas-laikipia-region.

30 Amnesty International, Nigeria: The Harvest of Death – Three Years of Bloody Clashes Between Farmers and Herders in Nigeria, December 2018, https://www.amnesty.org/download/Documents/AFR4495032018ENGLISH.PDF.

31 "Open Debate: 'Addressing the Impacts of Climate-Related Disasters on International Peace and Security,'" *What's In Blue*, 24 January 2019; and Theresa Krinninger, "Lake Chad: Climate Change Fosters Terrorism," *Deutsche Welle*, 7 December 2015, https://www.dw.com/en/lake-chad-climate-change-fosters-terrorism/a-18899499.

32 Joshua W. Busby, Todd G. Smith, and Kaiba L. White, "Locating Climate Insecurity: Where Are the Most Vulnerable Places in Africa?" *Robert S. Strauss Center for International Security and Law*, August 2010, 28.

33 Amnesty International, Dead Land: Islamic State's Deliberate Destruction of Iraq's Farmland, December 2018, https://www.amnesty.org/en/documents/mde14/9510/2018/en/.

34 Collin Douglas, "A Storm Without Rain: Yemen, Water, Climate Change, and Conflict," *The Center for Climate and Security – Briefer*, no. 40, 3 August 2016, 2.

35 Ibid, 2; and Rachel Furlow, "The US Can Decide to Worsen Yemen's Water Crisis or Alleviate it," *Atlantic Council*, 17 July 2017, https://www.atlanticcouncil.org/blogs/menasource/the-us-can-decide-to-worsen-yemen-s-water-crisis-or-alleviate-it. Qat, like cocaine or caffeine, enhances social interaction and masks fatigue and hunger.

36 Report of the United Nations High Commissioner for Human Rights containing the findings of the Group of Eminent International and Regional Experts and a summary of Technical Assistance provided by the Office of the High Commissioner to the National Commission of Inquiry, A/HRC/39/43, 17 August 2018, 5, https://documents-dds-ny.un.org/doc/UNDOC/GEN/G18/252/79/PDF/G1825279.pdf?OpenElement.

37 Douglas, "A Storm Without Rain: Yemen, Water, Climate Change, and Conflict," 3; Aasher Orkaby, "Yemen's Humanitarian Nightmare: The Real Roots of the Conflict," *Foreign Affairs*, 96, no. 6 (November/December 2017), 101; and Furlow, "The US Can Decide to Worsen Yemen's Water Crisis or Alleviate it."

38 UNICEF, "Drinking Water Systems Under Repeated Attack in Yemen," 1 August 2018, https://www.unicef.org/press-releases/drinking-water-systems-under-repeated-attack-yemen; and Kate Lyons, "Yemen's Cholera Outbreak Now Worst in History as One Millioneth Case Looms," *The Guardian*, October 2017, https://www.theguardian.com/global-development/2017/oct/12/yemen-cholera-outbreak-worst-in-history-1-million-cases-by-end-of-year.

39 UNDP, *Human Development Report 2011* (New York: United Nations, 2011), 59; and Lyal S. Sunga, "Does Climate Change Worsen Resource Scarcity and Cause Violent Ethnic Conflict?" *International Journal on Minority and Group Rights*, 21, no. 1 (2014), 13–14.

40 Marshall B. Burke, Edward Miguel, Shanker Satyanath, John A. Dykema, and David B. Lovell, "Warming Increases the Risk of Civil War in Africa," *Proceedings of the National Academy of Sciences of the United States of America*, 106, no. 49 (October 2009), 20670–20674; and Sunga, "Does Climate Change Worsen Resource Scarcity and Cause Violent Ethnic Conflict?" 1–24.

41 Mark Notaras, "Does Climate Change Cause Conflict?" *Our World*, 27 November 2009, https://ourworld.unu.edu/en/does-climate-change-cause-conflict.

6

THE FATE OF THE ROHINGYA AND THE FUTURE OF HUMAN RIGHTS

Contents

Over a five-month period between August and December 2017, hundreds of thousands of desperate ethnic Rohingya civilians fled across the border from Myanmar into Bangladesh. In just a few months the refugee camps registered 711,984 new arrivals.[1] The Rohingya were fleeing so-called clearance operations carried out by Myanmar's security forces in Rakhine State, including widespread killings, sexual violence and the systematic burning of more than 350 villages. The UN high commissioner for human rights, Zeid Ra'ad Al Hussein, initially called these attacks 'a textbook example of ethnic cleansing' and later described them as potential 'acts of genocide' that should be referred to the International Criminal Court for investigation. The UN special adviser on the prevention of genocide, Adama Dieng, concurred, describing how the intent appeared to be to destroy the Rohingya as a people, 'which, if proven, would constitute the crime of genocide'.[2] Meanwhile the UN Office for the Coordination of Humanitarian Affairs conveyed the unimaginable horror of the crisis from the point of view of those providing emergency assistance to the refugees:

> Not only has the pace of arrivals since 25 August made this the fastest growing refugee crisis in the world, the concentration of refugees in Cox's Bazar is amongst the densest in the world. Refugees arriving in Bangladesh – mostly women and children – are traumatized, and some have arrived with injuries caused by gunshots, shrapnel, fire and landmines. Entire villages were burned to the ground, families were separated and killed, and women and girls were gang raped. Most of the people who escaped are now severely traumatized after witnessing unspeakable atrocities.[3]

While the scale and ferocity of the violence was shocking, it was not surprising. The Rohingya – a mainly Muslim ethnic minority group in a predominately Buddhist country – had been persecuted for decades, with tensions and violence dating back to disputes between Burmese nationalists and colonial loyalists about which side to support during the Second World War: Britain or Japan? Independence from the British Empire in 1948 and an awkward postcolonial transition were followed by the imposition of military rule in Burma in 1962. The core of the military dictatorship was organised around the Bamar Buddhist majority, with significant ethnic and religious minorities largely marginalised from political and economic life. These divisions resulted in decades of armed conflict between the military junta and various ethnic armed groups, including those fighting on behalf of the Karen, Kachin and Shan peoples in different parts of the country. Burma's military rulers also changed the name of the country to Myanmar in 1989. Meanwhile, the country's 1982 Citizenship Law did not recognise the estimated one million Rohingya – who were concentrated in Rakhine State, bordering Bangladesh – as one of the country's 135 'national races', rendering most of them stateless.[4]

Despite a gradual move away from military rule after 2011, anti-Muslim sentiment and the persecution of the Rohingya intensified. Hate speech derided the Rohingya as 'Bengalis' – illegal interlopers from Bangladesh – despite the fact that the overwhelming majority of Rohingya were born in Myanmar and know no other home. Discriminatory laws restricted their freedom of movement and access to employment and education, with more than 120,000 Rohingya confined to displacement camps in Rakhine State following intercommunal violence in 2012. In 2014 the Rohingya were prohibited from self-identifying on the national census, the first to take place in the country since 1983. The so-called Race and Religion Protection Laws, which were passed in 2015 and place harsh restrictions on women and non-Buddhists, further constrained the fundamental religious freedoms of the Rohingya, as well as their reproductive and marital rights. In short, the conditions under which the Rohingya minority were forced to live in Myanmar constituted a uniquely Southeast Asian form of apartheid.[5]

Following an attack by Rohingya militants on several border posts in October 2016, a four-month 'counter-insurgency' campaign by Myanmar's security forces led to mass arrests, torture, sexual violence, extrajudicial killings and the widespread destruction of Rohingya homes and mosques. At least 73,000 Rohingya fled to refugee camps in Bangladesh. Although the UN criticised the widespread human rights violations committed during the security forces' operations, and described them as constituting possible crimes against humanity, an internal investigation conducted by Myanmar's military exonerated itself of any wrongdoing. Despite this blatant obfuscation, there was no follow-up from the UN Security Council or the Association of Southeast Asian Nations (ASEAN). Myanmar's major international donors and investors also turned a blind eye to the ongoing persecution. In many respects, the four-month campaign between October 2016 and February 2017 was a prelude to the expanded and deadlier offensive later that year.[6]

The military's August 2017 operations began as collective punishment for a coordinated attack on police and army barracks by Rohingya militants armed mainly with knives. The attacks on 25 August resulted in twelve members of the security forces being killed along with more than fifty of the attackers, who were members of the self-styled Arakan Rohingya Salvation Army. Two of Myanmar's light infantry divisions, the 33rd and 99th, had already been deployed to Rakhine State and were immediately unleashed in coordinated operations against at least twenty-two Rohingya villages. One week later, the commander of Myanmar's military, General Min Aung Hlaing, described the 'Bengali problem' as an 'unfinished job' left over from the Second World War. On 1 September the general's official Facebook page declared that there was 'no Rohingya race' in Myanmar. Under General Min Aung Hlaing's overall command, widespread atrocities committed by Myanmar's security forces against the Rohingya population after 25 August clearly constituted crimes against humanity under international law and also appeared to be genocidal in intent.[7]

No one knew precisely how many civilians were dead or displaced inside Myanmar, but according to research by Médecins Sans Frontières, at least 6,700 Rohingya were killed in Rakhine State between 25 August and 24 September alone. With burning villages and the desperate exodus of tens of thousands of Rohingya dominating the international media, attention then turned to the UN Security Council. The Council discussed Myanmar under 'any other business' on 30 August, 13 September and 26 September. UN Secretary-General António Guterres also briefed the Security Council about the crisis on 28 September, noting that the UN had received 'bone chilling accounts' regarding 'excessive violence and serious violations of human rights' in Rakhine State.[8]

On 8 September, just fifteen days after 'clearance operations' began, diplomats representing the majority of the Security Council also attended a private briefing where I and two other civil society representatives provided analysis, satellite evidence and eyewitness reports.[9] One of the briefers had just arrived from Bangladesh and read from interview notes with Rohingya survivors who had made it to the safety of the refugee camps. Council members also attended an Arria formula meeting on 13 October at which former UN secretary-general Kofi Annan spoke about the underlying sources of conflict and persecution in Rakhine State. There was no question, therefore, that given the multiple sources of intelligence available to them, the entire Council was aware of the scale and intensity of the atrocities that were underway.

Their response was tepid at best. It took ten weeks for the UN Security Council just to release a presidential statement on the crisis. That 6 November statement emphasised that the 'Security Council stresses the primary responsibility of the Government of Myanmar to protect its population including through respect for the rule of law and the respect, promotion and protection of human rights.'[10] Part of the reason for the delay was that China remains a powerful ally of the generals who still dominate Myanmar, and has extensive economic interests in the country.[11] But facing global outrage, China avoided having to veto a binding Security Council resolution by reluctantly agreeing to a unanimous presidential statement instead. Words, but no action.

Despite the Security Council's inertia, the flow of Rohingya refugees eventually ebbed. This was not because atrocities were halted, but because an estimated eighty percent of the Rohingya population had fled by the end of the year, with the total number of refugees in Bangladesh eventually reaching around 890,000.[12] Another report by ASEAN Parliamentarians for Human Rights, based upon findings by the Bangladesh government, calculated the approximate death toll during the so-called clearance operations to include 43,000 Rohingya adults. Meanwhile, the authorities in Myanmar began a campaign of bulldozing the remains of many burned and abandoned Rohingya villages.[13]

Undeterred by years of warnings about the threat of atrocities in Rakhine State, a number of governments had taken refuge in the idea that quiet diplomacy – including acquiescing to Myanmar's insistence on not publicly mentioning the Rohingya – would create space for gentle reform. Instead it had the reverse effect, encouraging those generals who desired a 'final solution' in Rakhine State and wanted to test the limits of Nobel Peace Prize winner Aung San Suu Kyi's moral authority. However, democracy in Myanmar cannot be built on the bones of the Rohingya. As an extremely critical report from the UK Parliament's International Development Committee subsequently argued:

> In fact, continuing engagement with Burma seems to have been interpreted as tacit acceptance of the treatment of the Rohingya, reinforcing the problem. There appears to have been over-optimism about the speed and breadth of democratic reform in Burma. The Rohingya have paid a heavy price for the lack of consensus amongst the international community on how and when to decide to act effectively to prevent or end emerging crises.[14]

It was due to the brave testimony of Rohingya survivors – as well as the efforts of journalists, humanitarian workers and civil society activists – that there was international awareness and outrage regarding the plight of the Rohingya. Partly in response, during October the United States suspended its training programs with Myanmar's military, and then in December it placed sanctions on Maung Maung Soe, the general responsible for overseeing operations in Rakhine State. France and the United Kingdom also suspended their training programs with Myanmar's military, while the European Union said it would maintain its arms embargo.[15] But these measures were not coordinated globally, nor were they mandated by the UN Security Council and therefore binding under international law.

Lowest-common-denominator diplomacy

Almost eight decades since the end of the Second World War, the UN Security Council is still the only legitimate body mandated with the maintenance of global peace and security. With regard to the prevention of mass atrocity crimes, the Council's recent failures have come in many forms. The most dramatic and tragic have been a result of the abuse of the veto, with fourteen vetoes since 2011 regarding the Syrian crisis (eight by China and Russia together, six by Russia alone). But another form of diplomatic failure has resulted from not even putting a draft resolution forward because a permanent member has used its 'silent veto' behind closed doors to delay or deny a vote. As a result, the Security Council is left looking powerless as atrocities and historic levels of civilian displacement threaten the multilateral system.

Despite the UN Security Council's failure to act regarding Myanmar, during September 2017 the government of Nigeria issued an official statement condemning atrocities committed against the Rohingya and calling upon 'the United Nations to invoke the principle of the "Responsibility to Protect" and intervene in Myanmar to stop the ongoing ethnic cleansing and create conditions for the safe return' of displaced Rohingya.[16] Similarly, Australia's foreign minister, speaking at the UN during September, argued that the 'Government of Myanmar has a responsibility to protect all citizens in its territory, and where human rights violations have taken place, those responsible must be held to account'.[17] Even Malaysia, an ASEAN member state that had previously been critical of R2P, issued a formal statement expressing 'grave concerns' over atrocities against the Rohingya, 'which have unleashed a full-scale humanitarian crisis that the world simply cannot ignore but must be compelled to act upon'.[18]

These sentiments were echoed in a joint appeal from eighty-one human rights, faith-based and humanitarian organisations to the UN Security Council. The appeal argued that the 'Myanmar government has the primary responsibility to protect its diverse population without discrimination and regardless of ethnicity, religion or citizenship status'. It also called for 'prompt, concerted and effective international action', including an arms embargo and targeted sanctions against 'senior officers responsible for crimes against humanity or other serious human rights abuses'.[19]

Responding to widespread criticism, on 28 September 2017 Myanmar's national security advisor, U Thaung Tun, spoke at the UN Security Council, stressing that the international community had been provoked by 'subjective and emotionally charged' accounts in the media. However, according to him, those with expert knowledge of Rakhine State and prior 'exposure to the propaganda tactics of terrorists' would be able to determine that 'there is no ethnic cleansing and no genocide in Myanmar'. It was noted by some onlookers that U Thaung Tun did not utter the word *Rohingya* once during his statement, referring only to an exodus of 'Muslim villagers'.[20]

One month later U Thaung Tun participated in a televised discussion in Myanmar, commenting that the concept of the responsibility to protect was 'very dangerous for our country'. Among other things, he noted that Myanmar had been listed as 'a red color country', meaning a country where atrocities were occurring and urgent international action was needed.[21] While arguing that China and Russia would defend Myanmar's interests at the UN Security Council and noting that 'international pressure did not hurt our sovereignty' in the past, U Thaung Tun worried that because of the R2P principle, 'it could this time'.[22]

U Thaung Tun's hopes, rather than his fears, were realised, as Chinese diplomats continued to insist in various private UN Security Council negotiations that they were prepared to veto a binding resolution on the crisis in Myanmar. A unanimous presidential statement censuring the government was one thing, but any attempt by the Council to adopt a formal resolution imposing sanctions or an arms embargo remained anathema.[23] In their intransigent backroom defense of Myanmar, Chinese diplomats exposed the enduring problem of a UN Security Council that is immobilised and unable to function when a permanent member threatens to use its veto power to protect the interests of a state that is committing atrocities. Syria, Yemen and Myanmar are all contemporary cases in point, despite the best efforts of 115 states who have signed the "Code of Conduct regarding Security Council action against genocide, crimes against humanity or war crimes."[24]

Australia's former foreign minister, Gareth Evans – who was a cochair of the international commission that developed the R2P principle – has written that the whole point of the exercise was 'to create a new norm of international behavior which states would feel ashamed to violate, compelled to observe, or at least embarrassed to ignore'.[25] Fundamentally, the Myanmar crisis was not just a failure of the UN Security Council to uphold its collective responsibility to protect, it was a failure to challenge the calculus of lowest-common-denominator diplomacy and defend the basic norms and principles of human rights and humanitarianism. In this context it is also worth recalling the words of the UN's first special adviser on the responsibility to protect, Edward Luck:

> Some norms do little more than codify existing patterns of behavior, while R2P, like other human rights and humanitarian norms, has an aspirational quality in that it challenges governments, groups, and individuals to do better and aim higher. Without some level of discomfort and dissatisfaction with current practice, we will never get better at prevention and protection.[26]

Eight months after so-called clearance operations began in Rakhine State, the UN Security Council did, however, undertake an official visit to the region. During April 2018, Council members visited Rohingya refugee camps in Bangladesh, and in Myanmar they met with political and military leaders, including de facto head of state Aung San Suu Kyi and senior general Min Aung Hlaing.

On the flight across Rakhine State, the ambassadors flew over scorched villages and several of them photographed the charred landscape below, noting that you could still see the outline where the huts and homes of the Rohingya had been.[27] The visit had a profound impact on several of the ambassadors, and although a group of states on the UN Security Council have worked to keep the issue of the Rohingya in the Council's focus, as of late 2020 – three years since the so-called clearance operations began – there has still not been a single resolution adopted to name the nature of the crime committed against the Rohingya or hold the perpetrators accountable.

Global progress versus perpetual crisis

The UN Security Council's failure to adequately respond to catastrophic crises, like in Myanmar, has led to an exponential increase in human suffering. One region in particular has borne the brunt of the resulting instability. In the words of a joint report by the World Bank and United Nations:

> The Middle East and North Africa have seen the most rapid expansion and escalation of violent conflict. Although home to only 5 percent of the world's population, in 2014 the region accounted for 45 percent of the world's terrorist incidents, 58 percent of battle-related deaths, 47 percent of internally displaced people, and 58 percent of refugees.[28]

By 2016 at least 17.5 million people were displaced in Yemen, Syria and Iraq alone.[29] Such statistics serve as a reminder that when conflicts metastasise they can destabilise entire regions and jeopardise millions of lives, throwing the entire international system into crisis and disrepute.

They also skew our perception of the world. Renowned psychologist Steven Pinker argues that the nature of human cognition and the immediacy of satellite news and social media combine to feed a 'negativity bias' in modern society. The horrific consequences of air strikes on civilians in Syria can be watched on an iPhone or satellite TV just moments after they occur. By comparison, incremental decades-long progress regarding human rights is never 'breaking news', and atrocities that are prevented cannot be broadcast, because they did not occur. Correspondingly, journalism that focuses on the horror of war can inspire human empathy and mobilise political action. But it can just as easily inculcate unbalanced pessimism regarding our ability to end human-created conflicts.[30]

In the words of the UN's 2018 Human Development Index, 'across the world, people are living longer, are more educated and have greater livelihood opportunities', with the average life span seven years longer now than it was in 1990. However, these global gains do not mean very much if you have the misfortune to be living in Syria or Yemen, where health, the economy and human security are all in precipitous decline. In this context, it is also worth keeping in mind that sixty-eight percent of all the refugees in the world in 2017 came from just five active conflict zones – Syria, Afghanistan, South Sudan, Myanmar and Somalia.[31]

Correspondingly, while 2017 will be remembered as the year that the UN Security Council failed to halt a genocide in Myanmar, in all likelihood the prevention of conflict in the tiny African country of the Gambia will be relegated to the footnotes of history. On 1 December 2016, Gambians voted and elected the opposition's presidential candidate, Adama Barrow. Despite initially accepting defeat, incumbent president Yahya Jammeh, who had held power since a 1994 military coup, refused to step down. Instead he started targeting opponents, declaring a state of emergency. According to Jaclyn Streitfeld-Hall:

> Jammeh had a long history of inciting divisions based on ethnicity, religion, and sexual orientation. In June 2016, he threatened to exterminate the entire Mandinka ethnic group, whom he did not consider authentic Gambians. He routinely endangered lesbian, gay, bisexual, and transgender people, notoriously threatening to 'slit the throats' of all gay men in the Gambia. In the weeks following his electoral defeat, some of his supporters blamed political instability in the country on gays and their alleged foreign supporters, signaling growing fractures in Gambian society that Jammeh could use to mobilize his political supporters.[32]

In late December and early January, Jammeh's 'disturbing and inflammatory rhetoric, his long history of human rights violations' and his determination to hold onto power 'combined to create a delicate and dangerous situation'.[33]

The response of the Economic Community of West African States (ECOWAS) was resolute. During December, ECOWAS sent a delegation comprised of the heads of state of Ghana, Liberia and Nigeria to reason with Jammeh. Alongside this initiative, an ECOWAS summit in Nigeria underlined its commitment to a democratic transfer of power. These efforts were supported by both the UN and the African Union. An ECOWAS military force was then mobilised on the Senegalese border (which surrounds the Gambia), mandated to remove Jammeh if he did not de-escalate tensions and respect the electoral result. With Senegalese troops eventually entering the country, Jammeh fled into exile on 21 January. Hardly a shot was fired, and there were no reported casualties.[34]

Reporting to the UN Security Council four days later, the head of the UN Office for West Africa and the Sahel described the Gambia as 'a success of preventive diplomacy that has been achieved through the mobilization of regional actors in perfect coordination with the international community'.[35] What was crucial was the unwavering role of ECOWAS, which consistently sought a diplomatic solution while maintaining a credible threat to militarily intervene if the situation continued to deteriorate. Senegal was serving as an elected member of the UN Security Council at the time, and also 'played a pivotal role in linking the actions of the United Nations and ECOWAS', keeping the Security Council engaged with the situation in a small, distant country that might otherwise not have received attention until too late.

After being sworn in, President Barrow attempted to repair the damage done by more than two decades of authoritarian rule. The new government initiated a constitutional review and announced its intention to establish both a truth and reconciliation commission and a national human rights commission. In January 2017 the Gambia requested assistance from the UN Peacebuilding Commission, and financial support was provided for security sector reform and transitional justice programs. The new government also rescinded Jammeh's decision to withdraw from the ICC. As a result, according to Freedom House's 2018 report *Freedom in the World*, at a time when the global trend was of 'emboldened autocrats' and a weakening of human rights, the Gambia 'secured one of the largest-ever improvements' in political rights and civil liberties in a single year.[36]

While cynics will argue that the Gambia is a small West African country, far from the nerve centre of global politics, it is worth recalling that Rwanda was a small country too. But international failure in Rwanda in 1994 not only resulted in a genocide, it directly contributed to years of instability and refugee flows across the entire Great Lakes region. Some of those conflicts continue to reverberate decades later. In short, ECOWAS' intervention in the Gambia played an important role in preventing another violent conflict with potentially disastrous consequences for the country and West Africa as a whole. It remains an example of how timely action can make all the difference in the world.

The price of prevention

All too often it appears that the international community still prefers solemn hand-wringing in the aftermath of mass atrocities to being accused of acting prematurely to avert them. The net effect has been to radically increase political rhetoric around the need for the UN system to improve its preventive capacity, combined with an unwillingness to actually invest in improving or utilising that capacity.

The price of failure has been exorbitant. In 2006, around eighty percent of international humanitarian assistance funding went to dealing with the consequences of natural disasters. By 2016, that same proportion was now going to the victims of human-created conflicts. The social and economic effects were ruinous. According to the UN and World Bank, countries lose 'an average 8.5 percentage points in economic growth in the first year of civil war and 4.5 percent in subsequent years', throwing people into unemployment, hunger and dependence upon emergency aid.[37]

Syria's GDP, for example, decreased by up to eighty percent between 2010 and 2016 as a result of the civil war – dramatically increasing poverty as the conflict displaced over twelve million people, destroyed entire cities and killed hundreds of thousands of civilians. By 2017 the World Bank estimated that the war had demolished one third of Syria's housing and half of its educational and medical facilities. In 2012, Syria was ranked 128 on the UN's Human Development Index, placing it in the middle grouping; by 2017, it had fallen twenty-seven places to 155 out of 189 surveyed countries and territories, placing it amongst the poorest and most underdeveloped and insecure countries on the planet.[38]

Overall, UN members states spent almost $8 billion on peacekeeping and $22.1 billion on humanitarian operations while responding to violent conflicts during 2016. Meanwhile, research by the World Bank and UN suggested that preventing the outbreak of violent conflict could potentially save over $34 billion in economic damage at the national level per year. Despite this reality, actual investment in prevention by donor governments still amounts to a miserly fraction of the amount spent on military aid or emergency relief. An analysis by Mercy Corps found that in 2014, donor governments spent only approximately one percent of their official development assistance funding on conflict prevention, conflict resolution and peacebuilding. Even in the most fragile states, the percentage spent on prevention or conflict mitigation programs only rose to four percent.[39]

In one of the most remarkable examples, in 2011 – three years before armed extremists from the so-called Islamic State swept across the Nineveh Plain – the United States spent $47 billion on military funding in Iraq. That same year, however, it spent a comparatively diminutive $184 million on 'democracy, human rights, conflict mitigation, and reconciliation programs'.[40] Given the poor return that the US got for its massive investment in Iraq's military (which retreated in the face of ISIL's offensive), one can only wonder if a greater investment in countering violent extremism and mediating tensions between Sunni, Shia and Kurdish communities might have helped prevent the bloodshed ISIL unleashed upon the country.

The failure to systematically invest in proximate efforts to prevent mass atrocities is definitely not the result of a paucity of information. Most conflicts where atrocities occur are situations that develop over years rather than days. These conflicts are often the result of deep structural problems rooted in protracted disputes over the use and abuse of power, such as Myanmar, where UN member states failed to adequately respond to years of early warning regarding the persecution of the Rohingya.[41]

Most importantly, prevention works. The international community successfully supported structural reforms in Kenya after the bloody 2007 election pitted ethnic and political rivals against one another. Measures to control and punish hate speech and ethnic incitement, as well as the implementation of constitutional reforms and the restructuring of governmental power, helped ease some of the underlying sources of conflict in Kenyan society, contributing to a largely peaceful election in 2013. Meanwhile, in Guinea, following a notorious stadium massacre in 2009, an election in 2010 paved the way for the country's first civilian government in five decades. The paid retirement of thousands of members of Guinea's bloated and abusive security forces was a key component of the overall effort to strengthen human rights.[42]

A key lesson of the current global crisis is that the infrastructure for both early warning and structural prevention is not being effectively mobilised where and when it is most desperately needed. As a result, when prevention fails it is often UN peacekeepers who are belatedly tasked with upholding the international community's responsibility to protect. However, in three of the most catastrophic conflicts in the world today – Syria, Yemen and Myanmar – UN peacekeeping is not a political option. In each of these cases one or more veto-wielding permanent members of the Council are allies of a party to the conflict and opposed to the involvement of UN peacekeepers. The prevention of further crimes in these countries will therefore require political imagination, including a determination to hold perpetrators accountable under international law.

Pursuing international justice

During November 2017 – while Myanmar's military was still conducting its 'clearance operations' in Rakhine State – the International Criminal Tribunal for the Former Yugoslavia (ICTY) found Ratko Mladić guilty of genocide, war crimes and crimes against humanity. As commander of the Bosnian Serb army during the 1992–1995 Bosnian War, Mladić appeared all-powerful and un-touchable, presiding over the genocide at Srebrenica and wantonly committing war crimes. His conviction at the ICTY means that he will now die in prison.

The Mladić verdict raises the uncomfortable question of whether we are doing enough to hold those responsible for atrocities today accountable for their crimes. In this regard, the International Criminal Court is still the most important in-stitutional development in the battle to end impunity for mass atrocity crimes. Of the 193 member states of the United Nations, more than 120 have ratified the Rome Statute, and the ICC is – to quote its chief prosecutor, Fatou Bensouda – the 'legal arm of the responsibility to protect'.[43]

As the ICC marked its twentieth anniversary in 2018, it had never been more needed, with thirteen situations currently under formal investigation. But the international battle against impunity is not restricted to the ICC. It includes the 2016 conviction for crimes against humanity of former Chadian dictator Hissène Habré at the Extraordinary African Chambers in Senegal. France, Germany and the Netherlands have also established specialised war crimes units that have utilised the principle of universal jurisdiction to prosecute Syrian per-petrators who have fled to Europe.[44] Meanwhile, Argentina, Brazil, Chile and Guatemala have all conducted domestic processes to confront crimes committed during times of dictatorship. This has included holding powerful politicians and military figures accountable for their role in atrocities, such as former Guatemalan president General Efraín Ríos Montt, whose historic 2013 conviction for geno-cide and crimes against humanity was later overturned on a legal technicality. An essential part of preventing a recurrence of atrocities in Latin America has been exposing the truth about the past and denying perpetrators the impunity and silence upon which they depend.

Despite the failure of the UN Security Council to act with regard to atrocities committed in Myanmar during late 2017, a myriad of civil society organisations – working with Rohingya survivors, journalists and legal advocates – continued to push for accountability. Partly in response, on 25 June 2018 the European Union and Canada imposed sanctions, including asset freezes and travel bans, on seven senior members of Myanmar's military and police. The sanctioned officials in-cluded General Maung Maung Soe, the former head of the army's Western Command. Following the announcement, the general was fired for alleged un-derperformance of duties.[45]

In the same way that metastasising conflicts and atrocities weaken international norms, justice can be contagious, and accountability in one country can deter potential perpetrators elsewhere. Even in the most desperate cases, with the Security Council immobilised and inert, the international community can pursue other options to ensure that international law is upheld. For example, on 21 December 2016 the UN General Assembly voted to establish an International, Impartial and Independent Mechanism (IIIM) to investigate and collect evidence of atrocities in Syria. While the IIIM has no prosecutorial power and is funded by voluntary contributions from concerned countries, its creation sent a message to the permanent members of the Security Council that the broader membership was not prepared to passively accept their failure.

Similarly, on 27 August 2018, one year after the 'clearance operations' in Rakhine State began, the Independent International Fact-Finding Mission on Myanmar (FFM), mandated by the Human Rights Council, reported that atrocities committed against the Rohingya amounted to four of the five prohibited acts in the Genocide Convention. The FFM's devastating 400-page report found evidence of 'genocidal intent', including discriminatory government policies designed to alter the demographic composition of Rakhine State and a premeditated plan to destroy Rohingya communities.[46] According to the FFM, Myanmar's authorities, including State Counsellor Aung San Suu Kyi, had not met their 'responsibility to protect the civilian population' and were complicit in the commission of crimes. The report called for several top military officers to be prosecuted for genocide, as well as for crimes against humanity and war crimes committed in Kachin and Shan states. The FFM also called upon the UN Security Council to refer the situation in Myanmar to the ICC or create an ad hoc international criminal tribunal.

With a possible Chinese, Russian or US veto making an ICC referral via the UN Security Council highly unlikely, the Human Rights Council then proposed an independent investigative mechanism. Like the IIIM for Syria, the mechanism could collect, preserve and analyse evidence of atrocities in Myanmar and help prepare potential cases against alleged perpetrators. Remarkably, on 27 September, thirty-five of the Human Rights Council's forty-seven members voted in favour of establishing an investigative mechanism for Myanmar, with only China, the Philippines and Burundi opposing. Pakistan's ambassador, commenting on the outcome, said that it showed that the 'UN works, the Human Rights Council works'.[47]

Following the Geneva vote, during October the FFM's chair, Marzuki Darusman, was invited to brief the UN Security Council in New York. Although China and Russia tried to block Darusman from speaking, this was subject to a procedural vote and not subject to a veto by one of the five permanent members. Nine of the Council's fifteen members supported the briefing, at which Darusman emphasised that 'national sovereignty is not a license to commit crimes against humanity or genocide' and that the 'Rohingya and all of Myanmar's people, in fact the entire world, is looking at [the Council] to take action'.[48]

Meanwhile, in response to the FFM's conclusion that Myanmar's military had displayed genocidal intent with regard to the Rohingya, it was reported that the European Union was considering trade sanctions that would deny Myanmar tariff-free access to the world's largest trading bloc. This was part of a process of escalating measures directed at those responsible for atrocities, including the targeted sanctions imposed by the EU and Canada in June and further sanctions imposed by the United States during August that focused on two military units, depriving their commanders of access to foreign financial assets. At the end of October, Australia, an important regional power, also imposed targeted sanctions on five senior officers from Myanmar's military.[49]

A number of states are now reviewing their trade, investment and development programs in Myanmar, ensuring that they do not reinforce discriminatory structures or enable perpetrators of genocide to profit from the seizure of Rohingya lands. In August 2018, Facebook was forced to take action after reporting by the FFM and in the media revealed how Myanmar's army had 'turned the social network into a tool for ethnic cleansing'. Facebook banned eighteen personal accounts, including that of senior general Min Aung Hlaing, and shut down fifty-two pages that promoted hate speech and disinformation. These accounts were followed by almost twelve million people, and had been proscribed, according to Facebook, to prevent them from being used to 'further inflame ethnic and religious tensions'. Finally, in late 2019, following a meeting of the Organization of Islamic Cooperation, it was announced that the Gambia would take Myanmar to the International Court of Justice (ICJ) for breaching the Genocide Convention. The public announcement of this historic case was made by the Gambia's justice minister, Abubacarr "Ba" Tambadou, at an event cohosted by Bangladesh and the Global Centre for the Responsibility to Protect on the margins of the UN General Assembly.[50]

When the case commenced at the ICJ in December 2019, the Gambia immediately submitted a request for the court to issue provisional measures in order to protect the Rohingya people and secure evidence of the crimes that had been committed against them. Minister Tambadou spoke movingly of the atrocities committed against the Rohingya and the conditions facing survivors in Rakhine State. Meanwhile, State Counsellor Aung San Suu Kyi came to the Hague to deny that a genocide had taken place and to defend the reputation of Myanmar's generals. When the ICJ accepted the arguments of the Gambia and issued a provisional-measures order in January 2020, the case received widespread global media attention.[51]

Altogether, the ICJ case and other bilateral measures imposed by UN member states on Myanmar sent a powerful message to the generals who still control much of the country's economy that they can no longer rely on 'business as usual'. It took more than two decades for the victims of Ratko Mladić to see their persecutors in a courtroom. Rohingya refugees and other victims of atrocities in the world today should not have to wait that long to see justice.

Conclusion

During 1994, the fifteen members of the UN Security Council adopted almost eighty resolutions, including on the peace processes in Mozambique and El Salvador, conflicts that consumed thousands of lives and shattered both countries. That year will forever be remembered, however, for the Security Council's historic failure to adequately respond to the genocide in Rwanda, a shame that eclipses any diplomatic achievements.

As the Security Council dithered, one million ethnic Tutsi were murdered in Rwanda between April and July 1994. Declassified diplomatic cables reveal that as early as 20 April, just thirteen days after the genocide began, New Zealand's ambassador, Colin Keating, who was serving as president of the UN Security Council, 'observed that it was becoming increasingly difficult to explain credibly why in the face of the most horrific killings the Council could remain formally silent'. After the presidency passed to Nigeria in May, their ambassador also lamented that the Council 'had to take some action very soon; otherwise it would become a laughing stock'.[52] History records that atrocities in Rwanda were not ended due to action by the Security Council but because the genocidal regime was eventually overthrown by armed rebels.

Two decades later, in April 2014, Keating was invited back to the Security Council to speak on the twentieth anniversary of the genocide. He detailed how the threat of the veto had been brandished by some permanent members to forestall action: 'I had the dreadful responsibility in April 1994 of presiding over a Council that refused to recognize that genocide was being perpetrated against the Tutsi in Rwanda and failed in its responsibilities to reinforce the United Nations peacekeeping mission in Rwanda in order to protect as many innocent civilians as possible.' He was, however, sanguine about a draft resolution before the Council on the issue of the prevention of genocide:

> I would like to add that the development of the principle of the Responsibility to Protect, which is referenced so clearly in the draft resolution before the Council today, gives further reason for hope. Recent Council practice in Mali and the Central African Republic and with the Force Intervention Brigade in the Democratic Republic of the Congo further demonstrates that some important lessons have been learned.[53]

Learned, but not always implemented. Twenty years from now, it is unlikely that the history books will commend current members of the Security Council for deliberately avoiding some discussions of how to protect vulnerable populations from atrocities in order to achieve faux unanimity and elude controversy. History will, however, definitely record that while over 700,000 Rohingya were being systematically displaced from Myanmar over a four-month period during 2017 – with hundreds of villages burnt down and tens of thousands of civilians killed – the

Council failed to pass a single resolution to halt these atrocities or to hold the perpetrators accountable.

If we want to avoid endlessly repeating the failures of the past, human rights and humanitarian principles cannot continue to be selectively applied or diluted and discarded. Norms, laws and institutions remain essential.[54]

The celebrated author and Holocaust survivor Primo Levi wrote movingly about his experience of Auschwitz during the final year of the Second World War. Less well known is the fact that before his transportation to the concentration camp, Levi was briefly an anti-fascist partisan in the mountains of Italy. After the war, Levi met other Jewish survivors who had fought in the forests of Nazi-occupied Eastern Europe. In 1982 he drew on these encounters in his final novel, a story of resistance titled *If Not Now, When?*

Levi's question seems like a fitting rejoinder to all those who say that it is too difficult in the current political climate to stand up for human rights and push back against the authoritarian tilt in global diplomacy. It is also a confutation of the politics of inaction and what Pope Francis has called 'the globalization of in-difference' with regard to refugees.[55] Levi reminds us that the work of those who created the Genocide Convention and crafted the Universal Declaration of Human Rights continues.

'Never again' was not intended as a silent prayer. It was a demand by the survivors of the Holocaust that we, the subsequent generations, actively prevent mass atrocities wherever or whenever they may be threatened, no matter how politically inconvenient it might be to do so. The historic campaign by the Gambia, working closely with international civil society, to hold Myanmar ac-countable for breaching the Genocide Convention should remind us that now is the time to prevent, halt and punish mass atrocity crimes. Because if not now, when?

Notes

1 UNHCR, "Bangladesh Refugee Emergency Fact Sheet," 15 August 2018, https://data2.unhcr.org/en/documents/download/65223. This chapter draws on research originally published as Simon Adams, "'If Not Now, When?': The Responsibility to Protect, the Fate of the Rohingya, and the Future of Human Rights," *GCR2P Occasional Paper*, no. 8, January 2019.

2 Statement by Adama Dieng, United Nations Special Adviser on the Prevention of Genocide, on his visit to Bangladesh to assess the situation of Rohingya Refugees from Myanmar, 13 March 2018, http://www.un.org/en/genocideprevention/documents/2018-03-13%20Statement_visit%20Rohingya%20Bangladesh_FINAL.pdf; "UN Human Rights Chief points to 'Textbook Example of Ethnic Cleansing' in Myanmar," *UN News*, 11 September 2017, https://news.un.org/en/story/2017/09/564622-un-human-rights-chief-points-textbook-example-ethnic-cleansing-myanmar; and Stephanie Nebehay and Simon Lewis, "'Acts of Genocide' Suspected against Rohingya in Myanmar: UN," *Reuters*, 7 March 2018, https://www.reuters.com/article/us-myanmar-rohingya-rights/acts-of-genocide-suspected-against-rohingya-in-myanmar-u-n-idUSKCN1GJ163. Although atrocities in Rakhine State continued into 2018, the main phase of atrocities and dis-placement was from 25 August until December 2017. By August 2018 the total population

in the Bangladesh refugee camps was 891,233 people. UNHCR, "Bangladesh Refugee Emergency Fact Sheet"; and Human Rights Watch, "Burma: 40 Rohingya Villages Burned Since October," 17 December 2017, https://www.hrw.org/news/2017/12/17/burma-40-rohingya-villages-burned-october.

3 United Nations Office for the Coordination of Humanitarian Affairs, "Rohingya Refugee Crisis," https://www.unocha.org/rohingya-refugee-crisis.

4 Myanmar has a population of approximately fifty-three million people, of whom around ninety percent are Buddhist. An estimated sixty-nine percent of the population are ethnically Bamar, while the Shan make up about nine percent, the Karen seven percent, and the Kachin 1.5 percent. Prior to the 'clearance operations', there were an estimated one million Rohingya, approximately 1.5 percent of the population. The issue of how many 'national races' or ethnic groups are officially recognised in Myanmar has been in constant flux – from 139 during British colonial rule, up to 144 under the military dictatorship in 1973 and then down to 135 by 1983. For more on the history of Muslims in Myanmar, see Francis Wade, *Myanmar's Enemy Within: Buddhist Violence and the Making of a Muslim 'Other'* (London: Zed Books, 2017). On Myanmar's various ethnicities, see Mae Sot, "Myanmar's Ethnic Problems," *IRIN News*, 29 March 2012, http://www.irinnews.org/report/95195/briefing-myanmar's-ethnic-problem.

5 Wade, *Myanmar's Enemy Within: Buddhist Violence and the Making of a Muslim 'Other'*.

6 UN Office of the High Commissioner for Human Rights, "Report of OHCHR Mission to Bangladesh: Interviews with Rohingyas fleeing from Myanmar since 9 October 2016," 3 February 2017, https://www.ohchr.org/Documents/Countries/MM/FlashReport3Feb2017.pdf; UNHCR, "Bangladesh Refugee Emergency Fact Sheet"; Fortify Rights, "'They Gave Them Long Swords': Preparations for Genocide and Crimes Against Humanity against Rohingya Muslims in Rakhine State, Myanmar," July 2018, https://www.fortifyrights.org/downloads/Fortify_Rights_Long_Swords_July_2018.pdf.

7 Amnesty International, "'We Will Destroy Everything': Military Responsibility for Crimes Against Humanity in Rakhine State, Myanmar," 27 June 2018, 157, https://www.amnesty.org.nz/we-will-destroy-everything-military-responsibility-crimes-against-humanity-rakhine-state-myanmar; and Simon Lewis, Zeba Siddiqui, Clare Baldwin, and Andrew R.C. Marshall, "The Shock Troops Who Expelled the Rohingya from Myanmar," *Reuters*, 26 June 2018, https://www.reuters.com/article/us-myanmar-rohingya-battalions-specialre/the-shock-troops-who-expelled-the-rohingya-from-myanmar-idUSKBN1JM1X7.

8 UN Secretary-General, "Remarks at open debate of the Security Council on Myanmar," 28 September 2017, https://www.un.org/sg/en/content/sg/statement/2017-09-28/secretary-generals-remarks-open-debate-security-council-myanmar; Médecins Sans Frontières, "MSF surveys estimate that at least 6,700 Rohingya were killed during the attacks in Myanmar," 12 December 2017, https://www.msf.org/myanmarbangladesh-msf-surveys-estimate-least-6700-rohingya-were-killed-during-attacks-myanmar.

9 The 8 September briefing was confidential but was chaired by the author.

10 "Security Council Presidential Statement Calls on Myanmar to End Excessive Military Force, Inter-communal Violence in Rakhine State," *UN News*, 6 November 2017, http://www.un.org/press/en/2017/sc13055.doc.htm.

11 Pieter D. Wezeman, Aude Fleurant, Alexandra Kuimova, Nan Tian, and Siemon T. Wezeman, "Trends in International Arms Transfers, 2017," *Stockholm International Peace Research Institute (SIPRI) Fact Sheet*, March 2018, https://www.sipri.org/sites/default/files/2018-03/fssipri_at2017_0.pdf.

12 UNHCR, "Bangladesh Refugee Emergency Fact Sheet."

13 The 43,000 figure was based upon interviews with Rohingya children at refugee camps in Bangladesh. At least 36,000 children reported having lost one parent, while 7,700 reported having lost both parents. It was noted that some unaccompanied children may

have simply been separated and lost contact with their families while fleeing. ASEAN Parliamentarians for Human Rights, "The Rohingya Crisis: Past, Present and Future – Summary Report of Findings from Fact-Finding Mission to Bangladesh," 2018, https://aseanmp.org/wp-content/uploads/2018/03/APHR_Bangladesh-Fact-Finding-Mission-Report_Mar-2018.pdf; and Amnesty International, "'We Will Destroy Everything': Military Responsibility for Crimes Against Humanity in Rakhine State, Myanmar."

14 United Kingdom House of Commons International Development Committee, "Bangladesh and Burma: the Rohingya Crisis," 15 January 201, 3, https://publications. parliament.uk/pa/cm201719/cmselect/cmintdev/504/504.pdf.

15 United States 115th Congress, Burma Human Rights and Freedom Act of 2017, DAV17189, 2 November 2017; United States Department of the Treasury, "United States Sanctions Human Rights Abusers and Corrupt Actors Across the Globe," 21 December 2017; Global Affairs Canada, "Canada imposes targeted sanctions in response to human rights violations in Myanmar," 16 February 2018, https://www. canada.ca/en/global-affairs/news/2018/02/canada_imposes_ targetedsanctionsinresponsetohumanrightsviolation.html; and *European Union Sanctions Map*, https://www.sanctionsmap.eu/.

16 Nigeria Ministry of Foreign Affairs, "Nigeria Condemns Human Rights Abuse in Myanmar," 12 September 2017, https://prnigeria.com/general/fg-condemns-human-right-abuse-myanmar/.

17 The Hon. Julie Bishop MP, Minister of Foreign Affairs of Australia, "Speech at Meeting on the Situation in Rakhine State," New York, 18 September 2017, https:// foreignminister.gov.au/speeches/Pages/2017/jb_sp_170918.aspx?w=tb1CaGpkPX %2FlS0K%2Bg9ZKEg%3D%3D.

18 Statement by the Minister of Foreign Affairs of Malaysia, Dato' Sri Anifah Aman, in Response to the ASEAN Chairman's Statement on the Humanitarian Situation in Rakhine State, 24 September 2017.

19 Joint Appeal to the UN Security Council to Act on Myanmar's Rohingya Crisis, 12 December 2017, http://www.globalr2p.org/publications/620. The signatories included Amnesty International, the Burma Human Rights Network, Darfur Women Action Group, Fortify Rights, the Global Centre for the Responsibility to Protect, Human Rights Watch, the International Federation for Human Rights, Physicians for Human Rights, Refugees International, Save the Children and the Syrian Network for Human Rights.

20 Statement by H.E. U Thaung Tun, National Security Advisor to the Union Government of Myanmar at the meeting on the situation in Myanmar in the United Nations Security Council, 28 September 2017, http://www.myanmarmissionnewyork. org/images/pdf/2017/Statements/NSA%20statement%20latest%2028%20sept.pdf.

21 U Thaung Tun attributed the 'red color' coding system to the UN, but he was almost certainly referring to the *R2P Monitor*, a bimonthly publication of the Global Centre for the Responsibility to Protect. Myanmar was listed under 'Current Crisis', which appears in red on the map. See, for example, http://www.globalr2p.org/media/files/r2p_ monitor_jan2018_final.pdf.

22 Lawi Weng, "Govt Frets UN Will Invoke Genocide Doctrine to Intervene in Rakhine," *Irrawaddy*, 27 November 2017, https://www.irrawaddy.com/news/burma/ govt-frets-un-will-invoke-genocide-doctrine-intervene-rakhine.html.

23 Based upon the author's confidential discussions with diplomats involved in Security Council discussions and negotiations concerning Myanmar.

24 Code of Conduct regarding Security Council action against Genocide, Crimes Against Humanity or War Crimes, 14 December 2015, https://www.globalr2p.org/resources/ code-of-conduct-regarding-security-council-action-against-genocide-crimes-against-humanity-or-war-crimes/.

25 G. Evans, "R2P: Looking Back, Looking Forward," Keynote address to International

Conference on The Responsibility to Protect at 10: Progress, Challenges and Opportunities in the Asia Pacific, Phnom Penh, Cambodia, 26 February 2015, http://www.gevans.org/speeches/speech568.html.

26 Edward C. Luck, "The Responsibility to Protect at Ten: The Challenges Ahead," Policy Analysis Brief, Stanley Foundation, May 2015, 3, https://www.stanleyfoundation.org/publications/pab/LuckPAB515.pdf.

27 Based upon the author's discussions with several ambassadors who were on the visit.

28 United Nations and World Bank Group, *Pathways to Peace: Inclusive Approaches to Preventing Violent Conflict: Main Messages and Emerging Policy Directions* (Washington DC: The World Bank, 2017), 7.

29 Ibid, 8–9.

30 Steven Pinker, *Enlightenment Now: The Case for Reason, Science, Humanism, and Progress* (New York: Viking Press, 2018), 41–42, 47–49.

31 United Nations Development Programme, Human Development Indices and Indicators: 2018 Statistical Update, 2018, 2–3, http://hdr.undp.org/sites/default/files/2018_human_development_statistical_update.pdf. Of the 25.4 million refugees in the world in 2017, 6.3 million were from Syria, 2.6 million from Afghanistan, 2.4 million from South Sudan, 1.2 million from Myanmar and 986,000 from Somalia. UNHCR, Global Trends: Forced Displacement in 2017, 3, http://www.unhcr.org/5b27be547.pdf.

32 Jaclyn Streitfeld-Hall, "Conflict Averted Without Anyone Firing A Shot," *Courier*, no. 89 (Spring 2017): 4, https://www.stanleyfoundation.org/resources.cfm?id=843&article=1.

33 Ibid.

34 Daniel Finnan, "Gambia: Senegalese Military Enters Banjul Safeguarding Barrow's Expected Arrival," *Radio France Internationale (RFI) English*, 23 January 2017, http://en.rfi.fr/africa/20170123-gambia-senegalese-military-enters-banjul-safeguarding-barrows-expected-arrival; and Christof Hartmann, "ECOWAS and the Restoration of Democracy in The Gambia," *Africa Spectrum*, 52, no. 1 (2017), 85–99.

35 Streitfeld-Hall, "Conflict Averted Without Anyone Firing A Shot."

36 International Peace Institute, "Toward a New Gambia: Linking Peace and Development," January 2018, 3, 10–11; Freedom House, Freedom in the World 2018, January 2018, 1, 7, https://freedomhouse.org/sites/default/files/FH_FITW_Report_2018_Final_SinglePage.pdf; and Ruth Maclean and Saikou Jammeh, "After beatings, black potions and brutality, the Gambia starts afresh," *The Guardian*, 10 May 2018.

37 UN and World Bank, *Pathways to Peace*, 8–9.

38 Ibid, 8–9; UNDP, Human Development Indices and Indicators: 2018 Statistical Update, 3; and Aron Lund, "As Syria looks to rebuild, US and allies hope money can win where guns lost," *IRIN News*, 22 May 2018, https://www.irinnews.org/analysis/2018/05/22/syria-looks-rebuild-us-and-allies-hope-money-can-win-where-guns-lost.

39 UN and World Bank, *Pathways to Peace*, 1–3; Mercy Corps, An Ounce of Prevention: Why increasing investment in conflict prevention is worth more than a 'pound of cure' in addressing the displacement crisis, September 2016, 3–4, 6–7, 10–11, 22, https://www.mercycorps.org/research-resources/ounce-prevention; United Nations, "General Assembly Approves Nearly $8 Billion for 15 Peacekeeping Missions in 2016/2017," 17 June 2016, https://www.un.org/press/en/2016/ga11794.doc.htm.

40 Mercy Corps, An Ounce of Prevention, 11.

41 Myanmar was listed in all thirty-four issues of the Global Centre for the Responsibility to Protect's bimonthly *R2P Monitor* between January 2012 and August 2017. Myanmar was listed as a 'serious concern' in sixteen issues and an 'imminent risk' in seven, and then analysed in eleven issues as a 'current crisis' where atrocities were being perpetrated. Myanmar was also the focus of various statements and reports by Human Rights Watch, Amnesty International, Fortify Rights and many other nongovernmental organisations, who made recommendations on how Myanmar's government, the UN and

the broader international community could avert the growing threat facing the Rohingya. There was also extensive public reporting from the UN special rapporteur on the human rights situation in Myanmar, Yanghee Lee, and her predecessors.

42 Jaclyn Streitfeld-Hall, "Preventing Atrocities in West Africa," *GCR2P Occasional Paper*, no. 6, September 2015, http://www.globalr2p.org/publications/389.

43 ICC Chief Prosecutor Fatou Bensouda, Address to Conference on R2P: The Next Decade, 18 January 2012, New York, http://www.stanleyfoundation.org/r2p.cfm.

44 On 26 September 2018, six countries wrote to the ICC prosecutor, invoking Article 14 of the Rome Statute and requesting that her office open a formal investigation into possible crimes against humanity in Venezuela. Argentina, Canada, Chile, Colombia, Paraguay and Peru made history as the first countries ever to refer a situation to the ICC for crimes that took place in another state. Matthew Pennington and Angela Charlton, "Canada, Latin American countries ask ICC to investigate Venezuela," *The Globe & Mail*, 26 September 2018. See also, Human Rights Watch, "The Long Arm of Justice: Lessons from Specialized War Crimes Units in France, Germany, and the Netherlands," September 2014, https://www.hrw.org/report/2014/09/16/long-arm-justice/lessons-specialized-war-crimes-units-france-germany-and.

45 European Union, Council Decision (CFSP) 2018/900 amending Decision 2013/184/CFSP concerning restrictive measures against Myanmar/Burma, 25 June 2018, https://eur-lex.europa.eu/legal-content/EN/TXT/?uri=uriserv:OJ.LI.2018.160.01.0009.01.ENG&toc=OJ:L:2018:160I:TOC.

46 United Nations, Report of the International Fact-finding Mission on Myanmar, A/HRC/39/64, 27 August 2018, http://ap.ohchr.org/documents/dpage_e.aspx?si=A/HRC/39/64.

47 Nick Cumming-Bruce, "Human Rights Council Ratchets Up Pressure on Myanmar," *New York Times*, 27 September 2018; and Tom Miles, "UN sets up body to prepare Myanmar atrocity prosecution files," *Reuters*, 27 September 2018, https://www.reuters.com/article/us-myanmar-rohingya-un/un-sets-up-body-to-prepare-myanmar-atrocity-prosecution-files-idUSKCN1M71W0.

48 "UN investigator says Myanmar genocide against Rohingya 'ongoing'," *Al Jazeera*, 25 October 2018, https://www.aljazeera.com/news/2018/10/investigator-myanmar-genocide-rohingya-ongoing-181025035804009.html.

49 Robin Emmott and Philip Blenkisop, "EU considers trade sanctions on Myanmar over Rohingya crisis," *Reuters*, 3 October 2018, https://www.reuters.com/article/us-myanmar-rohingya-eu-exclusive/exclusive-eu-considers-trade-sanctions-on-myanmar-over-rohingya-crisis-idUSKCN1MD28E; Edward Wong, "US Imposes Sanctions on Myanmar Military over Rohingya Atrocities," *New York Times*, 17 August 2018; and "Australia slaps sanctions on Myanmar army top brass," *Reuters*, 23 October 2018, https://www.reuters.com/article/us-australia-myanmar/australia-slaps-sanctions-on-myanmar-army-top-brass-idUSKCN1MX0O8.

50 Timothy McLaughlin, "Facebook Blocks Accounts of Myanmar's Top General, Other Military leaders," *Washington Post*, 27 August 2018; and Paul Mozur, "A Genocide Incited on Facebook, With Posts from Myanmar's Military," *New York Times*, 15 October 2018.

51 Global Justice Center and the Global Centre for the Responsibility to Protect, Q&A: The Gambia vs Myanmar, Rohingya Genocide at the International Court of Justice, 21 May 2020, https://www.globalr2p.org/publications/myanmarqav2/.

52 Diplomatic Cable from New Zealand Mission to the United Nations (New York) to Wellington, 20 April 1994, *National Security Archive*,https://nsarchive2.gwu.edu/NSAEBB/NSAEBB472/docs/Document%209.pdf; Diplomatic Cable to UN Secretary-General Boutros Boutros-Ghali regarding United Nations Security Council discussion on Rwanda, 5 May 1994, *National Security Archive*, https://nsarchive2.gwu.edu/NSAEBB/NSAEBB472/docs/Document%2016.pdf.

53 Statement of Former New Zealand Ambassador to the United Nations Colin Keating at

UN Security Council meeting on: "Threats to International Peace and Security: Prevention and the Fight Against Genocide," S/PV.7155, 16 April 2014, http://www.un.org/en/ga/search/view_doc.asp?symbol=S/PV.7155. The draft was adopted and became UN Security Council Resolution 2150.

54 Alex J. Bellamy and Edward C. Luck, *The Responsibility to Protect: From Promise to Practice* (Medford, CT: Polity Press, 2018), 184–186.

55 Alessandro Speciale, "Pope Francis decries 'Globalization of Indifference,'" *Washington Post*, 8 July 2013.

7

CONCLUSION

The mass graves that were not dug

Contents

In 2015 I was sitting on a dais inside the Human Rights Council chamber at the Palais des Nations in Geneva for an event celebrating the tenth anniversary of the adoption of the responsibility to protect. Under the blue hue of the brightly painted ceiling, with artistic stalactites dripping precariously above us, the packed chamber of more than 500 diplomats, human rights activists and global denizens listened to messages of support from the UN secretary-general and the high commissioner for human rights. I said a few words too, but it was a rhetorical question from Elisabeth Decrey Warner of Geneva Call, who was sitting beside me, that stayed with me afterwards: 'How do you prove how many women were not raped?'

Her point was that when it comes to exposing human rights abuses these days, the problem is rarely a dearth of information. Cell-phone cameras, satellite technologies, the internet and the proliferation of human rights organisations have taken care of that. But conversely, the problem with empirically measuring success in the world of atrocity prevention is that you are often asked to quantify something that did not happen. So how do you prove how many mass graves were not dug and filled? How do you show the schools that were not bombed or burned down? How do you count the child soldiers who were not recruited? How do you statistically measure how many people did not have to flee their homes in the dead of night, were not displaced and did not become refugees? And how do you prove how many women were not raped? These are not questions anyone can answer.

What we do know is that besides being morally reprehensible and posing an inherent threat to human security, atrocity crimes are a humanitarian and developmental catastrophe. For example, the 2011 conflict and atrocities in Côte d'Ivoire saw the country's GDP decline by six percent in just one year, and the UN has estimated that the war in Syria has wiped out gains in health and welfare made over the previous three and a half decades.[1]

According to UNICEF, in 2015 there were nearly twenty-four million children in twenty-two countries affected by conflict who were unable to attend school. Besides Syria, the worst case was South Sudan, where half of all primary and lower secondary schoolchildren were not being educated. After the civil war started in December 2013, both government-allied forces and rebel troops committed atrocities, including forcibly recruiting child soldiers and committing targeted killings of civilians from rival ethnic groups. Schools were requisitioned, damaged or destroyed during fighting. UNICEF's chief of education, Jo Bourne, argued that the net result was a generation of South Sudanese children who were facing the threat of being 'unable to learn even the basic reading and writing skills'.[2] This is why preventing atrocities must be a global development priority as well as a moral and political imperative.

A key argument of this book is that atrocities are neither natural nor normal. They are intentional crimes that require organisation. A key lesson of the last decade is that we need to get better at turning early warning about systemic human rights abuses and the threat of atrocities into timely action to actively prevent or disrupt these crimes. But how?

The British movement to abolish slavery was quite possibly the first global human rights campaign. The humble abolitionists who gathered together in London in 1787 went on to radically alter government policy and the laws of Britain, leading to the gradual destruction of a pernicious but profitable industry (including, eventually, through direct military intervention) and causing a fundamental shift in the way we regard slavery. The normative battle spanned decades and had many setbacks along the way, but the magnitude of the political change initiated by Thomas Clarkson, Olaudah Equiano, William Wilberforce and their multitude of collaborators is proven by the fact that selling human beings seems as unnatural and immoral to us today as it seemed essential and familiar to people of their age.[3]

When we talk of an 'international community' today, we are referring not just to states but also to intergovernmental organisations and institutions, as well as the vast variety of civil society organisations embedded in communities across the globe or lobbying and advocating in corridors of power around the world. If we look at other movements that have successfully changed the world – like the international struggle against apartheid, or even the global campaign to ban land mines – change comes from a combustible mixture of ideas, institutions and individuals. Without powerful ideas (like the universality of human rights or the responsibility to protect), you cannot fundamentally reshape people's views or inspire them to act. Without institutions, you cannot implement change. And without individuals who are prepared to utilise these ideas and institutions, the essential equilibrium shift will not occur. If we want to truly end mass atrocity crimes once and for all, there is much for us to do.

What the United Nations can do

Criticising the United Nations for its political ineffectiveness, its bloated bureaucracy and its celebrations of things like World Puppetry Day (21 March) has become *de rigueur* for political curmudgeons the world over. The political direction of the organisation is determined by the UN General Assembly and the bitterly divided Security Council. But what does the UN actually do?

The UN is made up of its secretariat, with departments that employ more than 40,000 people, and spans seventeen specialised agencies and fourteen funds. The UN has sent more than seventy peacekeeping and observer missions to conflict zones all over the world and helped mediate an end to deadly conflicts in Cambodia, Liberia, Sierra Leone and Timor-Leste, to name just a few. Since 1957, the International Atomic Energy Agency has inspected nuclear facilities the world over, and the International Civil Aviation Organization helps regulate all international air travel. The UN Development Programme works in 170 countries on projects to reduce poverty, and the Intergovernmental Panel on Climate Change is the global authority on climate science. Treaties negotiated at the UN form the backbone of international law, including conventions on genocide, refugees and chemical weapons, as well as the recent Arms Trade Treaty. Since 1951, more than sixty million displaced people have received help from the Office of the UN High Commissioner for Refugees, including food, shelter and medical assistance. Meanwhile, UNESCO preserves and protects humanity's cultural and natural heritage, and every year UNICEF vaccinates around half of all the children in the world. The World Health Organization has helped eradicate smallpox from the planet. All things considered, this is not a bad investment in time and money over the past 75 years.[4]

Moreover, with a core budget of around $5.4 billion and total annual expenditures of around $50 billion, the entire UN system is still considerably cheaper than the 2019 annual budget of New York City, which was $88.6 billion.[5] Even UN peacekeeping only costs around $9 billion a year, with peacekeepers protecting civilians in some of the most dangerous and deadly parts of the world.

For example, prior to 2013 and despite the country's name, many members of the UN Security Council could not have located the Central African Republic (CAR) on a map. The March 2013 overthrow of the venal government of President François Bozizé led to the collapse of the state. The new rulers from the predominately Muslim Séléka rebel alliance were unable to govern and were, in turn, forced out by so-called anti-balaka (anti-machete) militias formed mainly amongst the Christian population. The country's descent into ethno-religious violence accelerated. Murderous mobs 'cleansed' the capital, Bangui, of ninety percent of its Muslim population. The arrival of French and African Union peacekeepers in December failed to completely end the bloodletting. Sporadic attacks and terrifying machete killings still occasionally took place in broad daylight.

In response, between October 2013 and January 2018 the UN Security Council adopted ten resolutions aimed at halting atrocities in the CAR, urging the interim government to uphold its responsibility to protect and authorising the deployment of 10,000 UN peacekeepers to protect civilians. Moreover, unlike Rwanda in 1994, the UN stayed after the militias and predatory armed groups turned their guns against the peacekeepers. Between April 2014 and April 2019, the peacekeeping mission, MINUSCA, suffered eighty-two fatalities, and despite ongoing operational weaknesses, it has saved the lives of thousands of Central Africans.[6] In this sense the CAR is an example of what UN peacekeepers can do in even the worst situations, in one of the most remote parts of the world, if given the right mandate and resources by the UN Security Council. However, in this era of shrinking budgets and a retreat from multilateralism, such positive examples are increasingly rare.

The UN Security Council remains at the apex of the creaking and weary United Nations system, and its slow response to the crisis in the Central African Republic was due, in part, to many wasted months in which some permanent members privately argued that the former colony was France's problem, despite the fact that the country has been independent since August 1960. Since 2011, the crises in Syria, Yemen and Myanmar have exposed a more fundamental debility – the historic anachronism of five permanent members who can still veto (or privately threaten to veto) any attempt to stop mass atrocity crimes if doing so does not accord with their partisan interests.

This is one of the UN's main structural deficiencies as it confronts atrocities in our world. No UN member state today would openly proclaim that atrocities perpetrated behind sovereign borders are permissible. No government challenges the argument that the international community has an obligation to assist a state if it is struggling to protect its people. And yet timely and decisive political action is still the exception rather than the rule.

Nevertheless, it is worth noting that in the five years prior to the beginning of the Libya intervention in 2011, the Security Council passed only four resolutions that referenced R2P – two were thematic resolutions on the protection of civilians, and the other two concerned crises in the Democratic Republic of the Congo and Darfur, Sudan. By contrast, in the nine years following Resolution 1973, the Security Council adopted eighty-three resolutions that referenced R2P. A number of these were thematic (including one on the prevention of genocide, passed during the twentieth anniversary of the Rwandan genocide), but others concerned the threat of atrocities in Côte d'Ivoire, Yemen, Mali, Sudan, South Sudan, Somalia, Liberia, the Democratic Republic of the Congo and the Central African Republic.[7] The Council authorised peacekeepers and imposed a range of practical measures to help prevent or halt atrocities. Some resolutions were only partially implemented, and some actions were more successful than others, but that is the nature of praxis.

This also helps explain why, in a way that would have been almost inconceivable to the original framers of the organisation's charter, UN peacekeeping is now at the centre of atrocity prevention in the world today. But underresourcing can still swallow up even the best-intentioned mission. We need to expand the number of troop-contributing countries and, above all else, ensure that when vulnerable civilians see a blue helmet, they are certain that they will be vigorously protected.

Targeted sanctions and preventive diplomacy are other tools that, if strategically deployed by the UN Security Council, can have a huge impact. For example, sanctions imposed at the start of the conflict in Libya (before the military intervention) cut off nearly $36 billion in funds that Libya's eccentric dictator, Muammar al-Qaddafi, could not use to import more weaponry or hire more mercenaries. Despite legitimate criticisms regarding aspects of the Libyan intervention, there is little doubt that the civil war would have been longer and bloodier if Qaddafi had had access to these funds.[8]

Similarly, the proliferation of small arms is a recognised risk factor in the potential commission of mass atrocities. At the height of its power in 2015, ISIL's arsenal included 'more than 100 different types of arms and ammunition originally sourced from at least 25 countries', including weaponry stolen, traded or stockpiled from the Iran–Iraq War, the 2003 United States–led invasion and various other regional conflicts. In the words of a report by Amnesty International, this inventory was 'a textbook case of how reckless arms trading fuels atrocities on a massive scale'.[9] The ratification and enforcement of the UN's 2014 international Arms Trade Treaty and targeted arms embargoes are mechanisms by which the international community can effectively undermine the capacity of a state or armed group to commit atrocities.

In the most intractable cases, where a state is manifestly unwilling to protect its populations and it becomes necessary for the UN Security Council to authorise military intervention, we need to ensure that civilian protection mandates are not manipulated for opportunistic reasons of 'regime change'. That is a reason why Brazil's 2012 proposal that there is a 'responsibility while protecting' demanded serious attention.[10] However, most future mass atrocity situations will in all likelihood continue to look more like the Central African Republic than like Libya. That is to say, they will continue to require elements of both coercion and consent, with authorisation of the Security Council and active dialogue about how a state can uphold its responsibility to protect and how the Council can both assist and compel it to do so. In this regard, we have had too little intervention since 2011, not too much.

In order to make consistent progress, we also need a more representative and responsive Security Council. At the very least, all five of the permanent members of the Security Council should accept that they have a responsibility not to veto in any mass atrocity situation. The 'Code of Conduct regarding Security Council action against genocide, crimes against humanity and war crimes' has been signed by 115 UN member states, who pledge not to vote against any credible resolution aimed at preventing or halting mass atrocities. A French and Mexican initiative calling on the permanent members of the Council to restrain from using the veto in a mass atrocity situation also has more than ninety signatories.[11] Far-reaching reform of the UN Security Council's structure, membership and working methods is long overdue.

As for the UN itself, it is only ever as politically strong as its member states allow it to be. But with its considerable diplomatic 'soft power' and developmental infrastructure, the UN has unique resources at its disposal to prevent conflict and potential atrocities. Advancing the UN's Sustainable Development Goals will continue to be central in this regard. But other parts of the UN system should also be more than optional extras. The UN Peacebuilding Commission (PBC) and the Mediation Support Unit, for example, remain understaffed and undervalued. Meanwhile the UN's Human Rights Council, with its Special Procedures and Universal Periodic Review, is now an indispensable part of the global early warning system, as is the UN Office of the Special Advisers for the Prevention of Genocide and the Responsibility to Protect.

Despite the current grim reality of a deeply divided and dysfunctional UN Security Council, by strengthening the cohesiveness of different parts of the UN system a determined secretary-general can still move prevention beyond empty rhetoric to meaningful action. In the UN charter, human rights is one of the organisation's three pillars – along with development and peace and security. But the Office of the High Commissioner for Human Rights still receives less than four percent of the UN's regular budget. The funding of human rights needs to reflect the centrality that it holds to the fulfillment of the UN's global mission.[12] Otherwise, just like World Puppetry Day, the protection of human rights and the prevention of atrocity crimes will continue to be a marginal concern.

What governments can do

In the opinion of Leo Tolstoy, the genius author of *War and Peace*, 'government is an association of men who do violence to the rest of us'. While Tolstoy's prognosis is hopefully less prophetic today than it was during the golden age of European imperialism, governments – and the nation-states they control – remain the essential building blocks of the international system. The UN serves them and reflects their priorities. They remain the primary means by which populations are cohered and divided, and they oversee the institutions that implement policies and deliver services. They are also the vehicle by which atrocities are most often either prevented or perpetrated.

In September 2009 a notorious massacre took place in a stadium in Conakry, the capital of the West African country of Guinea, where the security forces killed more than 150 people and perpetrated mass rape. But just over a year later, in November 2010, Guinea transitioned to its first civilian government in fifty years. Shortly thereafter Guinea became the first state on the agenda of the Peacebuilding Commission to voluntarily request assistance. The PBC has supported Guinea since then, including by mobilising funds to help pay for the retirement of almost 3,000 officers from the country's dangerously abusive military as the country underwent serious security sector reform.[13]

Additionally, in recent years we have seen the steady development of domestic structures for preventing mass atrocities. In Washington, an interagency Atrocity Prevention Board was established after President Barack Obama declared that 'preventing mass atrocities and genocide is a core national security interest and a core moral responsibility' of the United States. Meanwhile the National Peace Council of Ghana is one of Africa's clearest examples of a strong national institution for addressing the root causes of conflict.[14]

Across regions and continents we have also seen the development of state-led communities of commitment, most notably the Global Network of R2P Focal Points, which now encompasses sixty diverse states (more than a quarter of the UN membership) from the Democratic Republic of the Congo and Côte d'Ivoire to Guatemala, the United States, the Netherlands and Australia. Two major regional organisations – the European Union and the Organization of American States – have also appointed an R2P Focal Point. An R2P Focal Point is a senior government representative mandated to strengthen domestic and regional commitment to preventing mass atrocities.

Ending impunity for past atrocity crimes is another means by which governments can help prevent their recurrence. The pursuit of truth and reconciliation regarding the past has enhanced peace and justice in Argentina, Guatemala and Chile, to name just a few. Genocide denialism in Turkey, by contrast, inhibits Ankara's ability to meaningfully engage with twenty-first-century debates about preventing mass atrocities. Turkey is not a state party of the International Criminal Court (ICC), and Article 301 of its criminal code still criminalises recognition of the Armenian genocide.

In short, all governments can implement policies that ensure they uphold their responsibility to protect, including the following:

- Rigorously uphold national laws recognising the universality of human rights and punishing incitement, genocide denial and hate speech. Encourage strategies for enhancing domestic human rights monitoring and actively support the constitutional protection of civil liberties.
- Ensure that all relevant international human rights instruments are ratified, including the Convention on the Prevention and Punishment of the Crime of Genocide; International Covenant on Civil and Political Rights and the Second Optional Protocol thereto (1989); Convention against Torture and Other Cruel, Inhuman or Degrading Treatment or Punishment; Convention on the Elimination of All Forms of Discrimination against Women; International Convention on the Elimination of All Forms of Racial Discrimination; Convention Relating to the Status of Refugees and the 1967 Protocol thereto; Rome Statute of the International Criminal Court; and Arms Trade Treaty.
- Support UN peacekeeping financially and by deploying national military, police and civilian personnel to missions operating under a protection-of-civilians or R2P mandate. Strengthen UN peacekeeping by endorsing the Kigali Principles on the protection of civilians and through the UN's Action for Peacekeeping initiative.
- Where relevant, encourage the formation of a national mechanism for preventing mass atrocities, such as the Atrocity Prevention Board in the United

States and the National Peace Council in Ghana. Appoint a national R2P Focal Point and develop a plan for the promotion of human rights and the prevention of atrocities.

- Support all international programs and targets, including the Paris Agreement, aimed at overcoming the effects of climate change. Particular attention should be paid to the conflict risks associated with climate change.
- Utilising the United States' Global Magnitsky Act as a template, tighten domestic laws in order to freeze or seize the locally held assets of foreign human rights abusers, including those accused of perpetrating mass atrocity crimes. Such laws should also be used to help the survivors of atrocities pursue financial compensation.

All governments should also acknowledge that accepting a fair share of refugees who are fleeing conflict, persecution and atrocities forms an essential part of upholding their responsibility to protect. They should ensure that the global refugee burden is not disproportionately borne by states that are themselves vulnerable to conflict.

And what of the irredeemable offenders? What to do when a government – usually a dictatorship or one-party state – is manifestly unwilling to uphold its responsibility to protect? How should the international community interact with a government that continues to perpetrate war crimes, genocide or crimes against humanity? History teaches us that the Democratic People's Republic of Korea, Syria and Eritrea are currently unlikely to implement any of these recommendations or enact policies to ease the suffering of their populations. Such states should, therefore, be treated as South Africa was during the peak years of apartheid – diplomatically isolated, with targeted sanctions imposed on their leadership and clear benchmarks established with regard to the need to end mass atrocity crimes in order to play a full and active role in the global economy and the United Nations. The UN is not a league of democracies, but all its member states are obligated to respect international law and uphold universal human rights.

What parliaments can do

On 16 June 2016, British parliamentarian Jo Cox was attacked and murdered by a neo-Nazi with a history of mental illness. Jo, who was elected only one year earlier as an opposition Labour Member of Parliament, viewed Parliament as an extension of her international human rights and humanitarian work. In a 12 October 2015 parliamentary debate, for example, she directly addressed the question of parliamentary responsibility with regard to atrocities in the world:

> Every decade or so, the world is tested by a crisis so grave that it breaks the mold. ... We have been tested by the second world war, the genocide in Rwanda and the slaughter in Bosnia, and I believe that Syria is our generation's test. Will we step up to play our part in stopping the abject horror of the Syrian civil war and the spread of the modern-day fascism of

ISIS, or will we step to one side, say that it is too complicated, and leave Iran, Russia, Assad and ISIS to turn the country into a graveyard? Whatever we decide will stay with us forever, and I ask that each of us take that responsibility personally."15

Around the world, parliamentarians are able to advocate on behalf of vulnerable populations. For example, in 2014, Vian Dakhil – who was Iraq's only female parliamentarian from the minority Yazidi community – argued in the Iraqi Council of Representatives for urgent military intervention to save thousands of Yazidis being targeted by ISIL as it advanced across northern Iraq. Dakhil's actions led to the parliament voting to initiate humanitarian airdrops over Mount Sinjar. President Barack Obama also referenced Dakhil's plea as influencing his decision to authorise air strikes against ISIL in northern Iraq.

Parliamentarians can also apply significant political pressure on governments to change policy, regardless of whether they are in the majority or not. In South Africa, for example, the Democratic Alliance (DA) control only around 20 percent of the seats in Parliament and are unable to pass legislation without the ruling party, the African National Congress. However, in 2016, when the government decided to withdraw South Africa from the International Criminal Court, the DA raised the issue in Parliament and initiated a wider public debate about the struggle against impunity for atrocity crimes. They also launched a legal challenge. The High Court ruled that the decision was unconstitutional and the government was forced to retract its letter of intent to withdraw from the ICC.

Where possible, parliamentarians who are committed to preventing atrocities should organise on a bipartisan basis. An All-Party Parliamentary Group for the Prevention of Genocide and Crimes against Humanity was established in the UK Parliament in 2005. The following year, Senator Roméo Dallaire founded a similar parliamentary group in Canada. Both groups have lobbied their governments around issues such as appointing an R2P Focal Point, improving the working methods of the UN Security Council in responding to atrocities and adopting domestic policies to strengthen human rights protection.

Meanwhile, external networks enable parliamentarians from different countries to raise human rights concerns. Notwithstanding huge variance in the efficacy of various networks, they are also important for the exchange of ideas. The Association of Southeast Asian Nations (ASEAN) Parliamentarians for Human Rights, for example, was one of the few high-level regional organisations in Asia to highlight the persecution of the Rohingya in Myanmar prior to the 2017 genocide. Other notable networks include the following:

- Parliamentarians for Global Action: This network has more than 1,400 members from 140 countries and has called for ratification of the Arms Trade Treaty and the Rome Statute of the International Criminal Court.
- Elie Wiesel Network – European Network of Parliamentarians for the Prevention of Genocide and Mass Atrocities and against Genocide Denial:

During June 2016, 184 parliamentarians from twenty-three national legislatures and the European Parliament formed the Elie Wiesel Network. The founding statement declares, 'We unite, in the name of our shared humanity, in preventing genocide and mass atrocities and fighting against genocide denial'.

- Inter-Parliamentary Union (IPU): With members from 171 parliaments and eleven associate members from regional organisations, in 2013 the IPU adopted a resolution on 'Enforcing the Responsibility to Protect: The Role of Parliament in Safeguarding Civilians' Lives'.

In Rwanda the buildings that house the parliament are still scarred by bullet and mortar rounds. The parliament itself has become a permanent memorial to the genocide against the Tutsi. While parliamentarians elsewhere do not work in such proximity to physical reminders of past atrocities, many have seen education as a key component of the struggle to make 'never again' a reality. In July 2016 the French Parliament amended and expanded laws that made it a crime to deny or 'trivialize' the Holocaust or the Armenian Genocide. A number of countries also annually commemorate the Holocaust on 27 January, providing an opportunity for parliamentarians to reflect on past atrocities. The European Parliament, representing 500 million people, is the largest parliament to officially recognise Holocaust Remembrance Day. In 2015 the Canadian Parliament also unanimously declared April to be Genocide Remembrance, Condemnation and Prevention Month.

However, in order to have a lasting impact, knowledge and awareness must be transformed into practical deeds. In May 2017 the Elie Wiesel Genocide and Atrocities Prevention Act was introduced in the United States Senate. The bill, which received bipartisan support, authorised a Mass Atrocities Task Force, established a Complex Crises Fund, and requires training for diplomats regarding early warning of atrocities and reporting from both the State Department and the director of national intelligence regarding situations where there is a serious risk of atrocity crimes. In January 2019 the bill was signed into law.[16]

As the institutional centre of any democracy, parliaments and parliamentarians can play an essential role in advocating, educating and legislating for the protection of human rights and the prevention of mass atrocities. While opportunities vary greatly depending upon national circumstances, the voices of parliamentarians matter.

What you can do

The role of civil society and human rights activists is also crucial. The preeminent academic scholar of the responsibility to protect, Alex Bellamy, has written that those who 'claim that R2P cannot be transformative because it does not change international law, exaggerate the transformative effects of law and undervalue the importance of politics'.[17] They also underestimate the influence of activism. The history of atrocities in the world, including examples discussed in this book, show that an individual decision to act – even in small ways that may seem futile at the time – can make a difference in the world. We all have an individual responsibility to protect.

Most people in European countries that were occupied by Germany during the Second World War did not actively collaborate in the Holocaust, but they also did not help rescue Jews or protect those persecuted by the Nazis. When the Nazis invaded Denmark in April 1940, the army put up little resistance. Instead, the Danish government consented to becoming a German protectorate. However, late in the summer of 1943, with the war going badly for the Nazis and popular resentment against the German occupiers growing, Denmark's semiautonomous government resigned. The Nazis declared martial law and ordered the deportation of Denmark's small Jewish population to concentration camps.

Raids of Jewish homes were planned for Friday, 1 October 1943. But on 28 September a German diplomat based in Copenhagen, Georg Duckwitz, leaked information concerning the impending Gestapo raids to a senior Danish Social Democrat politician, Hans Hedtoft. He in turn informed the Jewish community. The chief rabbi in Copenhagen, Marcus Melchior, instructed all Jews to go into hiding.[18]

Over the following three weeks, a mass escape of thousands of Jews was improvised, as entire families were smuggled from Copenhagen and other towns to the seaside. Danish fishermen hid Jews on their boats and transported entire families across the sea to neutral Sweden. Other Jews paddled or rowed their way to freedom. In all, more than 7,200 Danish Jews escaped. As a result, ninety-nine percent of Denmark's Jewish population survived the Holocaust.[19]

The campaign to help Jews escape had wide support in Denmark, with the underground resistance, church leaders, networks of university students, a fleet of willing fishermen and countless other people assisting the exodus in one way or another. Resistance rippled across a broad cross section of society, encouraging Danes to engage in thousands of little acts of defiance. As Michael Ignatieff has written, the lesson of the great Danish escape is that 'shared social and political understandings can make possible, in times of terrible darkness, acts of civil courage and uncommon decency'.[20]

There are many other examples from history of such acts. The international struggle against apartheid, for example, is now largely remembered for the international sporting boycott, the solidarity work of the 'frontline states' in Africa and angry protests held outside South African embassies around the world. But it has been forgotten that in the Western world, at least, for many decades the movement was led by a very small cadre of community activists and exiles. Moreover, in the pre-internet age, most anti-apartheid groups operated with activists having very little contact with their counterparts in other cities, countries or continents. And yet people persisted, sometimes with unexpected results.

On a Thursday during July 1984, at a Dunnes Stores shop on Henry Street in Dublin, Ireland, a twenty-one-year-old cashier called Mary Manning refused to sell two grapefruit from South Africa to a customer who had no idea from whence they came. Mary was abiding by a ban imposed by her union against handling fruit from South Africa as a protest against apartheid. Until then the ban had largely been symbolic. Mary and her union representative, Karen Gearon, were called into an office, where they were warned by management to end their pointless protest. They refused. The two young women were then suspended. Unbowed, Mary and Karen went on strike, and nine other union members joined them on the picket line outside.[21]

Initially, very few people supported the shopworkers, some of whom were still teenagers. The eleven strikers barely survived on union strike pay, and they faced abuse from irate shoppers as they sustained their picket line. But as the days extended into months, the strike started to gather sympathetic attention, including in distant South Africa. In 1985, Archbishop Desmond Tutu met with the Dunnes strikers on his way to Oslo to collect his Nobel Peace Prize. Politicians and celebrities eventually joined them on the picket line. The strikers educated themselves and others about the situation in South Africa and marched in front of large protests. Two of the Dunnes strikers were eventually invited to New York to speak to the UN Special Committee against Apartheid.

The strike lasted for two years and nine months. Finally, in April 1987, in response to a groundswell of public support, the Irish government became the first in Western Europe to completely ban the importation and sale of South African goods. Mary Manning and those two grapefruit had not changed the world, but together the eleven young Dunnes workers put a dent in the economy of apartheid South Africa. They also fundamentally altered the perception across Ireland of the efficacy of consumer boycotts and trade sanctions against apartheid.

While activism cannot guarantee success, it always makes a difference. The Save Darfur campaign, for example, was formed in July 2004 and was probably the largest modern campaign in the United States to protest against atrocities in a distant land – in this case, the vast western region of Sudan. The campaign began organising amongst academics, students, human rights activists and Sudanese émigrés but soon developed into a mass movement. The Save Darfur Coalition claimed that it eventually encompassed 'more than 190 faith-based, advocacy and human rights organizations with more than 1 million activists and hundreds of community groups committed to ending the genocide in Darfur'. At a major rally in Washington DC in April 2006, Senator Barack Obama and Elie Wiesel appeared in front of a crowd of tens of thousands of people to call for an end to atrocities. The Global Day of Action for Darfur saw demonstrations across Europe, Asia and Africa, with small solidarity protests even occurring in Cambodia and Rwanda.[22]

To state the obvious, the Save Darfur campaign did not actually save Darfur. But despite diverse motivations and the overblown expectations of some of its activists, the campaign elevated public awareness about Darfur in unprecedented ways and influenced US government policy, resulting in sanctions and divestment legislation. Although that didn't force President Omar al-Bashir of Sudan to halt atrocities, he was constrained. With increased international awareness, Sudan was sanctioned by the UN Security Council, peacekeepers were deployed to Darfur and Bashir was eventually indicted for genocide by the International Criminal Court. More than a decade later the conflict in Darfur continues, but not in the darkness and not at the same level. While some former Save Darfur activists were demoralised by their failure to completely halt atrocities or see Bashir arrested, others drew deeper lessons about how to build movements and carry out advocacy.[23]

In short, whether you live in a conflict zone where there is an immediate threat of mass atrocities or in a stable society where human rights are protected, everyone can be an active participant in civil society. Take, for example, the case of Colomba (name changed), who works for a small human rights organisation in Butembo in the North Kivu region of the Democratic Republic of the Congo. Colomba does human rights monitoring in the most difficult circumstances imaginable. Even in the midst of a deadly Ebola outbreak, he was still documenting attacks by former Mai Mai militias, helping reintegrate other militia members back into local society and advocating for the voiceless. By his own admission, 'for us as activists, we are in the bad situation and we can be killed at any time'.

When Colomba was arbitrarily arrested in late 2018, I feared the worst, but he was eventually released and returned to work. In May the following year, with the death toll from the Ebola outbreak already at more than 1,000 people, Colomba's wife gave birth to a beautiful baby girl. Just one day before, a Mai Mai militia had attacked the local Ebola treatment centre and nine people had been killed. Colomba emailed me details of the attack and pictures of the dead, and then in another email several hours later, a picture of his new baby. With characteristic understatement he wrote, 'We are safe my friend', but 'it is not easy'. Colomba still emails updates regarding extrajudicial killings and identity-based persecution in one of the most dangerous places on earth to be a human rights defender.[24]

Meanwhile, organisations like the Syrian Observatory for Human Rights (SOHR) and the Syrian Network for Human Rights (SNHR) have played an invaluable role in documenting atrocities and advocating for international action to hold the perpetrators accountable, while the White Helmets have saved thousands of lives and inspired people around the world. Mwatana for Human Rights has played a similar role to SOHR and SNHR with regard to the catastrophic war in Yemen, while Foro Penal and Centro de Justicia y Paz continue to document abuses in Venezuela despite economic collapse and the threat of arrest or disappearance.

In short, everywhere in the world where there is persecution and conflict, there are also people organising to end it. From the large international human rights organisations like Human Rights Watch, the Fédération international des ligues des droits de l'homme and Amnesty International to small local student organisations like STAND and the R2P Student Coalition, the world needs more activists. Wherever you happen to live, a vibrant civil society is essential for protecting human rights and preventing atrocities. We are all capable of acts of civil courage and uncommon decency. If Colomba can do it, so can you.

Conclusion

Twenty-five years after Rwanda, the international community is still struggling to consistently close the gap between words and decisive action when it comes to preventing atrocities. But to paraphrase UN scholar Thomas Weiss, at least there is now 'the double-standard of inconsistency', whereas previously there had been only a single standard of inaction and indifference.[25]

The idea that we all have a responsibility to protect, like all global principles and norms, will only ever be as effective as policy makers and practitioners make it. From Syria to Myanmar, or from Burundi to North Korea, those who commit atrocities would like nothing better than a return to the world of complacency, complicity and impunity. But R2P is not just another campaign to stop atrocities in a faraway place. This is a battle to change ideas, institutions and individuals. We need a movement of committed governments, parliamentarians, civil society organisations and dedicated activists — like the informal networks of local groups that helped end the slave trade during the nineteenth century, or the international movement against apartheid during the twentieth century — to transform the way that all states respond to atrocities, ensuring that these unconscionable crimes eventually become unimaginable.

The great American civil rights leader Martin Luther King Jr famously said that 'the arc of the moral universe is long, but it bends toward justice'. US President Barack Obama, who established his government's Atrocity Prevention Board, would often deploy this quote to argue that while one had to take a long view of the incremental advance of human freedom, further historical progress was not a fait accompli. More recently, the indomitable former UN high commissioner for human rights, Zeid Ra'ad Al Hussein, argued: 'All the fights worth fighting involve long-term struggles. ... The fights against apartheid, slavery, and colonialism have been fought over the long term, with battles both won and lost.'[26] Our collective attempt to end mass atrocity crimes will also be decades long. There will continue to be disappointments and defeats, but together we can bend the arc of history.

Notes

1 United Nations Development Programme, About Syria, http://www.sy.undp.org/content/syria/en/home/countryinfo.html.
2 UNICEF, Press Release: One in Four Children in Conflict Zones Are Out of School, 12 January 2016, http://www.unicef.org/media/media_89782.html.
3 Adam Hochschild, *Bury the Chains: Prophets and Rebels in the Fight to Free an Empire's Slaves* (New York: Mariner Books, 2006).
4 United Nations Seventieth Anniversary: 70 Ways the UN Makes a Difference, https://www.un.org/un70/en/content/70ways/index.html.

5 Chris McGreal, "70 Years and Half a Trillion Dollars Later: What Has the UN Achieved?," *The Guardian*, 7 September 2015; Fact Sheet: Mayor de Blasio Releases Preliminary Budget for Fiscal Year 2019, 1 February 2018, https://www1.nyc.gov/office-of-the-mayor/news/077-18/fact-sheet-mayor-de-blasio-releases-preliminary-budget-fiscal-year-2019#/0; Mattha Busby, "UN Is Running Out of Money and Member States Should Pay What They Owe, Warns Secretary-General," *The Independent* (UK), 27 July 2018.

6 MINUSCA Fact Sheet, https://peacekeeping.un.org/en/mission/minusca.

7 The period is from Resolution 1973 in March 2011 until Resolution 2514 in March 2020. Global Centre for the Responsibility to Protect – UN Security Council Resolutions Referencing R2P, https://www.globalr2p.org/resources/un-security-council-resolutions-and-presidential-statements-referencing-r2p/.

8 George A. Lopez, "Tools, Tasks and Tough Thinking: Sanctions and R2P," *GCR2P Policy Brief*, 3 October 2013, http://s156658.gridserver.com/media/files/lopez-sanctions-brief-1.pdf.

9 Amnesty International, Iraq: 'Islamic State' Atrocities fuelled by Decades of reckless Arms Trading, 8 December 2015. https://www.amnesty.org/en/latest/news/2015/12/islamic-state-atrocities-fuelled-by-decades-of-reckless-arms-trading/.

10 Letter dated 9 November 2011 from the Permanent Representative of Brazil to the United Nations addressed to the Secretary-General, A/66/551-S/2011/701, https://www.globalr2p.org/wp-content/uploads/2020/06/2011-RWP-Concept-Paper.pdf.

11 UN Security Council Code of Conduct.

12 OHCHR's Funding and Budget, https://www.ohchr.org/EN/AboutUs/Pages/FundingBudget.aspx.

13 Jaclyn Streitfeld-Hall, "Preventing Mass Atrocities in West Africa," *GCR2P Occasional Paper*, no. 6, September 2015, http://www.globalr2p.org/publications/389.

14 Todd F. Buchwald and Adam Keith, "By Any Other Name: How, When, and Why the US Government Has Made Genocide Determinations," US Holocaust Memorial Museum: Simon-Skjodt Center for the Prevention of Genocide, Washington DC, March 2019, 17; Streitfeld-Hall, "Preventing Mass Atrocities in West Africa."

15 All parliamentary speeches of Jo Cox available at http://myparliament.info/Member/4375/Speeches. The following section regarding parliamentarians draws on, "Advocate, Educate, Legislate: The Role of Parliamentarians in the Prevention of Mass Atrocities," *GCR2P Policy Brief*, May 2017.

16 S.1158 – Elie Wiesel Genocide and Atrocities Prevention Act of 2018, https://www.congress.gov/bill/115th-congress/senate-bill/1158.

17 Alex J. Bellamy, *The Responsibility to Protect: A Defense* (Oxford: Oxford University Press, 2015), 17.

18 Ellen Otzen, "The mass escape of Jews from Nazi-occupied Denmark," *BBC News*, 8 October 2013, https://www.bbc.com/news/magazine-24427637; Michael Ignatieff, "One Country Saved Its Jews. Were They Just Better People?," *The New Republic*, 14 December 2013; Ian Buruma, "Countrymen: The Untold Story of How Denmark's Jews Escaped the Nazis," *The Guardian*, 13 March 2014.

19 Otzen, "The mass escape of Jews from Nazi-occupied Denmark,"; Ignatieff, "One Country Saved Its Jews. Were They Just Better People?"; and Buruma, "Countrymen: The Untold Story of How Denmark's Jews Escaped the Nazis."

20 That is not to say that all people had purely altruistic motivations. Ignatieff, "One Country Saved Its Jews. Were They Just Better People?"

21 Rosita Boland, "How 11 Striking Irish Workers Helped to Fight Apartheid," *Irish Times*, 6 December 2013; Padraig Durnin, "Anti-Apartheid in Ireland: The Dunnes' Stores Strike, 1984-87," *History Workshop*, 17 July 2019, http://www.historyworkshop.org.uk/anti-apartheid-in-ireland-the-dunnes-stores-strike-1984-87/; "An 'boks amach': The Irish Anti-Apartheid Movement, *History Ireland*, 14, no. 4 (July/August 2016); Nemesha Balasundaram, "Dunnes Striker Liz Deasy on How Joining the Fight

Against Apartheid in South Africa Changed Her Life," *Irish Post*, 27 December 2015; and Ryle Dwyer, "State Archives: Dunnes Stores Strike Demonstrated Power of the Few,"*Irish Examiner*, 1 January 2016.

22 Justin Lynch, "Darfur Wasn't Saved," *Slate*, 11 October 2017, https://slate.com/news-and-politics/2017/10/why-couldnt-the-save-darfur-movement-stop-the-killing-in-sudan.html; United to End Genocide: Our History, http://endgenocide.org/who-we-are/history/; "Protesters around World Plead: Intervene in Darfur," *CNN*, 17 September 2006, http://www.cnn.com/2006/US/09/17/darfur.rally/.

23 Rebecca Hamilton, *Fighting for Darfur: Public Action and the Struggle to Stop Genocide* (New York: Palgrave Macmillan, 2011).

24 Emails from "Colomba" to S. Adams, 22 October 2018, 6 May 2019, 7 May 2019, 8 May 2018, 9 May 2019, 10 May 2019.

25 Thomas G. Weiss, "Military Humanitarianism: Syria Hasn't Killed It," *Washington Quarterly*, 37, no. 1 (2014), 7–20.

26 Zeid Ra'ad Al-Hussein, "Despite Setbacks, Fight Against Impunity Continues," International Center for Transitional Justice, 9 February 2015, https://www.ictj.org/debate/article/despite-setbacks-fight-against-impunity-continues.

EPILOGUE

Benjamin Ferencz's experience of war and genocide irrevocably altered his life. As a member of the US Army, Ben served in the headquarters of General George S. Patton and visited recently liberated Nazi concentration camps, where he walked amongst the corpses. He also listened to the stories of survivors. When the killing and dying ended, Ben was then called to Nuremburg, where he prosecuted twenty-two senior Einsatzgruppe commanders and sat in the courtroom in April 1948 as fourteen of them were sentenced to hang for war crimes and crimes against humanity. He was not even thirty years old at the time. Six decades later, in 2011, a now-elderly Ben spoke during the first case to be heard at the International Criminal Court in the Hague.

Ben is 100 years old now and stands only five feet tall, but there is nothing diminutive about him. Ben and the generation that survived the Second World War built the United Nations, compressed centuries of moral philosophy into a succinct Universal Declaration of Human Rights and had to come to terms – morally, politically and legally – with the horrors of Auschwitz. That generation not only prosecuted those responsible for the Holocaust, they outlawed the crime of genocide for the first time in human history.

Adopted at the Palais de Chaillot in Paris on 9 December 1948, one day before the Universal Declaration of Human Rights, the Convention on the Prevention and Punishment of the Crime of Genocide was the first international human rights treaty of the postwar era. The location of the 1948 UN General Assembly where the convention was adopted was especially poignant. In June 1940, Adolf Hitler had been photographed at the Palais with the Eiffel Tower behind him, celebrating his conquest of Paris.

Despite being the architect of the Genocide Convention, Raphael Lemkin's reflections of 9 December 1948 were muted by his emotional exhaustion following the interminable negotiations that preceded its adoption. In his memoir,

Lemkin briefly recalled that there 'were many lights in the large hall' that day, that the public galleries were full and that 'the delegates appeared to have a solemn radiating look'. An Australian, Herbert V. Evatt, presided over the meeting and described the Genocide Convention as 'an epoch-making concept'. It was officially adopted by the UN General Assembly with fifty-five votes in favour, no abstentions and no votes against. Afterwards, according to Lemkin, there was a 'storm of applause'. A story in the *New York Times* featured a picture of Lemkin with his tie askew and the line 'His Idea Adopted'. A few days later Lemkin checked himself into a Paris hospital; he would later comment that his years campaigning for the Genocide Convention 'almost destroyed me'.[1]

Exactly seventy years and one day after the convention's adoption, on 10 December 2018, the UN Security Council held an Arria formula meeting on the prevention of mass atrocity crimes in the world today. By then, more than six decades had passed since the UN had moved from its temporary home in Paris to its permanent headquarters in New York. The meeting was initiated by Poland, who were serving on the Council at the time, and the room was crowded with diplomats and civil society types.

Diplomatic protocol is strictly hierarchical, and so, in due course, various permanent representatives (ambassadors), deputy permanent representatives and other plenipotentiaries were called upon to make their national statements. With a few exceptions (most notably Russia), the diplomats spoke in favour of the enduring connection between the Genocide Convention, the Universal Declaration, R2P and the need for the UN to keep 'human rights up front' today. Several hours later, with the meeting running over time, I was given the floor and the last word on behalf of 'international civil society'.

It is not easy to make a durable impression with a three-minute speech, especially at the UN, where pallid language and unemotional delivery are considered signs of virtue. My general point was that the successful intervention to halt atrocities in Côte d'Ivoire was the counterpoint to international failure in Syria and Yemen. Timely conflict prevention in the Gambia was the counterpoint to the UN Security Council's inertia when confronted with a developing genocide in Myanmar. Civilian-protection operations carried by UN peacekeepers in South Sudan and the Central African Republic were the counterpoint to impunity and extrajudicial killings in Venezuela and Burundi. And I ended by directly addressing the UN Security Council members with the following words:

> Those to whom mass atrocities are not just words, but real acts that pose a direct threat to them, their families, and their communities, are looking to this Council. Some of you may be shy of the words, but those facing death need you to defend human rights and uphold your responsibility to protect. And they need you to do so without exception, and with consistency and courage.[2]

My point that day, and the core argument of this book, is that timely international action cannot guarantee success, but it is always better than passivity, diplomatic inertia and certain failure in the face of mass atrocity crimes.

When I turned off my microphone and the red light faded, I spared a thought for Raphael Lemkin, Ben Ferencz and all those who got us to this point in world history. There is a saying in the Irish language, the tongue of my disputatious ancestors: 'Ar scáth a chéile a mhaireann na daoine' – 'all people live in the shadow of one another'. When I wrote a book about the 1972 murder of a relative of mine in Belfast by undercover British soldiers, I used this phrase to try to convey that no matter what side of Ireland's conflict you came from, and despite death and diaspora, our lives were interconnected. These days I think of the saying's wider humanist implications regarding our collective responsibility to protect. You don't need to be a diplomat, international lawyer or government minister to help bend the arc of history.

In April 2018, a few months before the seventieth anniversary of the Genocide Convention and the Universal Declaration of Human Rights, Ben Ferencz gave possibly his last public speech at the United Nations. The wood-panelled room was at maximum capacity, and Ben's parting words were that from Nuremburg to today there were three things we needed to learn from his seven decades of campaigning for human rights and international justice: 'never give up, never give up, and never give up'.[3]

Notes

1 Donna-Lee Frieze, ed., *Totally Unofficial: The Autobiography of Raphael Lemkin* (New Haven, CT: Yale University Press, 2013), 177–179; "166 Organizations Urge Action Against Genocide," *New York Times*, 9 December 1948; "U.N. Votes Accord Banning Genocide," *New York Times*, 10 December 1948.

2 Remarks delivered at UN Security Council Arria Formula Meeting on 'Raising Effectiveness of Atrocity Crimes Prevention,' 10 December 2018, https://www.globalr2p.org/publications/remarks-delivered-at-un-security-council-arria-formula-meeting-on-raising-effectiveness-of-atrocity-crimes-prevention/.

3 Ferencz was possibly paraphrasing Winston Churchill's famous "Never Give In, Never, Never, Never," speech that he gave at Harrow School on 29 October 1941, https://www.nationalchurchillmuseum.org/never-give-in-never-never-never.html.

SELECTED BIBLIOGRAPHY

Bellamy, Alex J. *The Responsibility to Protect: A Defense* (Oxford, UK: Oxford University Press, 2015). *This book provides an academic analysis of the responsibility to protect one decade after its adoption at the UN World Summit. Bellamy argues that despite its shortcomings, R2P remains indispensable to the prevention of mass atrocities in the world today.*

Bellamy, Alex J., and Edward C. Luck, *The Responsibility to Protect: From Promise to Practice* (Medford, MA: Polity Press, 2018). *This book by two of R2P's leading academic champions confronts the gap between the promise inherent in the adoption of R2P at the 2005 UN World Summit and its practical implementation in the imperfect world of global diplomacy.*

Bloxham, Donald and Moses, A. Dirk., (eds), *The Oxford Handbook of Genocide Studies* (New York: Oxford University Press, 2010). *More than thirty leading scholars from around the world examine genocide through the ages and analyse the emergence of genocide as an international crime during the twentieth century. This multidisciplinary handbook provides essential background on the study of genocide.*

de Swaan, Abram *The Killing Compartments: The Mentality of Mass Murder* (New Haven, CT: Yale University Press, 2015). *A unique exploration of social psychology as a means of understanding why some humans commit mass atrocity crimes and other do not.*

Evans, Gareth *The Responsibility to Protect: Ending Mass Atrocity Crimes Once and For All* (Washington DC: Brookings Institution Press, 2008). *This 2008 book by one of the inventors of R2P was the emerging norm's defining text – it sought to explain what the responsibility to protect was, what it was not and how it could be implemented to prevent and halt war crimes, genocide, crimes against humanity and ethnic cleansing.*

Hamilton, Rebecca *Fighting for Darfur: Public Action and the Struggle to Stop Genocide* (New York: Palgrave Macmillan, 2011). *Hamilton offers a forensic analysis of the Save Darfur campaign, the grassroots political advocacy movement that began on university campuses in the United States and sought to end the campaign of atrocities perpetrated by the Sudanese government in the vast western region of that country.*

Puri, Hardeep Singh *Perilous Interventions: The Security Council and the Politics of Chaos* (New York: HarperCollins, 2016). *India's former permanent representative to the United Nations in New York offers a unique perspective on India's 2011–2012 tenure on the UN Security Council during the Arab Spring and the emerging civil wars in Libya and Syria.*

Thakur, Ramesh *Reviewing the Responsibility to Protect: Origins, Implementation and Controversies* (New York: Routledge, 2019). *Thakur, one of the original members of the international commission that developed the concept of R2P, offers an assessment of how the norm developed, why it has been so controversial and how it remains essential to international politics in the twenty-first century.*

Weiss, Thomas G. *Humanitarian Intervention: Ideas in Action* (Malden, MA: Polity Press, 2007). *Weiss, a leading international scholar of the UN system, analyses the use and abuse of the concept of humanitarian intervention and explains the intellectual and political origins of the concept of the responsibility to protect.*

INDEX

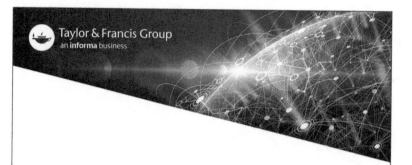